Tony Cliff

LENIN

Volume Three

Revolution Besieged

Pluto Press

Lenin Volume 3 : Revolution Besieged
First published 1978 by
Pluto Press Limited
Unit 10, Spencer Court
7 Chalcot Road, London NW1 8LH
Copyright © Pluto Press 1978
ISBN 0 904383 09 1 paperback
ISBN 0904383 10 5 hardback
Printed by Clarke, Doble & Brendon Ltd
Plymouth and London
Designed by Richard Hollis, GrR

Lenin Volume 1 : Building the Party
First published 1975 by Pluto Press

Lenin Volume 2 : All Power to the Soviets
First published 1976 by Pluto Press

Contents

Foreword

When on the morrow of the October insurrection Lenin calmly declared, 'We shall now proceed to construct the socialist order', he had behind him a quarter of a century of prison, exile, clandestine work and emigration, organizing, educating and leading a party of persecuted revolutionaries, very far from state power. Lenin now had before him five years as leader of the party, in charge of a revolutionary government and the head of a newly established Communist International.

In the long hard years of political work behind him Lenin had been sustained by a great dream – of a new socialist order. For twenty-five years he worked relentlessly towards a goal which seemed far more remote than it actually proved to be; as late as February 1917 he still did not believe that the revolution would come in his lifetime. After their dramatic ascent from obscurity to the summit of power, Lenin and the Bolsheviks faced a host of new, difficult tasks. They had to administer the state of a gigantic, backward country, whose economy was in ruins and which was under attack by 'fourteen armies'. The Bolsheviks had to create a workers' and peasants' army from scratch, and lead it against domestic and foreign armies far better equipped.

On coming to power the party had to change its mode of operation radically from agitating and organizing against a state, to administering a state and leading the workers in doing so. Lenin and the other Bolsheviks never doubted the crucial role of the proletariat in the revolution and its ability to rule, even though it was a class with no experience of power, no standing in society, and no wealth or culture to speak of. The Bolsheviks had great confidence in the creative abilities of the awakened working class. Relying on the iron discipline of the party, forged over many hard years of struggle, and the courage and heroism of the proletariat, Lenin unhesitatingly grasped the helm of the state.

Another new, heavy burden fell on Lenin's shoulders – that

of leading the newly founded Communist International. The Russian revolution had massive reverberations abroad. From tiny groups of revolutionary marxists, mass communist parties emerged in a number of countries. It was an extremely arduous task to educate and train the young, inexperienced parties.

The present work is the first of two volumes which span the period between Lenin's rise to power and his death. Of necessity its canvas has to be much broader than the previous two: Lenin's triple role as leader of the party, the government and of the International has to be documented and analysed.

The relationship between Lenin's biography and the history of the working class is an everchanging one. In Volume One I tried to show how Lenin influenced the party and the party influenced the proletariat, as well as how the proletariat created the party and the party shaped Lenin. The political biography of Lenin meshed in with the political history of the working class. The fusion of Lenin's activities with those of the party and the class reached its climax in the revolution of 1917, the subject of Volume Two. If in Volume One the strands of biography and of history did not harmonize completely it was because Lenin had to work his way towards implanting the party in the class, remoulding the party and himself in the struggle to change the working class and transform society. In 1917 the fusion of the biographical and the historical was complete, so that it seems as if Lenin merged completely with the party and the proletariat. He acquired his strength and greatness in 1917 from the strength and greatness of the workers.

In this third volume, the relationship between the biographical and the historical changes again. Following the October revolution, the grim reality of Russian backwardness and peasant conservatism, combined with the tardiness of the international revolution, led to an increasing impotence and inability of the Bolsheviks to shape reality. It was as if the march of events pushed Lenin to the periphery of social life. The biographical element appears very marginal compared with the historical. The weakness of Lenin and his party in the face of overwhelming forces makes this period of his life a tragic one; nevertheless, the sacrifices which he, the party and the proletariat made during this period were not made in vain.

Throughout the Promethean struggle Lenin never wavered in his conviction that the future belonged to Bolshevism. The relatively small proletariat of Russia, in the most difficult circumstances, provided a glimpse of what the international working class can achieve in its fight for freedom, for workers' power.

In the last few years of Lenin's life, the optimistic, heroic elements intertwine inextricably with the tragic: his grasp of the helm of state, party and International becomes weaker and weaker. Consequently, in this as well as the next volume the crucial dialectic of the biographical and historical elements causes the latter almost to obliterate the former.

Writing the present and succeeding volumes was extremely difficult, not only because of the conflict between the breadth of the subject – Russia in the international arena, the party, the state and the Communist International – but even more because it is hard to describe an historical tragedy intertwined with personal agony without descending to a pathos foreign to the subject of the book.

For dates before 1 (14) February 1918 I give two dates, the first according to the Julian or 'Old Style' calendar, the second (in parentheses) according to the Gregorian calendar, known as the 'West European' or 'New Style'. The Old Style was abolished and the New Style introduced in Russia on 1 (14) February 1918. For events occurring later only the Gregorian calendar applies.

Tony Cliff
London, July 1977

List of Abbreviations

Cheka	Chrezvychainaia Komissiia pri sovet Narodnykh Komissarov po borbe s kontrrevoliutsiei i sabotazhem (Extraordinary Commission for Combating Counter-revolution and Sabotage attached to the Council of People's Commissars)
Goelro	Gosudarstvennaia Komissiia po Elektrifikatsii Rossii (State Commission for the Electrification of Russia)
Gosplan	Gosudarstvennaia Obshcheplanovaia Komissiia (State General Planning Commission)
Kombedy	Komitety Bednoty (Committees of Poor Peasants)
NEP	Novaia Ekonomicheskaia Politika (New Economic Policy)
Rabkrin	Narodnyi Komissariat Rabochei i Krestianskoi Inspektsii (People's Commissariat of Workers' and Peasants' Inspection)
RKP(b)	Rossiiskaia Communisticheskaia Partiia (Bolshevikov) (Russian Communist Party (Bolsheviks))
RSFSR	Rossiiskaia Sotsialisticheskaia Federativnaia Sovetskaia Respublika (Russian Socialist Federal Soviet Republic)
Sovnarkom	Sovet Narodnykh Komissarov (Council of People's Commissars)
SR	Sotsial-Revoliutsioner (Social-Revolutionary)
SSSR	Soiuz Sovetskikh Sotsialisticheskikh Respublik (Union of Soviet Socialist Republics)
TsIK	Tsentralnyi Ispolnitelnyi Komitet (Central Executive Committee)
Vikzhel	Vserossiiskii Ispolnitelnyi Komitet Soiuza Zheleznodoro-zhnikov (All-Russian Executive Committee of Union of Railwaymen)
VSNKh	Vysshii Sovet Narodnogo Khoziaistva (Supreme Council of National Economy)
VTsIK	Vserossiiskii (Vsesoiuznyi) Tsentralnyi Ispolnitelnyi Komitet (All-Russian (All-Union) Central Executive Committee)

1
The Bolshevik Government's First Steps

On 25 October (7 November) the Bolsheviks took control in Petrograd. When Lenin came out of hiding after nearly four months, he said to Trotsky: 'You know, from persecution and life underground, to come so suddenly into power . . .' – he paused for the right word. 'Es schwindet (it makes one giddy)', he concluded, changing suddenly to German, and circling his hand around his head.[1]

Lenin himself was in doubt as to how long the Bolsheviks would be able to hold power. Capitalist, Menshevik and Socialist Revolutionary circles were convinced that they could not survive for more than a few days. 'We are absolutely certain that the Bolsheviks will not be able to organize state power,' wrote *Izvestiia*, the official paper of the Soviets, whose last issue, the day after the revolution, was still controlled by the Mensheviks and Socialist Revolutionaries.[2]

S.N.Prokopovich, a minister in the Kerensky government, recalled a few years later: 'In Moscow the Rightists said openly: "Only let the Bolsheviks overthrow the power of the provisional government, and then it will be easy for us to cope with them." ' And he added: 'In the camps of both the right and the left I saw almost open rejoicing during those days over the boldness of the Bolsheviks.'[3] Another eye-witness, Stankevich, the Commissar of the provisional government at army headquarters, wrote of the mood on the right in the days after the October revolution: 'The conviction grew with every hour that the Bolsheviks would soon be liquidated.'[4]

The conservative daily *Novoe Vremia* wrote on the morning after the Bolsheviks assumed control:

Let us suppose for a moment that the Bolsheviks do gain the upper hand. Who will govern us then: the cooks perhaps, those connoisseurs of cutlets and beefsteaks? Or maybe the firemen? The stableboys, the chauffeurs? Or perhaps the nursemaids will rush off to meetings of the Council of State between the diaper-washing sessions? Who then? Where are the statesmen? Perhaps the mechanics will run the theaters, the plumbers foreign affairs, the carpenters, the post office. Who will it be? History alone will give a definitive answer to this mad ambition of the Bolsheviks.[5]

One conservative historian remembered: 'I never met anyone who doubted that the overthrow of the Bolsheviks was imminent. The only question was how and when.'[6] *Delo Naroda*, the daily paper of the Socialist Revolutionaries, wrote three days after the insurrection: 'The Bolshevik adventure . . . , like a soap bubble, will burst at the first contact with hard facts.'[7] And John Reed, who moved in a wide variety of social circles, provides similar testimony: 'That the Bolsheviki would remain in power longer than three days never occurred to anybody – except perhaps to Lenin, Trotsky, the Petrograd workers and the simple soldiers.'[8]

The capitalists, Mensheviks and Socialist Revolutionaries miscalculated, because, as the reliable witness Sukhanov points out: 'the Bolsheviks acted with the full backing of the Petersburg workers and soldiers.'[9] Similarly, Martov wrote to Axelrod on 6 (19) November 1917: 'Understand, please, that before us after all is a victorious uprising of the proletariat – almost the entire proletariat supports Lenin and expects its social liberation from the uprising.'[10]

The October insurrection was accompanied by very little resistance from the bourgeoisie; first, because the latter could not bring itself to believe that its 'natural rule' could be challenged by the proletariat; secondly, because it felt so isolated and estranged from the masses. It required the intervention of the Western imperialist powers to give the Russian bourgeoisie faith in itself and to encourage its resistance to Bolshevism.

The Congress of the Soviets

On 26 October (8 November), the Second All-Russian Congress of the Soviets opened at 11.45 p.m. Its social composition was very different from that of the earlier one. The June Congress was made up very largely of petty bourgeois elements. Intellectuals and army officers had been prominent. The October Congress was both younger and much more proletarian. As John Reed describes it:

> I stood there watching the new delegates come in – burly, bearded soldiers, workmen in black blouses, a few long-haired peasants. The girl in charge – a member of Plekhanov's Edinstvo group – smiled contemptuously. 'These are very different people from the delegates to the first Sezd,' she remarked. 'See how rough and ignorant they look! The Dark People . . .' It was true; the depths of Russia had been stirred, and it was the bottom which came uppermost now.'[11]

The political composition of the second Congress was also very different from that of the first. Whereas the Socialist Revolutionaries and Mensheviks had predominated in the June Congress, now the majority of the delegates were followers of Bolshevism. The Bolsheviks held some 390 seats out of a total of 650. The strength of the Socialist Revolutionaries was estimated variously as between 160 and 190. But these figures are misleading, since the party had split and most of the SR delegates were suporters of the Left SR Party, which was pro-Bolshevik at the time. The Mensheviks, who in June had accounted for more than 200 delegates, were now reduced to a mere 60-70, and these split into a number of groups. The Right SR and Mensheviks could count on less than 100 votes.

The Congress elected a new Executive. This consisted of 14 Bolsheviks, 7 Socialist Revolutionaries, 3 Mensheviks and 1 United Internationalist (from Maxim Gorky's group). The Right SR and Mensheviks at once declared that they would refuse to share executive power with the Bolsheviks.

Martov then mounted the rostrum and declared that the most urgent problem was to overcome the current crisis by peaceful means. The Bolsheviks, recognizing the need to expose the real nature of SR and Menshevik policy, did not oppose Martov's statement, despite the anti-Bolshevik tenor of his speech. 'The Bolsheviks had absolutely nothing against it; let the question of a peaceable settlement of the crisis be made the first item on the agenda. Martov's motion was voted on: against it – nobody.'[12]

However, the Right Mensheviks and Right SR leaders bluntly rejected collaboration with the 'party of insurrection'. Following their statement the entire Right – Mensheviks, Right SR and Jewish Bund – walked out of the Congress.

Martov continued to argue as if nothing had happened, and went on to preach conciliation. Trotsky then rounded on him:

> Now we are told: renounce your victory, make concessions, compromise. With whom? I ask: with whom ought we to compromise? With those wretched groups who have left us or who are making this proposal? But after all we've had a full view of them. No one in Russia is with them any longer. A compromise is supposed to be made, as between two equal sides, by the millions of workers and peasants represented in this Congress, whom they are ready, not for the first time or the last, to barter away as the bourgeoisie sees fit. No, here no compromise is possible. To those who have left and to those who tell us to do this we must say: you are miserable bankrupts, your role is played out; go where you ought to be: into the dustbin of history!
>
> 'Then we'll leave,' Martov shouted from the platform amidst stormy applause for Trotsky.[18]

The meeting went on to elect a new Central Executive Committee of the Soviet Congress (VTsIK), i.e. a legislative committee to operate between sessions of the Congress. The Bolsheviks were allowed 67 seats, the Left SR 29; 20 seats were divided among minor groups, including 6 United Internationalists.

The Congress also set up a new government – the Council of People's Commissars (Sovnarkom). The Left SRs refused to join it, arguing that this would enable them to mediate between the Bolsheviks on the one side and the Right SRs and Mensheviks on the other, so as to promote a wider coalition.

The composition of the Sovnarkum was as follows:
Chairman of the Council – Vladimir Ulianov (Lenin)
People's Commissar of the Interior – A.I.Rykov
Agriculture – V.P.Miliutin
Labour – A.G.Shliapnikov
Army and Navy Affairs – a committee consisting of
V.A.Ovseenko (Antonov), N.V.Krylenko and P.Y.Dybenko
Commerce and Industry – V.P.Nogin

Education – A.V.Lunacharsky
Finance – I.I.Skvortsov (Stepanov)
Foreign Affairs – L.D.Bronstein (Trotsky)
Justice – G.I.Oppokov (Lomov)
Food – I.A.Teodorovich
Posts and Telegraphy – N.P.Avilov (Glebov)
Chairman of Nationalities Affairs – J.V.Dzhugashvili (Stalin)
The post of People's Commissar for Railways was deliberately left open in the hope of reaching an agreement with the Central Executive Committee of the Railway Workers' Union (Vikzhel), which was insistent on the formation of a broad all-socialist government.*

Decrees, Decrees, Decrees...

In the first few days and weeks after coming to power, Lenin dealt with the numerous problems of economic, political and cultural life, by issuing a series of decrees. Eighteen months later, on 23 March 1919, he told the Eighth Congress of the party:

> Decrees are instructions which call for practical work on a mass scale. That is what is important. Let us assume that decrees do contain much that is useless, much that in practice cannot be put into effect; but they contain material for practical action, and the purpose of a decree is to teach practical steps to the hundreds, thousands and millions of people who heed the voice of the Soviet government. This is a trial in practical action in the sphere of socialist construction ... If we treat matters in this way we shall acquire a good deal from the sum total of our laws, decrees and ordinances. We shall not regard them as absolute injunctions which must be put into effect instantly and at all costs.[14]

Lenin's energy knew no bounds.

> Untiringly, he presided, five or six hours at a stretch, over the meetings of the Council of People's Commissars, which at that period took place every day; he directed the debates passing from subject to subject ... As a rule, the topics of discussion were put on the agenda without any previous preparation, and ... always demanding extreme urgency. Very often neither the

---

* See, further, Chapter 2 below.

chairman nor the commissars were familiar with the essentials of a problem until it became the subject of the debate.[15]

Lenin was a strict chairman of Sovnarkom meetings. To this end he drafted the following standing orders:

1. For those making reports – 10 minutes.
2. For speakers, the first time 5 minutes, the second time 3 minutes.
3. To speak not more than twice.
4. On a point of order, 1 for and 1 against, each for one minute.
5. Exceptions by *special* rulings of the Sovnarkom.[16]

At these meetings Lenin had a habit of sending scribbled notes on tiny bits of paper to members of the government asking for information on this or that point. His summary of the discussion was usually the basis for the subsequent decree. Trotsky quite rightly wrote: 'The collection of Soviet decrees forms in a certain sense a part, and not a negligible part, of the Complete Works of Vladimir Ilyich Lenin.'[17]

As there were no precedents, improvisation played a central role in drafting the decrees. Lenin's creative imagination was indispensable to the legislative work. This huge task was carried out under extremely difficult conditions, the founder of the new state having not even the most ordinary facilities for work. Typewriters were a great rarity in Smolny (the headquarters of the Soviets). There were no shorthand writers. The People's Commissars had to write out their decrees and proclamations in their own hand.

Everybody was extremely inexperienced. For instance, the newly appointed Director of the State Bank, S.S.Pestovsky, describes in his memoirs how he happened to get the job. A non-Bolshevik and former member of the SR party, he was visiting Smolny. He entered a room.

The room was rather large. In one corner the Secretary of the Sovnarkom, Comrade N.P.Gorbunov, was working at a small table . . . Farther on, Comrade Menzhinsky, looking very tired, was lounging on a sofa . . . over [which] was the sign: 'The People's Commissariat of Finance'.
I sat down near Menzhinsky and began to talk with him. In the most innocent way he started to question me about my earlier career and became curious in regard to my past studies.

I answered . . . that I had worked at the University of London, where, among other subjects, I had studied finance.

Menzhinsky suddenly arose, fixed his eyes upon me, and categorically declared: In that case we shall make you the director of the State Bank.

I was frightened and answered . . . that I had no desire to hold this position, since it was entirely 'outside my line'. Saying nothing, Menzhinsky asked me to wait, and left the room.

He was gone for some time, and then returned with a paper signed by Ilyich [Lenin] on which it was stated that I was the director of the State Bank.

I became even more dumbfounded, and began to beg Menzhinsky to revoke the appointment, but he remained inflexible on this point.[18]

And what were the qualifications of Menzhinsky himself to be People's Commissar of Finance? It seems 'he had once been a clerk in a French bank.'[19]

The qualifications of the Secretary of the Council of People's Commissars were also questionable. N.P.Gorbunov, a young man of 25, describes how one day he was called by V.D.Bonch-Bruevich, Lenin's secretary.

I went to him and, without any explanation, he dragged me upstairs to the third floor into the small corner room where Vladimir Ilyich worked in those first days . . . I saw Vladimir Ilyich who greeted me and to my astonishment, said, 'You will be the secretary of the Sovnarkom'. I received no instructions from him at that time. I knew absolutely nothing about my job or about secretarial duties in general. Somewhere I commandered a typewriter on which, for quite a long time, I had to bang out documents with two fingers; no typist could be found.

The office furniture consisted of one desk. Lenin called him into the first cabinet meeting to take the minutes even though he knew no shorthand and his spelling was imperfect.[20]

One result of the rush to issue decrees and proclamations was that formalities were abandoned. As Iu.Larin, a member of VTsIK and chief of the Bureau of Legislation of Sovnarkom, remembers:

Of the first fifteen decrees which are found in No.1 of the Collection of Laws (Sobranie Uzakonenii i Rasporiazhenii Rabochego i Kristianskogo Pravitelstva) only two were actually

B

considered by the Sovnarkom . . . I remember Lenin's astonishment when he first saw . . . the decree No.12, under his signature, which conferred legislative powers on the Sovnarkom (the Congress of Soviets granted only executive powers).[21]

The Decree on Peace

The first decree drafted by Lenin, which was issued the day after the insurrection by the newly formed government, was the decree on peace. The new workers' and peasants' government

> calls upon all the belligerent peoples and their governments to start immediate negotiations for a just, democratic peace.
> . . . by such a peace the government means an immediate peace without annexations (i.e. without the seizure of foreign lands, without the forcible incorporation of foreign nations) and without indemnities . . .
> The government considers it the greatest of crimes against humanity to continue this war over the issue of how to divide among the strong and rich nations the weak nationalities they have conquered, and solemnly announces its determination immediately to sign terms of peace to stop this war on the terms indicated, which are equally just for all nationalities without exception . . .
> The government abolishes secret diplomacy, and, for its part, announces its firm intention to conduct all negotiations quite openly in full view of the whole people. It will proceed immediately with the full publication of the secret treaties endorsed or concluded by the government of landowners and capitalists from February to 25 October 1917. The government proclaims the unconditional and immediate annulment of everything contained in those secret treaties insofar as it is aimed, as is mostly the case, at securing advantages and privileges for the Russian landowners and capitalists and at the retention, or extension, of the annexations made by the Great Russians.[22]

The Decree on Land

Another decree of world historical importance, that on land, was issued on the same day as the decree on peace. This was also drafted by Lenin.

> *Private ownership of land shall be abolished for ever*; land shall not be sold, purchased, leased, mortgaged, or otherwise alienated.

All land, whether *state, crown, monastery, church, factory, entailed, private, public, peasant, etc., shall be confiscated without compensation* and become the property of the whole people, and pass into the use of all those who cultivate it . . .

Lands on which *high-level scientific* farming is practised – orchards, plantations, seed plots, nurseries, hothouses, etc. – *shall not be divided up, but shall be converted into model farms,* to be turned over for exclusive use *to the state or to the communes,* depending on the size and importance of such lands . . .

The right to use the land shall be accorded to all citizens of the Russian state (without distinction of sex) desiring to cultivate it by their own labour, with the help of their families, or in partnership, but only as long as they are able to cultivate it. The employment of hired labour is not permitted . . .

Land tenure shall be on an equality basis, i.e. the land shall be distributed among the working people in conformity with a labour standard or a subsistence standard, depending on local conditions.[23]

Lenin's tactical adaptability shows itself at its best in the Decree on Land Reform. Unashamedly he adopted the SR programme:

The Socialist Revolutionaries fumed and raved [Lenin wrote], protested and howled that 'the Bolsheviks had stolen their programme', but they were only laughed at for that; a fine party, indeed, which had to be defeated and driven from the government in order that everything in its programme that was revolutionary and of benefit to the working people could be carried out![24]

The Right of the Peoples of Russia to Self-Determination

Another long-standing element in the programme of Bolshevism was the right of oppressed nations to freedom. On 2 (15) November, Sovnarkom issued a decree, to this effect, including the following principles:

1. Equality and sovereignty of the peoples of Russia.
2. The right of the peoples of Russia to free self-determination, up to secession and formation of an independent state.
3. Abolition of all and any national and national-religious privileges and restrictions.
4. Free development of national minorities and ethnic groups inhabitating Russia.[25]

The Decree on Workers' Control

A decree on workers' control was drafted by Lenin and issued by Sovnarkom on 14 (27) November:

> In order to provide planned regulation of the national economy, workers' control over the manufacture, purchase, sale and storage of produce and raw materials and over the financial activity of enterprises is introduced in all industrial, commercial, banking, agricultural, cooperative and other enterprises which employ hired labour or give work to be done at home.
>
> Workers' control is exercised by all the workers of the given enterprise through their elected bodies, such as factory committees, shop stewards' councils, etc., whose members include representatives of the office employees and the technical personnel.
>
> In every city, *guberniia* and industrial district a local workers' control council is set up which, being an agency of the Soviet of Workers', Soldiers' and Peasants' deputies, is composed of representatives of trade unions, factory and office workers' committees, and workers' cooperatives . . .
>
> Decisions of workers' control bodies are binding upon the owners of enterprises and may be revoked only by higher workers' control bodies . . .
>
> The All-Russia Workers' Control Council works out general plans of workers' control, issues instructions and ordinances, regulates relationships between district workers' control councils, and serves as the highest instance for all matters pertaining to workers' control.[26]

Many, Many Other Decrees

On 21 November (4 December) a decree on the right of recall, also drafted by Lenin, was issued by Sovnarkom:

> No elective institution or representative assembly can be regarded as being truly democratic and really representative of the people's will unless the electors' right to recall those elected is accepted and exercised. This fundamental principle of true democracy applies to all representative assemblies without exception.[27]

On 22 November (5 December) Sovnarkom issued a decree on the judiciary. The old judges were removed from office and replaced by new ones who were to be elected either by the Soviets or by popular vote. Former laws were to be valid 'only inasmuch as they are not abolished by the revolution and do not contradict revolutionary consciousness and a revolutionary sense of right'. This statement was supplemented by a provision to the effect that all laws that conflicted with decrees of the Soviet government and with the minimum programme of the Bolshevik and Socialist Revolutionary Party should be considered invalid.

Two decrees dated 16 (29) and 18 (31) December swept aside the marriage and divorce laws. According to these decrees only civil marriage was to be recognized by the state; children born out of wedlock were to be given the same rights as the offspring of marriage; divorce was to be had for the asking by either spouse. The new laws emphasized the full equality of men and women.[28]

The complete separation of church from state and school from church was decreed by a law promulgated on 2 February 1918. Under this law every Soviet citizen was free to profess any or no religion; no religious ceremonies were to be performed in connection with any state function; religious teaching was forbidden in schools; churches and religious societies were denied the right to own property.[29]

Alongside decrees on subjects of major importance, one finds Lenin dealing with a vast quantity of regulations affecting details of local administration, such as the uniting of some suburbs with the town of Bogorodsk, the assignment of 450,000 rubles (a negligible sum at the time) for the needs of the population of Kremenchug County in Ukraine which had suffered a flood, and the appointment and dismissal of individual officials.[30]

He involved himself with the most trivial affairs. Thus in March 1918 he asks why the clerks in the Moscow post office are required to work such long hours.[31] Then comes a string of complaints at the arbitrary requisitioning of property. In July 1918, as the war clouds gather in the east, he writes to one Ivanov, in a village between Kazan and the Urals: 'It is alleged that you have requisitioned some writing materials, including a table, belonging to the stationmaster. Return these objects at once. Telegraph your explanations.'

History, unfortunately, does not record the fate of the stationmaster's table, nor that of the bicycle belonging to the pharmacist at Zhlobin, which calls for two letters from the solicitous

Lenin.[32] At the time Lenin had at his disposal only the most rudimentary secretarial organization, and his communications system was likewise primitive; he was forever complaining about his malfunctioning telephone.

The Soviet Government Fighting for Survival

The stream of legislation was a product of the immediate struggle of the new regime for survival. There is no doubt that the decrees on peace and land won the new government mass popularity. However, the pen of the legislator had to be accompanied by the sword of the soldier, and for days, weeks, months, even years, the fate of the new regime hung in the balance.

During the week following the seizure of power the Bolsheviks had to face an uprising of the cadets at the military school in Petrograd, and to defend the capital against the movement of troops which Kerensky was trying to organize, which got under way while the Second Congress of Soviets was still in session.

On 26 October (8 November) General P.N.Krasnov, Commander of the Third Cavalry Corps, which had participated in Kornilov's luckless adventure, started to march on Petrograd on Kerensky's orders. Next day his forces occupied Gatchina, 27 miles from Petrograd. The day after, early in the morning, Krasnov advanced on Tsarskoe Selo, 15 miles from the capital.

On 30 October (12 November) Krasnov's Cossacks met strong resistance from a Bolshevik-led unit of sailors on the Pulkovo Heights, just outside the city limits. The Bolsheviks achieved the first military victory in the civil war, and Krasnov was forced to retreat to Gatchina.

On 2 (15) November Bolshevik troops stormed Gatchina. Krasnov was arrested and brought to Smolny under guard. The revolution was still a mild one at this stage. Krasnov was soon released, after giving his word not to take arms against the government again. (He broke his promise, and made his way to the Don where the following spring he became leader of the Cossack White Army movement.)

But even with military victory assured in Petrograd, Bolshevik rule was still limited to a tiny area of Russia – taking power in Moscow was much more difficult. After the Bolshevik victory in

Petrograd on 25 October, it took another eight long days to achieve power in Moscow, by means of a very bloody battle. Before October, for various reasons, Moscow was more difficult to win over to Bolshevism than Petrograd. It was more isolated from the front, it did not have Petrograd's rebellious soldiers and sailors, it suffered much less from food shortages. The Moscow proletariat was dispersed among smaller factories compared with the huge plants in Petrograd.[38] In the years when Bolshevism became a mass workers' party (1912-1914) Moscow lagged far behind Petrograd. As late as October 1917, the Socialist Revolutionaries had a large following among the workers of Moscow, while their influence among the workers of Petrograd was practically non-existent.

The most brilliant Bolshevik leaders, including Lenin and Trotsky, were in Petrograd. The Moscow leadership was split (as indeed was that of Petrograd). Bukharin took the same line as Lenin and Trotsky, while Nogin and Rykov hesitated and vacillated. It was only on 25 October (7 November) that a Military Revolutionary Committee was established in Moscow, and this consisted at first of 4 Bolsheviks, 2 Mensheviks and 1 United Internationalist. The Mensheviks openly declared that they were joining the Military Revolutionary Committee in order to obstruct its work. (They soon withdrew from it.) Only on 26 October (8 November) did a conference of representatives of the garrison convene. Hesitations and delays cost the Moscow proletariat dear. While only five people died in Petrograd during the insurrection, many hundreds of soldiers and workers lost their lives in the struggle in the ancient capital of Moscow.

Moscow was the only place in central and northern Russia where the Bolshevik seizure of power met persistent and violent resistance. Elsewhere the course of the transfer of power to the Soviets varied from place to place depending on such factors as the proportion of industrial workers in the population, the mood of the local garrison and the strength of the local Bolshevik Party organization.

In the central industrial region and the Urals the Bolsheviks took control quickly and easily straight after the October insurrection in Petrograd. Thus in Ivanovo-Voznesensk, 'the Russian Manchester', the Bolsheviks achieved their objectives 'in the most painless manner . . . without firing a single shot or shedding a single drop of blood'. The news of the Petrograd coup was announced to an enthusiastic meeting of the town's municipal council and the revolutionary council was established.[34]

At Cheliabinsk and Ekaterinburg and other cities the Bolsheviks took over almost without meeting any resistance.[35] In such middle and lower Volga towns as Nizhni Novgorod, Samara and Saratov, as well as those on the Trans-Siberian railway (Krasnoiarsk, Irkutsk), 'the October days . . . took the form of a brief confrontation'.[36] In the north west, in White Russia, the troops were solidly Bolshevik and the transfer of power was very smooth indeed.

In non-industrial provincial centres, such as Penza and Simbirsk, the setting up of an unambiguously Bolshevik regime took place slowly and was only completed in December.

In the industrialized eastern and south eastern regions of the Ukraine, where the Russian population was quite large and Ukrainian nationalism had few roots, the Bolsheviks seized power quite easily. On 31 November (7 December), the Soviet of Kharkov, the largest city in eastern Ukraine, passed a resolution demanding an All-Ukrainian Congress of Soviets to be the repository of power. In the western part of the Ukraine, whose capital was Kiev, and where the industrial working class and Bolshevik organization were relatively weak and nationalism strong, power remained in the hands of the petty bourgeoisie of the Rada.

When at the Third Congress of Soviets (8 (21)-18 (31) January 1918) the Bolsheviks proclaimed the establishment of the Russian Federated Soviet Republic (RSFSR) they were actually in control of only a fragment, albeit a substantial fragment, of the former empire. They held the two capitals, the central and northern part of European Russia, and, more precariously, a few towns in Siberia and central Asia.

In the west the armies of the Central Powers occupied a vast area stretching from the Dniester to beyond the Gulf of Riga. Further north, in Finland, a bourgeois government was waging a bloody civil war against the revolt of the Social Democrats, who were aided by the Bolsheviks. In the south a newly formed nationalist bourgeois government of the Caucasus and the Trans-Volga regions was fighting the extension of Bolshevik power with varying degrees of success. In the south east the first White Guards, under the command of Kornilov, Kaledin, Alekseev and Denikin, moved into action on the Don; and the Cossacks of Orenburg rose under Ataman Dutov.

Fighting Sabotage

While the Bolsheviks had to deal with the external threat of General Krasnov's march on Petrograd, those inside the capital had to deal with another enemy no less dangerous – the saboteurs within. On 27 October (9 November) a general strike of all state employees was called in Petrograd, and almost all the officials and clerks of public institutions came out.

The employees of the Ministries of Agriculture, Labour, Posts and Telegraphs, Food, Finance and Foreign Affairs went on strike. So did the teachers. By 15 (28) December, more than 30,000 Petrograd teachers were on strike. They were joined by the workers in the public libraries and the People's Houses and by 50,000 bank clerks. These strikes confronted the new rulers with grave difficulties.

The telegraphists and telephonists also stopped work. Telegraphy was the only quick means of communication across the huge distances of Russia. These workers were very much under the influence of the Mensheviks and Socialist Revolutionaries. Most of the telegraphists refused to work for the Bolshevik intruders, so it was left to a group of sailors from Kronstadt to struggle with the apparatus in an attempt to inform the country about Lenin's first decrees on peace and land. They soon found that they could not cope with the tasks: some of the machinery and the supply of current had been sabotaged.

The Bolsheviks put up a large placard outside the telegraph office, explaining what had happened and asking for assistance. Eventually, after angry Bolshevik sympathizers from the factories had arrived and intimated the telegraphists, some of them returned to their posts.[37]

Similar difficulties were encountered at the telephone offices. According to John Reed, 'Smolny was cut off, and the Duma and the Committee for Salvation were in constant communication with all the *yunker* schools and with Kerensky at Tsarskee.'[38] The Bolsheviks found it was very difficult to operate the telephone system.

> Only half a dozen trained operators were available. Volunteers were called for; a hundred responded, sailors, soldiers, workers. The six girls scurried backwards and forwards, instructing, helping, scolding . . . So, crippled, halting, but *going*, the wires began to hum. The first thing was to connect Smolny with the barracks and the factories; the second, to cut off the Duma and the *junker* schools.[39]

Another group of workers who threatened to sabotage Bolshevik rule was the one million railwaymen. The social composition of the railway employees was complex and hierarchical. At the top of the hierarchy were the civil service employees in the administrative headquarters of the railway networks, and the owners and managers of the private companies. Next came the engineers, planners, statisticians and the less important office workers. These two groups represented between 16 and 17 per cent of all those employed on the railways.[40]

The group which ran the railway union was the Vikzhel. Its composition was: 12 senior administrative staff, 10 engineers and technicians, 3 lawyers, 2 doctors, 3 office workers, 2 engine crew and 8 clerical staff and workers.

Thus Vikzhel's support came chiefly from the middle and higher ranks of the railway employees, who were influenced by the two main moderate socialist parties, the SRs and the Mensheviks. The Bolsheviks were an insignficant minority. The members included 2 Bolsheviks, 14 Socialist Revolutionaries, 7 Mensheviks, 3 Socialist-Populists and 11 non-party representatives, many of whom supported the Cadets.[41]*

The railwaymen, who had played a central role in crushing the Kornilov coup, now, after the October insurrection, presented the Bolsheviks with an ultimatum: unless they entered a coalition

---

* The main group of railwaymen supporting the Bolsheviks were those working in railway workshops and depots – who made up 35 per cent of all railwaymen – but they had opted out of the All-Russian Union by joining the more radical trade unions of the metal workers and joiners.[42]

with the Socialist Revolutionaries and Mensheviks the Vikzhel would launch a general strike, whose consequences could have been very grave indeed (as we shall see later).

It was only after 78 days (on 13 (26) January 1918) that the strike of public employees in Petrograd came to end. In Moscow the strike of the 16,000 municipal employees was to last four months.

The Beginning of Red Terror

The military cadets whom the Bolsheviks had released on parole from the Winter Palace on 26 October (8 November) betrayed their trust two days later and staged an uprising. Similarly mild treatment was shown to General Krasnov, which he also repaid with treason.

Lenin wrote on 5 (18) November:

> We are accused of resorting to terrorism, but we have not resorted, and I hope will not resort, to the terrorism of the French revolutionaries who guillotined unarmed men. I hope we shall not resort to it, because we have strength on our side. When we arrested anyone we told him we would let him go if he gave us a written promise not to engage in sabotage. Such written promises have been given.[48]

Victor Serge, in his *Year One of the Russian Revolution* wrote of the events in Moscow:

> The Whites surrendered at 4 p.m. on 2 [15] November. 'The Committee of Public Safety is dissolved. The White Guard surrenders its arms and is disbanded. The officers may keep the sidearms that distinguish their rank. Only such weapons as are necessary for practice may be kept in the military academies ... The MRC [Military Revolutionary Committee] guarantees the liberty and inviolability of all.' Such were the principal clauses of the armistice signed between Reds and Whites. The fighters of the counter-revolution, butchers of the Kremlin, who in victory would have shown no quarter whatever to the Reds – we have seen proof – *went free.*

And Serge comments:

> Foolish clemency! These very Junkers, these officers, these students, these socialists of counter-revolution, dispersed themselves throughout the length and breadth of Russia, and there organ-

ized the civil war. The revolution was to meet them again, at Iaroslavl, on the Don, at Kazan, in the Crimea, in Siberia and in every conspiracy nearer home.[44]

These were the early days of revolutionary innocence. But Lenin was not a pacifist. The morning after the October insurrection, on Kamenev's initiative and in Lenin's absence, the death penalty was abolished. When he learned about this first piece of legislation, Lenin was very angry. 'How can one make a revolution without firing squads? Do you think you will be able to deal with all your enemies by laying down your arms? What other means of repression do you have? Imprisonment? No one attaches any importance to this during a civil war when each side hopes to win.'

'It is a mistake,' he went on, 'an inadmissible weakness, a pacifist illusion', and much more. 'Do you really think that we shall come out victorious without any revolutionary terror?'[45]

At the Fifth Congress of Soviets (July 1918) he repeated the point: 'a revolutionary who does not want to be a hypocrite cannot renounce capital punishment. There has never been a revolution or a period of civil war without shootings.'[46]

To organize the struggle against counter-revolution, on 7 (20) December 1917 Sovnarkom established the Cheka, the All-Russian Extraordinary Commission to fight Counter-revolution and Sabotage. At first its staff was small, its resources very limited, and the few death sentences it passed were on common criminals. M.I.Latsis, member of the Cheka in 1918, states that during the first six months of its existence, the Cheka had 22 people shot.[47]

The revolutionary terror in Russia, like its predecessor in France during *its* great revolution, was a reaction to foreign invasion and the immensity of the threat to the revolution. The Paris terror of 2 September 1793 followed the Duke of Brunswick's proclamation threatening foreign invasion and ruthless repression of the revolution.

It was foreign invasion, starting with the victories of the Czechoslovak troops over the Red Army in June 1918, that threatened the greatest danger to the Soviet republic. On 20 June the popular Bolshevik orator, Volodarsky, was assassinated by counter-revolutionaries. On 30 August an attempt was made on Lenin's life. He was badly wounded and for a few days was in a critical condition. Another Bolshevik leader, Uritsky, the President of the Petrograd Cheka, was murdered. The Red terror was unleashed in retaliation. On 2 September 500 hostages were shot in Petrograd. Whereas between September 1917 and June 1918 the Cheka had executed 22 people, in the second half of 1918 more than 6,000 executions took place.[48] September 1918, writes E. H. Carr, 'marked the turning-point after which the terror, hitherto sporadic and unorganized, became a deliberate instrument of policy.'[49]

Compared with the White terror, however, the Red terror was mild. Thus in Finland alone, in April 1918 between 10 and 20,000 workers were slaughtered by the counter-revolutionaries.[50] With complete justification Lenin told the Seventh Congress of Soviets on 5 December 1919:

> The terror was forced on us by the terror of the Entente, the terror of mighty world capitalism which has been throttling the workers and peasants, and is condemning them to death by starvation because they are fighting for their country's freedom.[51]

One should not exaggerate the effectiveness of the Cheka and the Red terror during the civil war. The following incident illustrates this. On 19 January 1919, Lenin was in a car with his sister Maria, driven by his chauffeur, S.K.Gil, who tells the story. The car was moving slowly through the snow, when they heard a shout, 'Stop'. Gil accelerated. A few blocks further on, several men were standing in the middle of the road with revolvers in their hands, and shouted, 'Halt!' Gil, seeing this was not a patrol, drove straight at them. 'Stop, or we shoot,' one of the men yelled. Gil wanted to speed past, but Lenin told him to stop.

'Halt! Stop the car!' the men ordered.

Lenin opened the door and said, 'What's the matter?'

'Get out, shut up,' came the reply.

He grabbed Lenin by his sleeve and pulled him out. Lenin showed his pass, with photograph and name and said, 'What's the matter comrades? Who are you?'

One of the armed men searched Lenin's pocket and took his wallet and a small Browning. Maria exclaimed, 'What right have you to search him? Why, he is Comrade Lenin. Show your papers!'

'We don't need papers,' somebody replied, 'We can do anything.'

Gil, who had remained at the wheel, with his revolver cocked, did not dare use it.

The hold-up group now asked Gil to leave the car. When he obeyed, they all got in and drove off.

Nearby stood the building of the Sokolniky Soviet. They walked over to phone the Kremlin for a car. But the watchman would not let them in. He asked Lenin for his pass.

'I am Lenin,' Lenin said, 'but I cannot prove it. I have just been robbed of my pass.'

The watchman looked sceptical. Gil showed his identification, which served for all of them. Inside they found nobody. In a small room they awakened a sleeping telephone operator, who rang the Kremlin. A car came.[52]

Relying on the Initiative of the Masses

The enormous legislative activity associated with the urgent task of self-defence against counter-revolution, and the creation of effective armed forces and an organ of revolutionary terror in the midst of total chaos, were possible only because Lenin and the Bolshevik leaders knew that their actions merged completely with those of the masses in shaping a new historical epoch.

'Miracles of proletarian organization must be achieved.' This idea of Lenin's was central to the actions of the Government, the party and the proletariat. The initiative of the masses was the most important factor. Lenin wrote:

> One of the most important tasks today, if not the most important, is to develop this independent initiative of the workers, and of all the working and exploited people generally, develop it as widely as possibly in creative *organizational* work . . . There is a great deal of talent among the people. It is merely suppressed. It must be given an opportunity to display itself. It *and it alone*, with the support of the people, can save Russia and save the cause of socialism.[53]

'We must be guided by experience; we must allow complete freedom to the creative faculties of the masses', Lenin declared to the Second Congress of the Soviets the day after the October revolution.[54] 'Creative activity at the grass roots is the basic factor of the new public life . . . living, creative socialism is the product of the masses themselves.'[55] One should not worry at all about mistakes. The mistakes of the masses were in themselves creative. 'Let there be mistakes—they would be the mistakes of a new class creating a new way of life . . . There was not and could not be a definite plan for the organization of economic life. Nobody could provide one. But it could be done from below, by the masses, through their experience.'[56] The building of a new society, Lenin declared at the Third Congress of Soviets on 11 (24) January 1918,

> will entail many difficulties, sacrifices and mistakes; it is something new, unprecedented in history and cannot be studied from books. It goes without saying that this is the greatest and most difficult transition that has ever occurred in history.[57]
> . . . socialism . . . for the first time creates the opportunity for employing it on a really *wide* and on a really *mass* scale, for actually drawing the majority of working people into a field of labour in which they can display their abilities, develop the capacities, and reveal those talents, so abundant among the people whom capitalism crushed, suppressed and strangled in thousands and millions.[58]

Above all Lenin made it clear that the strength of a workers' state is rooted in the strength of the proletariat. 'Our idea is that a state is strong when the people are politically conscious. It is strong when the people know everything, can form an opinion of everything and do everything consciously,' Lenin said to the Second Congress of Soviets, summing up the debate on the Decree on Peace.

The Close Relationship of
the Leaders and the Mass of Workers
The closeness of the relationship between the masses and the leadership is well conveyed in a scene described by John Reed. Trotsky was reporting to the Petrograd Soviet on the progress of the fighting:

> 'The cruisers, *Oleg*, *Avrora* and *Respublika* are anchored in the Neva, their guns trained on the approaches to the city . . .'

'Why aren't you out there with the Red Guards?' shouted a rough voice.

'I'm going now!' answered Trotsky, and left the platform.[59]

Another scene illustrates how the leaders had to accommodate the feelings of the masses: V.A.Antonov-Ovsenko, Joint People's Commissar of War and Navy, needed a car to go and inspect the revolutionary front on 28 October (10 November) 1917.

Antonov stood in the middle of the street and signalled a passing machine, driven by a soldier.

'I want that machine,' said Antonov.

'You won't get it,' responded the soldier.

'Do you know who I am?' Antonov produced a paper upon which was written that he had been appointed Commander-in-Chief of all the armies of the Russian Republic, and that everyone should obey him without question.

'I don't care if you're the devil himself,' said the soldier, hotly. 'This machine belongs to the First Machine-Gun Regiment, and we're carrying ammunition in it, and you can't have it.'[60]

2
The Consolidation of Power

At the Congress of Soviets on 29 October (11 November), the representative of the All-Russian Executive Committee of the Union of Railway Workers (Vikzhel), which contained a majority of Mensheviks and Socialist Revolutionaries, declared its opposition to the seizure of power by the Bolsheviks; he demanded a government composed of all socialist parties; declared Vikzhel's intention to keep control of the railways, and threatened that if a coalition government were not constituted it would call a general strike throughout the country.

At this critical moment a number of leading comrades in his own party ranged themselves against Lenin, demanding that the Bolsheviks should relinquish power to a coalition of all socialist parties. Before the October insurrection, the leaders of the right wing of Bolshevism (Zinoviev, Kamenev, Rykov, Nogin, Lunacharsky) had argued that the uprising was premature and would meet defeat. After the victorious insurrection they argued that the Bolsheviks would not be able to retain power unless they entered a coalition with the Mensheviks and Socialist Revolutionaries.

At the insistence of the Right Bolsheviks, negotiations were begun with these parties immediately after the insurrection. The parties overthrown by the October insurrection demanded a majority for themselves, and the exclusion from power of Lenin and Trotsky, as those responsible for the October 'adventure'. These conditions amounted to a demand for the Bolsheviks to declare the October revolution null and void, and to excommunicate the inspirer and the organizer of the insurrection. The Right Bolshevik leaders were inclined to accept these demands.

Lenin did not oppose the negotiations with the Mensheviks and Socialist Revolutionaries, on condition that the Bolsheviks were assured a stable majority, and that these parties recognized the Soviet state, the peace decree, the land decree, and so on. He was convinced that nothing would come of the negotiations, and that they could serve as an important lesson for those who had illusions about the soft option of a coalition government.

At a meeting of the Central Committee of the Bolsheviks, from which Lenin and Trotsky were absent, it was decided unanimously 'that the base of the government has to be widened and that some changes in its composition are possible'.

The question of whether to accept the Vikzhel's ultimatum – including the exclusion of Lenin and Trotsky from the government – was put to the vote. Four voted for: Kamenev, Miliutin, Rykov and Sokolnikov; and seven against: Ioffe, Dzerzhinsky, Vinter, A.Kollontai, Ia.Sverdlov, A.Bubnov, M.Uritsky.[1] The Committee then elected a delegation to attend the conference called by Vikzhel; significantly this consisted of three right-wing Bolsheviks: Kamenev, Sokolnikov and Riazanov.

On 1 (14) November the Bolshevik representative at the negotiations reported that the negotiations were going to a conference of the Central Committee, the Petrograd Committee and representatives of the military organization and the trade unions. Kamenev reported the demand of the Mensheviks, Socialist Revolutionaries and Vikzhel that the Central Executive Committee of the Soviets (TsIK) should be enlarged by the addition of a strong contingent of bourgeois representatives (the municipal councils [dumas] of Petrograd and Moscow), a demand which called into question the Soviet character of the new regime. The other condition, noted above, was the exclusion of Lenin and Trotsky from membership of the government.

> The Central Committee split wide open. Trotsky declared:
> 'One thing is clear from the report, and that is that the parties which took no part in the insurrection want to grab power from the people who overthrew them. There was no point in organizing the insurrection if we do not get the majority; if the others do not want that, it is obvious they do not want our programme. We must have 75 per cent. It is clear that we cannot give a right of objection, just as we cannot yield on Lenin's chairmanship; such a concession is completely unacceptable.'

Dzerzhinsky asserted that 'the delegates did not observe the CC's instructions. The CC definitely decided that the government must be responsible to the TsIK . . . We also stated definitely that we would not allow objections to Lenin and Trotsky. None of this was implemented and I propose an expression of no confidence in the delegation and that they be recalled and others sent.' The same hard line was taken by Uritsky. He considered that 'the CC has taken a firm stand on the position of all power to the Soviets and that means there can be no question of supplementation.'

He objected:

> to representation from the Dumas and considers that a majority of Bolsheviks in the TsIK is obligatory. This must be established conclusively. The same for ministerial posts; we must have a solid majority . . . there is no doubt that we must not yield on either Lenin or Trotsky, for in a certain sense this would be renunciation of our programme; there is no need to insist on the others.

Lenin then stated:

> it is time to make an end of vacillation. It is clear that Vikzhel is
> on the side of the Kaledins and the Kornilovs. There can be no
> wavering. The majority of the workers, peasants and army are
> for us. No one here has proved that the rank and file are against
> us; choose between Kaledin's agents and the rank and file. We
> must rely on the masses, and send agitators into the villages.

The right-wingers on the Central Committee, however,
were unyielding in their fight for a coalition. Rykov declared:
'. . . there is a gap between us . . . If we break off [the negotiations]
we will lose the groups which are supporting us as well and we
will be in no position to keep power. Kamenev conducted the
talks absolutely correctly.'

Miliutin raised 'the question of whether we are going to
insist on keeping power exclusively in our own hands . . . if we
do not get carried away . . . it will become clear to us that we
cannot sustain a long civil war.' Riazanov stated that he

> went in to these talks as a way out of the position we involun-
> tarily find ourselves in. Even in Peter, power is not in our hands
> but in the hands of the Soviet, and this has to be faced. If we
> abandon this course, we will be utterly and hopelessly alone. We
> made a mistake when we headed the government and insisted
> on names; if we had not done this, the middle levels of the
> bureaucracy would have supported us . . . If we reject agreement
> today, we will be without the Left SRs, without anything . . . an
> agreement is unavoidable.

After heated discussion the question, whether to break off
the talks or not, was put to the vote. The result was: for breaking
off 4; against 10. The intransigent Lenin, Trotsky and Sverdlov
found themselves in a minority,[2] and the Bolshevik delegates continued their efforts to form a coalition government.

On the same day as this debate in the enlarged Central Committee meeting, a debate on the same subject took place in the
Petersburg Committee of the party. Here again Lenin did not
mince his words:

> now, at such a moment, when we are in power, we are faced
> with a split. Zinoviev and Kamenev say that we will not seize
> power [in the country as a whole]. I am in no mood to listen to
> this calmly. I view this as treason . . . Zinoviev says that we are

not the Soviet power. We are, if you please, only the Bolsheviks, left alone since the departure of the Socialist Revolutionaries and the Mensheviks, and so forth and so on. But we are not responsible for that. We have been elected by the Congress of the Soviets ...

As for conciliation, I cannot even speak about that seriously, Trotsky long ago said that unification is impossible. Trotsky understood this, and from that time on there has been no better Bolshevik.

They [Zinoviev, Kamenev and co.] say that we will be unable to maintain our power alone, and so on. But we are not alone. The whole of Europe is before us. We must make the beginning.

Lenin went on to say, 'Our present slogan is: No compromise, i.e. for a homogeneous Bolshevik government.' He did not hesitate to use the threat, which he meant seriously, to 'appeal to the sailors': 'If you get the majority, take power in the Central Executive Committee and carry on. But we will go to the sailors.'

Opposing Lenin's views, Lunacharsky argued that a coalition government was a necessity. He pointed to the sabotage caried out by technical personnel as proof of the need for the Bolsheviks to join a coalition. 'We cannot manage with our own forces. Famine will break out.'

Similar arguments were used by Nogin. 'The Socialist Revolutionaries left the Soviets after the revolution; the Mensheviks did likewise. But this means that the Soviets will fall apart. Such a state of affairs in the face of complete chaos in the country will end with the shipwreck of our party in a very brief interval.'

Trotsky came out strongly in support of Lenin's point of view: against conciliation, against a coalition government with the Mensheviks and Socialist Revolutionaries.

We have had rather profound differences in our party prior to the insurrection, within the Central Committee as well as in the broad party circles. The same things were said, the same expressions used then as now in arguing against the insurrection as hopeless. The old arguments are now being repeated after the victorious insurrection, this time in favour of a coalition. There will be no technical apparatus, mind you. You lay the colours on thick in order to frighten, in order to hinder the proletariat from utilizing its victory ...

The bourgeoisie is aligned against us by virtue of all its class interests. And what will we achieve against that by taking to the road of conciliation with Vikzhel? . . . We are confronted with armed violence which can be overcome only by means of violence on our own part . . .

The sum total of what the Chernovs can contribute to our work is: vacillation. But vacillation in the struggle against our enemies will destroy our authority among the masses. What does conciliation with Chernov mean? . . . It means an alignment with Chernov. This would be treason.[3]

The Right Bolshevik leaders displayed their differences with Lenin to the outside world. In the Central Executive Committee of the Soviets, Kamenev, the chairman of this body, proposed that the Council of People's Commissars should resign and be replaced by a coalition government. He was supported by Nogin, a member of the Central Committee of the party and People's Commissar for Industry and Commerce; Rykov, also a member of the Central Committee and People's Commissar for Internal Affairs; Miliutin, Member of the Central Committee and People's Commissar for Agriculture; and Teodorovich, People's Commissar for Food, as well as by Zinoviev. The Bolshevik conciliators, together with non-Bolshevik members of VTsIK, voted against their own party. This produced a serious crisis in both government and party. The rule that party members in office should follow party instructions was openly flouted.

Lenin was so angry that next day, on 2 (15) November, he moved a resolution at the Central Committee decisively denouncing a coalition government. He achieved a majority for his position only after a long and bitter debate. His resolution was put to the vote a number of times. In the first vote there were 6 for Lenin's motion and 6 against; the second gave 7 for and 7 against; in a third Lenin emerged as the victor by one vote: 8 for, 7 against.[4]

The next day he got the majority of the Central Committee to issue an ultimatum to the Rightists: 'we demand a categorical reply in writing to the question: does the minority undertake to submit to party discipline . . . If the reply to this question is in the negative or is indeterminate, we will make an immediate appeal to the Moscow Committee, the Bolshevik group in the TsIK, the Petrograd City Conference and to a special party congress.'

If the opposition were not ready to abide by majority decision, let them leave the party. 'A split would be a very regrettable fact, of course. But an honest and open split now is incomparably better than internal sabotage, the blocking of our own decisions, disorganization and prostration.'

Unrepentant, the opposition reiterated its stand, and declared its decision to resign from the Central Committee. On 4 (17) November a statement by Kamenev, Rykov, Zinoviev and Nogin declared:

> We consider that a government [of all Socialist parties] has to be created to avoid further bloodshed and impending starvation, to prevent Kaledin's men destroying the revolution . . . We cannot take responsibility for [the] fatal policy of the CC, pursued contrary to the will of a vast proportion of the proletariat and soldiers, who gave a speedy end to the bloodshed between the different sections of the democracy.
>
> For that reason we relinquish the title of members of the CC so that we can have the right to state our view frankly to the masses of the workers and soldiers and appeal to them to support our call.[5]

The same day four People's Commissars – Nogin, Rykov, Miliutin and Teodorovich – resigned from the government, and Shliapnikov, People's Commissar for Labour, declared his political solidarity with them, but did not resign.

However, when it became clear that Lenin and his close colleagues would not vacillate, the opposition collapsed. On 7 (20) November, Zinoviev capitulated and asked to be taken back on to the party's Central Committee. In words foreshadowing his future more tragic surrenders, Zinoviev appealed to his friends:

> we remain attached to the party, we prefer to make mistakes together with millions of workers and soldiers and to die together with them than to step to one side at this decisive, historic moment.[6]

Three weeks later, on 30 November (12 December) similar statements were issued by Rykov, Kamenev, Miliutin and Nogin. Thus a very threatening split in the party at a critical moment of history was averted.

The logic of the class struggle was far too strong to be

blocked by the conciliatory attitude of the right-wing Bolsheviks. Not only did Lenin oppose them, but the Menshevik and Socialist Revolutionary leaders pulled the carpet from beneath them, by putting forward demands more appropriate for victors rather than for the vanquished. On 29 October (11 November),

> the SRs and Mensheviks had amplified their position by demanding, (1) that the Red or Workers' Guard be disarmed, (2) that the garrison be placed under orders of the city council, and (3) that an armistice be declared, offering for their part to secure a pledge that the troops of Kerensky on entering the city would not fire a shot or engage in search and seizure. A socialist government would then be constituted, but without Bolshevik participation.[7]

At the Vikzhel conference on 1 (14) November,

> The Mensheviks said that one should talk to the Bolsheviks with guns . . . and the Central Committee of the Socialist-Revolutionaries was against an agreement with the Bolsheviks.[8]

One positive outcome of the negotiations was that the Left Socialist Revolutionaries, resentful of the attitude of the Mensheviks and Right Socialist Revolutionaries, decided to join Lenin's party in the government.

3
The Dissolution of the Constituent Assembly

After resolving the crisis in the Bolshevik leadership over coalition with the Mensheviks and the Right Socialist Revolutionaries, the regime had to face a new problem. The Bolsheviks had to decide whether elections to a Constituent Assembly should be allowed. If the result of such elections was to create a body whose composition was radically different from that of the Soviet, what could be done about it?

The demand for the convocation of a Constituent Assembly had been one of the main planks of the programme of the Russian Social Democratic Labour Party since its foundation. Since 1905 Lenin had repeatedly referred to this demand as 'one of the three pillars of Bolshevism'. (The other two were the nationalization of land and the 8-hour day.) This slogan was put forward even more immediately and urgently between the February and October revolutions. The Bolsheviks pressed constantly for a Constituent Assembly to be called and the delay in doing so was one of the many charges they laid at the door of the provisional government. Again and again between April and October Lenin reiterated that the Bolsheviks, and only the Bolsheviks, would ensure its convocation without delay. They were fighting at the time simultaneously for power for the Soviets and the convening of the Constituent Assembly. They asserted that unless the Soviets took power the Constituent Assembly would not be convened.

In early April 1917 Lenin set out the Bolshevik attitude to the question of whether the Constituent Assembly should be convened. 'Yes,' he said, 'as soon as possible. But there is only one way to assure its convocation and success, and that is by increasing the number and *strength* of the Soviets and organizing and *arming* the working-class masses. That is the only guarantee.'[1]

On 12-14 (25-27) September he wrote: 'Our party alone, on taking power, can secure the Constituent Assembly's convocation; it will then accuse the other parties of procrastination and will be able to substantiate its accusations.'[2]

On 24 September (7 October) the Bolshevik daily *Rabochii Put* accused the Cadets of 'secret postponement and sabotage of the Constituent Assembly'.[3]

For many months the Bolsheviks had posed the question not of Soviets *or* Constituent Assembly, but of Soviets *and* Constituent Assembly. In a fiery speech at the Kerensky-convened State Council on 7 (20) October Trotsky, leading the Bolshevik fraction out of the meeting, said in conclusion: 'Long live an immediate, honest, democratic peace. All power to the Soviets. All land to the people. Long live the Constituent Assembly.'[4]

On 29 November (12 December) Bukharin, using precedents from English and French history, proposed that once the Constituent Assembly was convoked the Cadets should be expelled from it, and that the Assembly should declare itself a revolutionary convention. Bukharin hoped that in the Assembly the Bolsheviks and Left Socialist Revolutionaries would command an overwhelming majority, which would give the truncated Assembly legitimacy. Trotsky supported Bukharin's plan of action. Stalin argued that Bukharin's tactic would not work. No-one suggested the dispersal of the Constituent Assembly.

The fact is that the Bolsheviks, who campaigned strongly for the convocation of the Constituent Assembly, were completely unprepared for a conflict between the Assembly and the Soviets. At the same time they were quite clear that the future masters of Russia would be the Soviets, the revolutionary organizations of the proletariat and peasantry. If they did not consider the possibility of conflict between the Constituent Assembly and the Soviet, it was because then it was the provisional government which stood in opposition to both the Soviets and the Constituent Assembly.

Immediately after the October insurrection, Lenin was clearly worried about the results of elections to the Constituent Assembly and wanted them to be postponed, the voting age to be lowered to 18 years, the electoral list revised, and the Cadets and Kornilov supporters outlawed. Other Bolshevik leaders said that postponement was unacceptable, especially since the Bolsheviks had often reproached the provisional government with this very crime.

> 'Nonsense!' objected Lenin. 'Deeds are important, not words. In relation to the provisional government the Constituent Assembly represented, or might have represented, progress; in relation to the regime of the Soviets, and with the existing electoral lists, it will inevitably mean retrogression. Why is it inconvenient to postpone it? Will it be convenient if the Constituent Assembly turns out to be composed of a Cadet-Menshevik-Socialist Revolutionary alliance? ...
> Sverdlov, who more than others was connected with the provinces, protested vehemently against the adjournment.
> Lenin stood alone. He kept on shaking his head, dissatisfied, and went on repeating:

'You are wrong; it's clearly a mistake which can prove very costly. Let us hope that the revolution will not have to pay for it with its life.'[5]

In the event, the Bolsheviks permitted the election to be held.

The Results of the Elections

The elections took place over a period of a few weeks. One study gives the following results:

The vote by parties for the whole country

Socialist Revolutionaries	15,848,004
Ukrainian Socialist Revolutionaries	1,286,157
Mensheviks	1,364,826
Cadets	1,986,601
Bolsheviks	9,844,637
Others	11,356,651
Total	41,686,876[6]

For the seats in the Constituent Assembly, the archives of the October Revolution have assembled a list of 707 deputies, divided into the following groupings:

Socialist Revolutionaries	370
Left Socialist Revolutionaries	40
Bolsheviks	175
Mensheviks	16
Popular Socialists	2
Cadets	17
National groups	86
Unknown	1[7]

The Socialist Revolutionaries achieved a clear majority, both of the popular vote and of the seats in the Assembly. While the Bolshevik vote was about a quarter of the total, in some key areas they predominated. In the two capitals, the Bolshevik vote was four times larger than that of the Socialist Revolutionaries, and nearly 16 times larger than that of the Mensheviks.

What about the troops?

If the districts were remote from the metropolitan centers, and specifically from the influence of the Petrograd Soviet and the Bolshevik party organization, the SRs carried the day, and the farther removed the district was, the greater their degree of success; but on the Northern and Western Fronts the old-line agrarian appeal of the Socialist Revolutionary Party had been overbalanced by intensive propaganda in favour of immediate peace and immediate seizure of the estates, so that here the SRs sustained a crushing defeat and Lenin's party won a great victory. The contrast is seen in the accompanying tabulation:

	Western Front	Rumanian Front
Bolsheviks	653,430	167,000
Socialist Revolutionaries	180,582	679,471
Mensheviks	8,000	33,858
Ukrainian Socialist Bloc	85,062	180,576
Cadets	16,750	21,438
Residue	32,176	46,257
Total	976,000	1,128,600[8]

If we take the northern and western fronts, the vote polled by the Bolsheviks amounted to over a million, compared with 420,000 votes polled by the Socialist Revolutionaries. However, the strength of Bolshevism waned steadily as the influence of the metropolitan centres receded. Not only the Socialist Revolutionaries, but also the Mensheviks, were helped by distance: thus on the western front Menshevism was already virtually extinct by the time of the election, whereas on the Rumanian front it still retained a following, albeit a modest one.[9]*

'The conclusion is inescapable, that only time was needed to make the more remote fronts resemble the Petersburg garrison,' writes Radkey, historian of the Socialist Revolutionary Party.[10]

Summing up the general position in the country, Radkey writes:

The Bolsheviks had the center of the country – the big cities, the industrial towns, and the garrisons of the rear; they controlled those sections of the navy most strategically located with reference to Moscow and Petrograd; they even commanded a strong following among the peasants of the central, White Russian, and northwestern regions. The Socialist Revolutionaries had

---

* The same is true of the navy. The Bolsheviks overwhelmed the Socialist Revolutionaries three to one in the Baltic fleet, only to succumb by a margin of two to one in the Black Sea fleet.

the black-earth zone, the valley of the Volga, and Siberia; in general they were still the peasants' party, though serious defections had taken place. Particularist or separatist movements had strength in the Ukraine, along the Baltic, between the Volga and the Urals, and in the Transcaucasus; of these movements by all odds the most robust was Ukrainian nationalism. Menshevism was a spent force everywhere save in the Transcaucasus, where it was entwined with Georgian nationalism.[11]

The Bolsheviks Decide
to Disperse the Constituent Assembly

So, contrary to Bolshevik expectations, the Right Socialist Revolutionaries dominated the Constituent Assembly. Lenin used a number of arguments to explain this. First, the elections were held under an obsolete law that gave undue weight to the Rights among the Socialist Revolutionary candidates:

> as is well known, the party which from May to October had the largest number of followers among the people, and especially among the peasants – the Socialist Revolutionary Party – produced united election lists for the Constituent Assembly in the middle of October 1917, but split in November 1917, after the elections and before the Assembly met.
>
> For this reason, there is not, nor can there be, even a formal correspondence between the will of the mass of the electors and the composition of the elected Constituent Assembly.[12]

Radkey, who was far from being partial to the Bolsheviks, confirms this evaluation of Lenin's.[13]

However, the main reason for the conflict between the Assembly and the Soviets was more fundamental. The catchment area covered by the Constituent Assembly was far wider than that of the Soviet. While the Second Congress of Soviets represented about twenty million people, the number of votes for the Constituent Assembly was more than forty million. The Bolsheviks, together with the Left Socialist Revolutionaries, represented the overwhelming majority of the urban proletariat, the peasantry in the neighbourhood of the industrial centres, and the troops in the north and northwest. These were the most energetic and enlightened elements of the masses, on whose active support the revolution depended for survival. The Socialist Revolutionaries who dominated the Constituent Assembly represented the political confusion and indecision of the petty bourgeoisie in the towns and the millions of peasants relatively distant from the capital and the industrial centres.

To consider the Constituent Assembly in isolation from the class struggle was impossible. The interests of the revolution had to take precedence over the formal rights of the Constituent Assembly. At the Second Congress of Russian Social Democracy, Plekhanov had already answered in the affirmative the question he himself posed: whether the proletariat, on coming to power, would be justified in suppressing democratic rights.[14]

The Constituent Assembly met on 5 (18) January 1918. Sverdlov, in the name of VTsIK read a 'Declaration of the Rights of the Toiling and Exploited People' written by Lenin. It summed up the main decrees of the Soviet government: all power to the Soviets, the decree on land, the decree on peace, workers' control over production. Sverdlov's proposal that the Assembly should endorse the declaration was rejected by 237 votes to 136. This sealed the fate of the Assembly. After one day of existence it was dissolved.

Unlike the disagreement among the Bolshevik leadership on the question of coalition government, the decision to dissolve the Constituent Assembly led to little dissension in the party. There were, however, some difficulties.

On 13 (26) December, *Pravda* published Lenin's 'Theses on the Constituent Assembly', in which final form was given to the Bolshevik tactics. Starting from the principle that 'revolutionary Social Democracy has repeatedly emphasized, ever since the beginning of the Revolution of 1917, that a republic of Soviets is a higher form of democracy than the usual bourgeois republic with a Constituent Assembly', Lenin argued that the election returns did not correspond with the actual will of the people. Since the October revolution the masses had moved further to the left, a change not reflected in the Assembly. The civil war then beginning had 'finally brought the class struggle to a head, and destroyed every chance of settling in a formally democratic way the very acute problems with which history has confronted the people of Russia'. If therefore, the Constituent Assembly would not declare that 'it unreservedly recognizes Soviet power, the

Soviet revolution, and its policy on the question of peace, the land and workers' control', then 'the crisis in connection with the Constituent Assembly can be settled only in a revolutionary way, by Soviet power adopting the most energetic, speedy, firm and determined revolutionary measures.'[15]

Lenin used two arguments to justify the dispersal of the Constituent Assembly. The basic one was that the Constituent Assembly was a bourgeois parliament and had become the rallying point for the forces of counter-revolution; the second, that for a number of contingent reasons (the split within the SRs, the timing of the elections, etc.) the composition of the Constituent Assembly did not adequately reflect the actual balance of forces within the country.

Ballots and Bullets

In our times there is not a single issue which can be decided by ballots. In the decisive class battles bullets will prevail. The capitalists count the machine guns, the bayonets, the grenades at their disposal, and so does the proletariat. Lenin expressed this very clearly in his article 'The Constituent Assembly Elections and the Dictatorship of the Proletariat'. While in terms of voting power the countryside outweighed the towns, in real social, political power, the towns were far superior. 'The country cannot be equal to the town under the historical conditions of this epoch. The town inevitably *leads* the country. The country inevitably *follows the town*.' Controlling the capitals gave the Bolsheviks a great 'striking power':

> An overwhelming superiority of forces at the decisive point at the decisive moment – this 'law' of military success is also the law of political success, especially in that fierce, seething class war which is called revolution. Capitals, or, in general, big commercial and industrial centres (here in Russia the two coincided, but they do not everywhere coincide), to a considerable degree decide the political fate of a nation, provided, of course, the centres are supported by sufficient local, rural forces, even if that support does not come immediately.[16]

The Bolsheviks had '(1) an overwhelming majority among the proletariat; (2) almost half of the armed forces; (3) an overwhelming superiority of forces at the decisive moment at the decisive points, namely: in Petrograd and Moscow and on the war fronts near the centre.'

Not only could elections not replace force in achieving the dictatorship of the proletariat, but this dictatorship itself must be 'an instrument for winning the masses from the bourgeoisie and from the petty bourgeois parties'.[17]

Lenin poured ridicule on the reformist leaders who argued

the proletariat must first win a majority by means of universal suffrage, then obtain state power, by the vote of that majority, and only after that, on the basis of 'consistent' (some call it 'pure') democracy, organize socialism. But we say on the basis of the teachings of Marx and the experience of the Russian revolution:
the proletariat must first overthrow the bourgeoisie and win *for itself* state power, and then use that state power, that is, the dictatorship of the proletariat, as an instrument of its class for the purpose of winning the sympathy of the majority of the working people.[18]

The petty-bourgeois democrats . . . are suffering from illusions when they imagine that the working people are capable, under capitalism, of acquiring the high degree of class-consciousness, firmness of character, perception and wide political outlook that will enable them to decide, *merely by* voting, or at all events, to *decide in advance*, without long experience of struggle, that they will follow a particular class, or a particular party . . .
Capitalism would not be capitalism if it did not, on the one hand, condemn the *masses* to a downtrodden, crushed and terrified state of existence, to disunity (the countryside!) and ignorance, and if it (capitalism) did not, on the other hand, place in the hands of the bourgeoisie a gigantic apparatus of falsehood and deception to hoodwink the masses of workers and peasants, to stultify their minds, and so forth.[19]

From Constituent Assembly to Civil War

Under the banner of the Constituent Assembly reaction assembled its forces. Long before, Engels had explained the role of 'pure democracy' in a letter to Bebel (11 December 1884) on 'pure democracy'.

pure democracy . . . when the moment of revolution comes, acquires a temporary importance . . . as the final sheet-anchor of the whole bourgeois and even feudal economy . . . Thus between March and September 1848 the whole feudal-bureaucratic mass strengthened the liberals in order to hold down the revolutionary masses . . . In any case our sole adversary on the day of the crisis and on the day after the crisis will be the whole of the reaction which will group around pure democracy, and this, I think, should not be lost sight of.[20]

And Marx elaborated: 'from the first moment of victory, and after it, the distrust of the workers must not be directed any more against the conquered reactionary party, but against the previous ally, the petty bourgeois democrats, who desire to exploit the common victory only for themselves.'[21]

Throughout the years of the civil war in Russia (1918-1920), the slogan of the Constituent Assembly served as a screen for the dictatorship of the landowners and capitalists. Admiral Kolchak's banner was that of the Constituent Assembly, carried for him by the Socialist Revolutionaries (until he suppressed them). The South-eastern Committee of the Members of the Constituent Assembly, overwhelmingly Socialist Revolutionary in composition, called for recruits to the Volunteer Army of Generals Denikin and Alekseev. At Archangel, in Siberia, on the Volga, Socialist Revolutionary leaders raised the banner of the Constituent Assembly, under which recruits could be mobilized for the White Armies.

4

The Peace of Brest-Litovsk

One of the first problems for the newly established Bolshevik Government was the issue of war or peace with Germany.

For a number of years Lenin argued that if the proletariat came to power in Russia it would have to launch a revolutionary war against the imperialist powers. Thus in an article published on 13 (26) October 1915, he wrote that, if the revolution put the proletariat in power in Russia, it would immediately offer peace to all the belligerents on condition that all oppressed nations be freed. Of course no capitalist government would accept these terms. 'In that case, we would have to prepare for and wage a revolutionary war.' And, 'We would raise up the socialist proletariat of Europe for an insurrection against their governments . . . There is no doubt that a victory of the proletariat in Russia would create extraordinarily favourable conditions for the development of the revolution in both Asia and Europe.'[1] He used similar arguments a number of times after the February revolution.

On 3 (16) December armistice negotiations were opened with representatives of the Germans and the Austro-Hungarian empire, which led to the signing of an armistice. On 9 (22) December peace negotiations began at Brest-Litovsk. The leader of the Bolshevik delegation was Trotsky. He was accompanied by Karl Radek, who had just arrived in Russia and was the editor of the German paper *Die Fackel* (The Torch), which was distributed in the German trenches. On arriving at Brest-Litovsk Radek, under the eyes of the officers and diplomats assembled on the platform to greet the Soviet delegation, began to distribute revolutionary pamphlets among the German soldiers.

On 14-15 (27-28) December the German representative read out the draft of a harsh annexationist peace treaty. Trotsky broke off negotiations and left for Petrograd.

In critical situations Lenin was in the habit of expressing his views in the condensed form of a thesis. Now, facing an utterly new situation, demanding in his view a radical change of strategy, he did the same. On 7 (20) January 1918 he wrote 'Theses on the Question of the Immediate Conclusion of a Separate and Annexionist Peace':

> That the socialist revolution in Europe must come, and will come, is beyond doubt. All our hopes for the *final* victory of socialism are founded on this certainty and on this scientific

prognosis. Our propaganda activities in general, and the organization of fraternization in particular, must be intensified and
extended. It would be a mistake, however, to base the tactics
of the Russian socialist government on attempts to determine
whether or not the European, and especially the German,
socialist revolution will take place in the next six months (or
some such brief period). Inasmuch as it is quite impossible to
determine this, all such attempts, objectively speaking, would be
nothing but a blind gamble.

One cannot make war without an army, and Russia had no
army to speak of. 'There can be no doubt that our army is
absolutely in no condition at the present moment to beat back
a German offensive successfully.'

The socialist government of Russia is faced with the question –
a question whose solution brooks no delay – of whether to
accept this peace with annexations now, or to immediately
wage a revolutionary war. In fact, no middle course is possible.

One should not derive the necessary tactics directly from a
general principle. Some people would argue:

'such a peace would mean a complete break with the fundamental principles of proletarian internationalism.'
This argument, however, is obviously incorrect. Workers who
lose a strike and sign terms for the resumption of work which
are unfavourable to them and favourable to the capitalists, do
not betray socialism.

Would a peace policy harm the German revolution, asked Lenin.
And answered:

The German revolution will by no means be made more difficult
of accomplishment as far as its objective premises are con-
cerned, if we conclude a separate peace ...
A socialist Soviet Republic in Russia will stand as a living
example to the peoples of all countries, and the propaganda and
revolutionizing effect of this example will be immense.

He disdainfully rejected a 'heroic' attitude to the solution of life
and death questions facing the proletariat.

Summing up the arguments in favour of an immediate revolutionary war, we have to conclude that such a policy might
perhaps answer the human yearning for the beautiful, dramatic
and striking, but that it would totally disregard the objective

balance of class forces and material factors at the present stage of the socialist revolution now under way.[2]

Lenin unfortunately met with very tough resistance in the party ranks. His supporters of the October days were by and large surprised and shocked by his stand. On the whole the Right that opposed him in the days of October now came to his support. The most extreme enthusiast for immediate peace was Zinoviev, while the Left, which had supported Lenin during the revolution, was practically unanimous in opposing his peace policy.

The first formal discussion of Lenin's Thesis took place at the Central Committee meeting of 8 (21) January, with a number of lesser party leaders also present.

Wide sections of the party, including the great majority of the Petersburg Committee and of the Moscow Region Bureau, were in favour of a revolutionary war. The views of many of the rank and file could be summed up in the phrase used by Osinsky (Obolensky), a member of the Moscow Regional Bureau: 'I stand for Lenin's old position.' Even Trotsky did not support Lenin.

At this meeting Trotsky reported on his mission to Brest-Litovsk and presented his conclusion: 'Neither war nor peace.' Lenin argued for the acceptance of the German terms. Bukharin spoke for 'a revolutionary war'. The vote brought striking success to Bukharin. Lenin's motion received only 15 votes. Trotsky's position obtained 16 votes. 32 votes were cast for Bukharin's stand.[3]

Shortly after the meeting Lenin wrote:

The state of affairs now obtaining in the party reminds me very strongly of the situation in the summer of 1907 when the overwhelming majority of the Bolsheviks favoured the boycott of the Third Duma and I stood side by side with Dan in favour of participation and was subjected to furious attacks for my opportunism. Objectively, the present issue is a complete analogy; as then, the majority of the party functionaries, proceeding from the very best revolutionary motives and the best party traditions, allow themselves to be carried away by a 'flash' slogan and *do not grasp the new* socio-economic and political situation, do not take into consideration *the change in the conditions* that demands a speedy and abrupt change in tactics.[4]

At the next session of the Central Committee, on 11 (24) January, Dzerzhinsky reproached Lenin with timidity, with surrendering the whole programme of the revolution: 'Lenin is doing in a disguised form what Zinoviev and Kamenev did in October.'

To accept the Kaiser's *diktat*, Bukharin argued, would be to stab the German and Austrian proletariat in the back. In Uritsky's view Lenin approached the problem 'from Russia's angle, and not from an international point of view'. Lomov argued that 'by concluding peace we capitulate to German imperialism'. On behalf of the Petrograd organization Kosior harshly condemned Lenin's position.

The most determined advocates of peace were Zinoviev, Kamenev, Sverdlov, Stalin and Sokolnikov. Stalin said: 'There is no revolutionary movement in the west, nothing existing, only a potential, and we cannot count on a potential.' As in October, Zinoviev saw no ground for expecting revolution in the west. No matter, he said, that the peace treaty will weaken the revolutionary movement in the west: 'of course . . . peace will strengthen chauvinism in Germany, and for a time weaken the movement everywhere in the west'.

Lenin hastened to repudiate these two clumsy supporters. 'Can't take into account?' Lenin exclaimed on Stalin's position. It was true the revolution in the west had not yet begun. However, 'if we were to change our tactics on the strength of that . . . then we would be betraying international socialism'. Against Zinoviev he declared that it was wrong to say

> that concluding a peace will weaken the movement in the west for a time. If we believe that the German movement can immediately develop if the peace negotiations are broken off, then we must sacrifice ourselves, for the power of the German revolution will be much greater than ours.[5]

Lenin did not for a moment forget the revolutionary potential in the west.

> Those who advocate a revolutionary war point out that this will involve us in a civil war with German imperialism and in this way we will awaken revolution in Germany. But Germany is only just pregnant with revolution and we have already given birth to a completely healthy child, a socialist republic which we may kill if we start a war.[6]

However, he was willing to let Trotsky try playing for time. Against Zinoviev's solitary vote, the Central Committee decided to 'do everything to drag out the signing of a peace'.[7]

On 2 (15) January a group of Central Committee members and People's Commissars issued a statement demanding an immediate convocation of a party conference, declaring: 'in the event of a peace treaty being *signed . . . without such a conference having been called*, the undersigned find it necessary whatever happens to leave such posts of responsibility in the Party and governmental organs as they may hold.' The signatories were: 'Member of the CC RSDLP G.Oppokov (A.Lomov); People's Commissar V.Obolensky (N.Osinsky); V.Iakovleva, Sheverdin, N.Krestinsky, V.Smirnov, M.Vasilev, M.Savelev; Commissar of the State Bank Georgii Piatakov; Member of the CC RSDLP and ed. *Pravda* N.Bukharin; Member of the Urals Regional Committee and the TsIK Preobrazhensky.'

On the same day the Executive Commission of the Petersburg Committee of the party issued a denunciation of Lenin's peace policy, describing it as

> the abdication of our positions in full view of the coming international revolution and the sure death of our party as the vanguard of the revolution . . . If the peace policy is continued . . . it threatens to split our party. With all this in mind, the Executive Commission demands, in the name of the Petersburg organization, that a special party conference be convened immediately.[8]

On 11 (24) January the Moscow Committee of the party unanimously passed a resolution sharply condemning Lenin's peace policy.

> Acceptance of the conditions dictated by the German imperialists goes contrary to our whole policy of revolutionary socialism, would objectively involve renouncing a consistent line of international socialism in both foreign and internal policy and could lead to opportunism of the worst kind.[9]

For six weeks a sharp internal debate took place in the Bolshevik party and, as in previous crises, nearly split it. On 21 January (3 February) the Special Conference took place. It came to no clear conclusion. When the decisive question was put:

'Should the peace be signed if a German ultimatum were received?' the great majority abstained.[10]

With the party leadership in disarray, Trotsky continued with his policy of procrastination. On 29 January (10 February) he broke off negotiations with the Central Powers, declaring that while Russia refused to sign the annexationist peace, it also simultaneously declared the war to be at an end.

On 13 February Trotsky gave a detailed account of the negotiations at Brest and explained the reasons for his policy at a meeting of the Central Committee. In conclusion he said:

> I do not want to say that a further advance of the Germans against us is out of the question. Such a statement would be too risky, considering the power of the German Imperialist party. But I think that by the position we have taken up on the question we have made any advance a very embarrassing affair for the German militarists.

Sverdlov proposed a resolution which was passed unanimously, approving 'the action of its representatives at Brest-Litovsk.'[11]

On 18 February the Germans resumed their military offensive. The Central Committee met again. This time Lenin's proposal to offer peace immediately was defeated by 7 votes to 6. Trotsky voted against.[12] On the evening of the same day the Central Committee met again. Now the mood changed. The news had come that the Germans had captured Minsk and were advancing in the Ukraine, and apparently meeting with no resistance. The Central Committee passed a resolution to 'send the German Government an offer straight away to conclude peace immediately'; 7 (Lenin, Smilga, Stalin, Sverdlov, Sokolnikov, Zinoviev and Trotsky), voted for this resolution, and 5 (Uritsky, Ioffe, Lomov, Bukharin, Krestinsky) against; there was 1 abstention (Stasova).[13]

To add to the disarray in the leadership's ranks, a new factor intervened. On 22 February Trotsky reported to the Central Committee an offer by France and Britain to give military aid to Russia in a war against Germany. The majority of the 'Left Communists' were opposed in principle to accepting aid from such imperialist quarters. Trotsky came out clearly in favour of accepting aid, from whatever source. 'The "Left Communists" arguments do not stand up to criticism. The state is forced to do what the party would not do. Of course the imperialists want to take advantage of us and if we are weak, they will do so; if we are strong, we will not allow it.'

As the party of the socialist proletariat which is in power and conducting a war against Germany, we mobilize every means through state institutions to arm and supply our revolutionary army in the best way possible with all necessary resources and, for that purpose, we obtain them where we can, including therefore from capitalist governments. In doing this, the Russian Social-Democratic Labour Party retains full independence in its external policy, gives no political undertakings to capitalist governments and examines their proposals in each separate case according to what is expedient.

Lenin, who had not been present at the meeting of the Central Committee, added the following statement to the minutes of the session: 'Please add my vote *in favour* of taking potatoes and weapons from the Anglo-French imperialist robbers.'[14]

To explain his readiness to use the conflict between the imperialist powers in the interests of the proletariat in power, Lenin wrote, on 22 February, an article entitled 'The Itch'.

Let us suppose Kaliaev,* in order to kill a tyrant and monster, acquires a revolver from an absolute villain, a scoundrel and robber, by promising him bread, money and vodka for the service rendered.
Can one condemn Kaliaev for 'dealing with a robber' for the sake of obtaining a deadly weapon? Every sensible person will answer 'no'. If there is nowhere else for Kaliaev to get a revolver, and if his intention is really an honourable one (the killing of a tyrant, not killing for plunder), then he should not be reproached but commended for acquiring a revolver in this way. But if a robber, in order to commit murder for the sake of plunder, acquires a revolver from another robber in return for money, vodka or bread, can one compare (not to speak of identifying) *such* a 'deal with a robber' with the deal made by Kaliaev?[15]

---

* A member of the combat group of the Socialist Revolutionary Party, who took part in a number of terrorist acts. On 4 (17) February 1905 he assassinated the Governor General of Moscow, the Grand Duke S.A.Romanov, uncle of Nicholas II. He was executed at Schlüsselburg on 10 (23) May.

In a postscript to the article, Lenin added:

> The North Americans in their war of liberation against England at the end of the eighteenth century got help from Spain and France, who were her competitors and just as much colonial robbers as England. It is said that there were 'Left Bolsheviks' to be found who contemplated writing a 'learned work' on the 'dirty deal' of these Americans.[16]

In the end, however, nothing came of the offer of aid from Britain and France.

On 22 February, the German reply to the Russian peace offer was received. It was followed by a revolt in the Bolshevik Party. When the severe German terms became known, both the Petersburg Committee and the Moscow Regional Bureau combined to oppose Lenin's peace policy, in even more extreme terms than hitherto. On the same day Bukharin decided to resign from the Central Committee and from his post as editor of *Pravda*. The following jointly offered their resignation from all responsible posts held by them, and reserved their rights to 'freely agitate both within the Party and outside it': Lomov, Uritsky, Bukharin and Bubnov (members of the Central Committee); V.M.Smirnov, Iakoleva, Piatakov, Stukov and Pokrovsky of the Moscow Regional Bureau; and Spunde of Petrograd. The declaration accompanying the resignation was a harsh condemnation of Lenin's policy:

> the advance contingent of the international proletariat has capitulated to the international bourgeosie. By demonstrating to the whole world the weakness of the dictatorship of the proletariat in Russia, it strikes a blow at the cause of the international proletariat . . .
> The surrender of the proletariat's positions abroad inevitably prepares the way for surrender internally, too.[17]

On 21 February Lenin launched a public campaign in the press for his peace policy, with an article in *Pravda* called 'The Revolutionary Phrase'. He was relentless in his criticism of the Left Communists:

> the revolutionary phrase about a revolutionary war might ruin our revolution. By revolutionary phrase-making we mean the repetition of revolutionary slogans irrespective of objective circumstances at a given turn in events.

The Bolsheviks must face the fact that 'The old army does not exist. The new army is only just being born.'[18]

It was empty talk to suggest helping the German revolution by sacrificing Soviet power in Russia.

> It is one thing to be certain that the German revolution is maturing and to do your part towards helping it mature, to serve it as far as possible by *work*, agitation and fraternization, anything you like, but help the maturing of the revolution by *work*. That is what revolutionary proletarian internationalism means.
>
> It is another thing to declare, directly or indirectly, openly or covertly, that the German revolution is *already mature* (although it obviously is not) and to base your tactics on it.[19]

> We must fight against the revolutionary phrase, we have to fight it, we absolutely must fight it, so that at some future time people will not say of us the bitter truth that 'a revolutionary phrase about revolutionary war ruined the revolution'.[20]

Lenin was frequently forced to reiterate the basic Marxist tenet that one cannot identify the specific with the general, that the concrete is not the same as the abstract. As he wrote in his *Pravda* article of 25 February, 'A Painful But Necessary Lesson':

> It is indisputable that 'every strike conceals the hydra of the social revolution'. But it is nonsense to think that we can stride directly from a strike to the revolution. If we 'bank on the victory of socialism in Europe' in the sense that we guarantee to the people that the European revolution will break out and is certain to be victorious within the next few weeks, certainly before the Germans have time to reach Petrograd, Moscow or Kiev, before they have time to 'finish off' our railway transport, we shall be acting, not as serious internationalist revolutionaries, but as adventurers.[21]

On 16 February Germany declared that as from noon of 18 February it considered itself at war with Russia. At the time announced, German forces went on the offensive along the whole front, and met no resistance at all.

On 23 February the Central Committee discussed the new German terms. According to these, Soviet Russia was to lose all the Baltic territory, and part of Belorussia; it was also proposed that the towns of Marz, Batum and Ardagan be surrendered to Turkey. Under the conditions of the ultimatum, Russia would have to completely demobilize the army immediately, withdraw forces from Finland and the Ukraine and conclude peace with the Ukrainian People's Republic, i.e. with the bourgeois-nationalist Central Rada. The German government demanded that the terms it had set out be adopted within 48 hours, that plenipotentiaries be dispatched immediately to Brest-Litovsk and that a peace be signed in three days.

Lenin insisted that the terms must be accepted, and to drive the point home he threatened to resign from all his positions in government and party. The members of the Central Committee reacted in various ways. Lomov was unmoved. 'If Lenin threatens resignation, there is no reason to be frightened. We have to take power without V.I. [Lenin]. We have to go to the front and do everything we can.' However, other members, above all Trotsky, gave way under Lenin's pressure. Although not convinced by his arguments, Trotsky declared he was not ready to oppose Lenin's policy any more.

> We cannot fight a revolutionary war when the Party is split . . . The arguments of V.I. [Lenin] are far from convincing: if we had all been of the same mind, we could have tackled the task of organizing defence and we could have managed it. Our role would not have been a bad one even if we had been forced to surrender Peter and Moscow. We would have held the whole world in tension. If we sign the German ultimatum today, we may have a new ultimatum tomorrow. Everything is formulated in such a way as to leave an opportunity for further ultimatums. We may sign a peace; and lose support among the advanced elements of the proletariat, in any case demoralize them.

A similar attitude of abstention was taken by Krestinsky, Ioffe and Dzerzhinsky.*

---

* It is interesting to note that vacillation did not leave the pro-peace camp in the Central Committee untouched. Thus Stalin, at just this moment, found it possible to state: 'It is possible not to sign but to start peace negotiations.' And Lenin had to come down sharply against the vacillation of his own supporters: 'Stalin is wrong when he says it is possible not to sign. These terms must be signed. If you do not sign them, you will be signing the death sentence of Soviet power in three weeks.'

The outcome was that Lenin just got his way. There were 7 votes for his position (Lenin, Stasova, Zinoviev, Sverdlov, Stalin, Sokolnikov and Smilga), 4 against (Bubnov, Uritsky, Bukharin and Lomov) and 4 abstentions (Trotsky, Krestinsky, Dzerzhinsky and Ioffe).

Immediately after this session Bukharin, Uritsky, Lomov, Bubnov, Iakovleva, Piatakov and Smirnov declared they were 'resigning from all responsible party and Soviet posts and retaining complete freedom to campaign both within the party and outside it for what we consider to be the only correct positions'. Stalin raised 'the issue of whether leaving a post does not in practice mean leaving the party'. Lenin hastened to avoid bloodletting. He indicated that 'resigning from the CC does not mean leaving the party'.[22]

On 24 February the Moscow Regional Bureau unanimously adopted a resolution of no confidence in the Central Committee. In explanation it stated:

> The Moscow Regional Bureau considers a split in the party in the very near future hardly avoidable, and it sets itself the aim of helping to unite all consistent revolutionary communists who equally oppose both the advocates of the conclusion of a separate peace and all moderate opportunists in the party. *In the interests of the world revolution, we consider it expedient to accept the possibility of losing Soviet power, which is now becoming purely formal.*

The Bureau made it clear that it was not going to abide by the discipline of the Central Committee.

Lenin's reaction was most patient and tolerant. The party was still deeply democratic.

> In all this there is not only nothing appalling, but also nothing strange. It is completely natural for comrades who differ sharply with the Central Committee on the issue of a separate peace to reprimand the Central Committee sharply and express their conviction on the inevitability of a split. All this is the legal right of members of the party, and this is fully understandable.[23]

On 24 February a Soviet peace delegation left for Brest-Litovsk. Peace negotiations were resumed on 1 March, and on 3 March the treaty was signed. The Soviet delegates made it quite clear that they were signing it under duress. Thus, before signing, the Russian delegation issued a statement saying:

> Under the circumstances Russia has no freedom of choice . . .
> The German proletariat is as yet not strong enough to stop the
> attack [of German imperialism]. We have no doubt that the
> triumph of imperialism and militarism over the international
> proletarian revolution will prove to be temporary and ephem-
> eral. Meanwhile the Soviet government . . . unable to resist the
> armed offensive of German imperialism, is forced to accept the
> peace terms so as to save revolutionary Russia.[24]

The Harsh Terms of the Peace Treaty

It was estimated that by this treaty Russia lost territories and resources approximately as follows: 1,267,000 square miles, with over 62,000,000 population, or one-fourth of her territory and 44 per cent of her population; one-third of her crops and 27 per cent of her state income; 80 per cent of her sugar factories; 73 per cent of her iron and 75 per cent of her coal. Of the total of 16,000 industrial undertakings, 9,000 were situated in the lost territories.[25]

Opposition to Lenin's peace policy now spread widely among the masses. In February a referendum of the views of 200 Soviets was held. Of these a majority – 105 – voted for war against Germany. In the industrial city Soviets the majority in favour of war was overwhelming. Only two large Soviets – Petro-grad and Sebastopol – went on record as being in favour of peace. On the other hand several of the big centres (such as Moscow, Krondstadt, Ekaterinburg, Kharkov, Ekaterinoslav, Ivanovo-Voznessensk), voted against Lenin's policy with overwhelming majorities. Of the Soviets of 42 provincial cities that were con-sulted, 6 opted for peace, 20 for war; 88 county towns and villages opted for peace, 85 for war.[26]

However, the debate in the party came to an end with a specially convened Seventh Congress on 6-8 March. The day before it opened, a new daily, *Kommunist*, 'Organ of the St Peters-burg Committee and the St Petersburg Area Committee of the RSDLP' appeared. It was edited by Bukharin, Radek and Uritsky, with the collaboration of a number of prominent Party leaders:

Bubnov, Lomov, Pokrovsky, Preobrazhensky, Piatakov, Kollontai, Inessa Armand and others. The list of names gives some idea of the strength and quality of *Kommunist*.

After a bitter debate, the Seventh Congress resolved to support Lenin's policy by 30 votes to 12, with four abstentions. Local party organizations followed this line, either immediately or after a time.

By 7 March a Petrograd Party Conference had adopted a resolution condemning the Left Communists and calling upon them to stop their 'independent organizational existence'. As a result of this resolution *Kommunist* was soon forced to cease publication in Petrograd and was transferred to Moscow, where it reappeared in April under the auspices of the Moscow Regional Bureau. On 15 May Lenin was able to win the stronghold of the Left Communists, the Moscow region; after a debate with Lomov at a party conference his line was adopted by 42 votes to 9.

In some places the Left Communists continued to prevail. Thus in Ivanovo-Voznessensk, a district party conference held on 10 May, having heard a report by Bukharin, voted 12 to 9 with 4 abstentions for Bukharin's policy.[27]

The final ratification of the treaty took place at the Fourth Congress of Soviets on 15 March, 1918, by a vote of 748 to 261 with 115 abstentions. Among the latter were 64 Left Communists.

From then on the Left Communists lapsed into silence regarding the war question (although, as we shall see later, they continued to oppose Lenin's policy in a different sphere – that of economic affairs). But the Left Socialist Revolutionaries voiced their opposition to the peace policy all the more loudly and impatiently. Immediately after the ratification of the peace they withdrew from the Council of People's Commissars.

Trotsky's Position

As Stalinist historiography exaggerates beyond recognition the differences between Lenin and Trotsky regarding the Brest-Litovsk negotiations, it is important to elaborate somewhat on Trotsky's position.

Throughout the debate on Brest-Litovsk there was not the slightest disagreement between Lenin and Trotsky about the *im-*

possibility of a revolutionary war. Thus, for instance, in a speech on 8 (21) January Trotsky said : 'It is clear as day that if we wage revolutionary war, we shall be overthrown.'[28] He explains his position at the time thus :

> It was obvious that going on with the war was impossible. On this point, there was not even a shadow of disagreement between Lenin and me. We were both equally bewildered at Bukharin and the other apostles of a 'revolutionary war'. But there was another question, quite as important. How far could the Hohenzollern government go in their struggle against us? . . . Could Hohenzollern send his troops against revolutionaries who wanted peace? How had the February revolution, and, later on, the October revolution, affected the German army? How soon would any effect show itself? To these questions, no answer could as yet be given. We had to try to find it in the course of the negotiations. Accordingly we had to delay the negotiations as long as we could. It was necessary to give the European workers time to absorb properly the very fact of the Soviet revolution, including its policy of peace.[29]

Lenin's suggested tactics for the peace negotiations in Brest-Litovsk proved to be correct in practice. This, however, does not mean to say that Trotsky's position must inevitably have been wrong. Possibly the tactic he suggested of 'neither war nor peace' would have worked. From the memoirs of Ludendorff and various statements made by German representatives at Brest-Litovsk, it is clear that the Austrian and German leaders hesitated before launching their offensive against Russia.

The Austrian monarchy especially was almost desperate. On 4 (17) January the Foreign Minister of Austria, Czernin, got a mesage from the Austrian Emperor which stated :

> I must once more earnestly impress upon you that the whole fate of the monarchy and of the dynasty depends on peace being concluded at Brest-Litovsk as soon as possible . . . If peace be not made at Brest, there will be revolution.[30]

While Trotsky was on his way to Brest-Litovsk on 15 (28) January a wave of strikes and outbreaks spread through Germany and Austria. Soviets were formed in Berlin and Vienna. Hamburg, Bremen, Leipzig, Essen and Munich took up the cry. 'All Power to the Soviets' was heard in the streets of Greater Berlin, where half a million workers downed tools. In the forefront of the demands were the speedy conclusion of peace without annexations or indemnities, on the basis of the self-determination of peoples in accordance with the principles formulated by the Russian People's Commissars at Brest-Litovsk, and the participation of workers' delegates from all countries in the peace negotiations.[31]

The Austrians were supported in their attempts to achieve unconditional peace by the Bulgarians and the Turks, and, even more important, by the German Foreign Minister, Baron Von Kühlmann, and Prime Minister, von Hertling.

Ludendorff's and Kühlmann's memoirs make it clear that for days there was a balance between the war party, headed by the German general staff (Hindenburg, Ludendorff, Hoffmann), and the peace party, headed by von Kühlmann and von Hertling. The latter argued repeatedly that the situation on the home front did not permit a military offensive against the Russians. But the German supreme command remained adamant and in the end, with the Kaiser's backing, won the day.

Thus Trotsky's position during the Brest negotiations was based not on sheer idealism, but also on a great deal of realism. When events proved that Lenin was right, Trotsky was generous in acknowledging this. On 3 October 1918, at a session of the Central Executive Committee, he declared:

> I feel it my duty to say, in this authoritative assembly, that when many of us, including myself, were doubtful as to whether it was admissible for us to sign the Brest-Litovsk peace, only Comrade Lenin maintained stubbornly, with amazing foresight, and against our opposition, that we had to go through with it, to tide us over until the revolution of the world proletariat. We must now admit that we were wrong.[32]

Realism and Principled Politics

Lenin's strength in the fateful days of war and peace was his strictly uncompromising adherence to principles, combined with his readiness to adapt his tactics to the changing objective circumstances.

With full recognition of the need to retreat in the face of the imperialist pressure, he insisted on the necessity of adhering to the internationalist principle of subordinating everything, including the fate of Russia, to the needs of the world revolution. While arguing at the Seventh Party Congress for immediate ratification of the peace treaty, he did not for a moment lower the international sights of the revolution.

> Regarded from the world-historical point of view, there would doubtlessly be no hope of the ultimate victory of our revolution if it were to remain alone, if there were no revolutionary movements in other countries. When the Bolshevik Party tackled the job alone, it did so in the firm conviction that the revolution was maturing in all countries.[33]

> it is the absolute truth that without a German revolution we are doomed.[34]

Despite the harshness of the steps he had to take, Lenin did not for a moment try to pull the wool over the eyes of the workers. On the contrary, the truth had to be told to them, however unappetizing it might be. He always stuck to the rule that any manoeuvring that replaces the *real* struggle may destroy the revolutionary morale of the masses. In all the changes of direction imposed on revolutionary leaders, they must never hide the basic truth from the workers. As Trotsky put it:

> The essence of the matter is that Lenin approached the Brest-Litovsk capitulation with the same inexhaustible revolutionary energy which secured the party's victory in October. Precisely this intrinsic, and as if organic, combination of October and Brest-Litovsk, of the gigantic sweep with intrepidity and circumspection, of both boldness and foresight, gives a measure of Lenin's method and of his power.[35]

Principled politics combined with ruthlessly clear realism were the decisive traits of Lenin's behaviour during the Brest affair. He emerged with enormous moral credit from the controversy. Having the courage of his convictions enabled him to defy the prevailing mood in the party. His extraordinary powers of persuasion enabled him finally to change party opinion.

5

The Transition from Capitalism to Socialism

Lenin hoped for a breathing space after the signing of the Brest-Litovsk peace treaty. In a speech to the Moscow Soviet on 23 April 1918 he said:

> We can say with confidence that in the main the civil war is at an end. There will be some skirmishes, of course, and in some towns street fighting will flare up here or there, due to isolated attempts by the reactionaries to overthrow the strength of the revolution – the Soviet system – but there is no doubt that on the internal front reaction has been irretrievably smashed by the efforts of the insurgent people.[1]

Lenin's writings during this period all demonstrate his belief that the destructive phase of the revolution was largely over, and that the main task now was to learn how to operate industry, how to advance a measure of economic construction. However, the revolution was to be denied a breathing space of any appreciable length. Less than three months elapsed between the signing of the Brest treaty and the outbreak of a fierce civil war.

The Marxist Heritage

Lenin always looked to his teachers, Marx and Engels, to help him find his way forward. He used the international experience of the workers' revolutionary movement from 1848 to 1871 and onwards, as analysed by Marx and Engels, to prepare himself for 1905 and 1917. What did he learn from these masters about the transition from capitalism to socialism, after taking power?

In *The Civil War In France* Marx explained that the workers had 'no ready-made Utopias', that they had 'no ideals to realize', but 'to set free the elements of the new society with which the old collapsing bourgeois society itself is pregnant.' The workers well know that 'they will have to pass through long struggles, through a series of historic processes, transforming circumstances and men'.[2]

Marx referred with contempt to the imposition on the proletariat of schemes independent of its own experience. To offer a theoretical analysis of a future economic order before experience provided the material for it would be daydreaming. 'In Marx,' observed Lenin in *State and Revolution*, 'there is no trace of any attempt to construct Utopias, to guess in the void about what cannot be known.'

But the few general remarks by Marx and Engels scattered through *Capital*, *The German Ideology*, *The Critique of the Gotha Programme* and their correspondence could not be readily and directly applied to the Russian revolution. Marx and Engels assumed that the overthrow of capitalism would begin in the most advanced capitalist countries, where powerful industry and a massive and cultured working class existed, and would take place in several key countries at once. Instead the revolution broke out in only one country, and that a very backward one. In such conditions socialist tasks are bound to be outweighed by pre-socialist tasks, and the implementation of both complicated by the pressures and interference of encircling imperialism.

Lenin was hard put to it to find guidelines for the building of a new society. Could he draw any lessons for the construction of socialism from the rise of capitalism? Unfortunately, there are radical differences between the way capitalism developed and the way socialism will arise.

Firstly, while the political revolution – the coming of the proletariat to power – precedes the economic and cultural evolution of socialism, the economic and cultural development of the capitalist system preceded the bourgeois revolution.

Capitalism developed from simple commodity production in the cracks and crannies of the feudal economy. Important elements of capitalism were created in the womb of the old society. Only after hundreds of years of growth did capitalism become the predominant economic form, and place its imprint on the whole of society, delineating the general trend of development.

> They [the bourgeoisie] did not build capitalism, it built itself [Bukharin wrote]. The proletariat will build socialism as an organized system, as an organized collective subject. While the process of the creation of capitalism was spontaneous, the pro-

cess of building communism is to a significant degree a conscious, i.e. organized process.[3]

The Communist Manifesto made it clear that the act of bringing the proletariat to power was an act of revolution. But once the proletariat was in power, its programme of action was a transitional one, which would *gradually* lead to socialism. The social–political revolution would open the door to a prolonged process of reform whose final result would be fully-fledged socialism (or communism). Before the revolution, the communist uses reforms to develop the self-confidence, consciousness and organization of the proletariat, so as to prepare it for the revolution, i.e. breaking the capitalist framework of political, economic and social power. After the revolution, on the foundation of a new class rule, socialist reforms are called for.

Once the dictatorship of the proletariat is established, a programme of economic transformation is to be implemented :

> The proletariat will use its political supremacy in order, by degrees, to wrest all capital from the bourgeoisie, to centralize all the means of production into the hands of the state (this meaning the proletariat organized as ruling class), and, as rapidly as possible, to increase the total mass of productive forces.

The Communist Manifesto goes on to spell out ten measures that the proletariat should take on coming to power, to transform the economy and society. None of these measures abolishes capitalism straight away; each constitutes a partial intervention by the state in the economic mechanism of capitalism, and only in the *totality*, and *over time*, are they deemed to undermine capitalism completely. Thus, for instance, the measure 'a vigorously graduated income tax' assumes that under the dictatorship of the proletariat there would still be marked differences in incomes – that the capitalist would not be expropriated at a stroke. 'During the revolution, the gigantic increase in the scope of taxation may serve as an attack on private ownership; yet even in such a case taxation must be a stepping stone to fresh revolutionary measures, otherwise there will be a return to the erstwhile bourgeois conditions.'[4]

Again, the measure 'abolition of the right of inheritance' assumes the existence of private property in the means of production, and so forth. The measures suggested make it clear that Marx and Engels regarded the transition from capitalism to socialism not as a single step, but as a process spread over a more or less lengthy historical period.

It must be emphasized that there is a *fundamental* difference between the way Marx and Engels posed partial demands and the way reformists put them. 'Inroads upon the rights of property' caried out by a workers' government are radically different from reforms under a bourgeois government. In the first case the partial demands will be outstripped, leading to further encroachment upon the rights of property. In the second they are mere adjustments to capitalism and are containable within it. For Marx and Engels transitional demands were such that each constituted an essential structural change in its own right, and all together added up to the transformation of capitalism into socialism.

Changing 'Human Nature'

For Marx, the agent for the transition from capitalism to socialism, a transition that must take not years but a whole historical epoch, was the active and conscious working class. While capitalism developed spontaneously over centuries in the heart of feudal society, socialism *does not* grow within capitalism; however, the proletariat, which is potentially able to create socialism, does. The clear implication is that capitalism as such does not create socialism, but that the revolutionary struggles of the proletariat to overthrow capitalism produces men with the will and ability to construct socialist society. This ability is developed in the struggle against capitalism, and is the *only* foundation of the new society. The centrality of the human element was made clear by Marx when he pointed out the differences between the propaganda of his group in the German Communist League and that of an opposing minority group:

> What we say to the workers is: 'You will have 15, 20, 50 years of civil war and national struggle and this not merely to bring about a change in society but also to change yourselves and prepare yourselves for the exercise of political power.' Whereas you say on the contrary: 'Either we seize power at once, or else we might as well just take to our beds.' While we are at pains to show the German worker how rudimentary the development of the German proletariat is, you appeal to the patriotic

feelings and the class prejudice of the German artisan, flattering him in the grossest way possible, and this is a more popular method, of course.[5]

It is essential for the creation of a socialist society that the proletariat should not only change social relations, but also change itself, so as to be able to carry out this historical task. To emphasize this, Marx wrote elsewhere: 'The tradition of all the dead generations weighs like a nightmare on the brain of the living.' The working class is an essential part of capitalism, and *potentially* the victor over it. Hence the concluding sentences of the first section of *The Communist Manifesto*: 'What the bourgeoisie therefore produces, above all, are its own gravediggers. Its fall, and the victory of the proletariat, are equally inevitable.'

The key to becoming the builder of a new society from being the subordinate class under capitalism is the proletariat's revolutionary prowess. The changes in social human relations necessary for this transformation are dialectically united by revolutionary practice. As Marx put it in the *Theses on Feuerbach*:

> The materialistic doctrine that men are products of circumstances and upbringing, and that therefore changed men are the product of other circumstances and changed upbringing, forgets that it is men who change circumstances and that the educator must himself be educated . . . The coincidence of the changing of circumstances and human activity can be conceived and rationally understood only as *revolutionizing practice*.

The difficulties of a proletarian government will be not so much in the domain of property, but rather in that of production, and of overcoming human nature as shaped by the old society. The field in which the difficulties will be most acute will be that of work discipline. The workers work because of the discipline of hunger and the threat of the sack. Of course in an advanced stage of socialist society, where working hours will be reduced to a reasonable limit and the unpleasant aspects of the process of labour eliminated, where the workplace will be hygienic and attractive, where the monotony of labour will largely be done away with, where the material inducement will be lavish, workers will work from force of habit and from the desire to serve the needs of fellow human beings. But it will take a whole historical period to change labour from a burden to a joy. How will labour discipline, so necessary for the continuation of production, be established immediately after the social revolution, with the proletariat still affected by the customs of capitalism?

Lenin on the Eve of the October Revolution

Lenin, like Marx and Engels, believed that the conquest of state power by the proletariat would have to be followed by a whole series of reforms taking place over a long period.

On the eve of the October revolution, he drew up a detailed plan for the measures to be put into effect by a Bolshevik government if it came to power in the near future. He wrote in *The Impending Catastrophe and How to Combat it*:

> These principal measures are:
> 1. Amalgamation of all banks into a single bank, and state control over its operations, or nationalization of the banks.
> 2. Nationalization of the syndicates, i.e. the largest, monopolistic capitalist associations (sugar, oil, coal, iron and steel, and other syndicates).
> 3. Abolition of commercial secrecy.
> 4. Compulsory syndication (i.e. compulsory amalgamation into associations) of industrialists, merchants and employers generally.
> 5. Compulsory organization of the population into consumers' societies, or encouragement of such organization, and the exercise of control over it.[6]

These measures are designed to achieve not the once-for-all destruction of capitalist property relations, but to start off a more or less lengthy process for their gradual undermining.

The nationalization of the banks is not to be confused with their expropriation.

> nationalization of the banks . . . would not deprive any 'owner' of a single kopek . . . If nationalization of the banks is so often confused with the confiscation of private property, it is the bourgeois press, which has an interest in deceiving the public, that is to blame for this widespread confusion . . .
> Whoever owned fifteen rubles on a savings account would continue to be the owner of fifteen rubles after the nationalization of the banks; and whoever had fifteen million rubles would con-

tinue after the nationalization of the banks to have fifteen million rubles in the form of shares, bonds, bills, commercial certificates and so on ...

Only by nationalizing the banks *can* the state *put itself in a position* to know where and how, whence and when, millions and billions of rubles flow. And only control over the banks, over the centre, over the pivot and chief mechanism of capitalist circulation, would make it possible to organize real and not fictitious control over all economic life.[7]

The nationalization of the banks will be a serious invasion of capitalist property relations and will meet tough resistance from the capitalists.

As to the state, it would for the first time be in a position first to *review* all the chief monetary operations, which would be unconcealed, then to *control* them, then to *regulate* economic life, and finally to *obtain* millions and billions for major state transactions, without paying the capitalist gentlemen sky-high 'commissions' for their 'services'. That is the reason – and the only reason – why all the capitalists . . . are prepared to fight tooth and nail against nationalization of the banks.

The nationalization of the syndicates (point 2 of Lenin's programme) would also help 'the regulation of economic activity'. No blanket expropriation is suggested, only encroachment on the wealth of the syndicates by fining heavily those which sabotage the national measures: 'war must be declared on the oil barons and shareholders, the confiscation of their property and punishment by imprisonment must be decreed for delaying nationalization of the oil business, for concealing incomes or accounts, for sabotaging production, and for failing to take steps to increase production'.[8]

Point 3 – abolition of commercial secrecy – is another encroachment on capitalist property relations, but it does not abolish them. The abolition of commercial secrecy will mean

compelling contractors and merchants to render accounts public, forbidding them to abandon their field of activity without the permission of the authorities, imposing the penalty of confiscation of property and shooting for concealment and for deceiving the people, organizing verification and control *from below*, democratically, by the people themselves, by unions of workers and other employees, consumers, etc.

The establishment of workers' control will increase the power of the proletariat as against that of the bourgeoisie, while in no way at a stroke liquidating the latter as a class.

> In point of fact, the whole question of control boils down to who controls whom, i.e. which class is in control and which is being controlled . . . We must resolutely and irrevocably, not fearing to break with the old, not fearing boldly to build the new, pass to control *over* the landowners and capitalists *by* the workers and peasants.

Point 4, 'compulsory syndication (i.e. compulsory amalgamation into associations) of industrialists, merchants and employers generally', again does not abolish capitalist property relations. 'A law of this kind does not directly, i.e. in itself, affect property relations in any way; it does not deprive any owner of a single kopek.'[9]

The spirit of the transitional programme elaborated by Lenin in *The Impending Catastrophe and How to Combat It* is the same as that of the *Communist Manifesto*. Once workers' power has been established, the transition from capitalism to socialism, the 'leap', is seen as a more or less prolonged process of evolution. Capitalism, which grew up over centuries, is going to be replaced by socialism, which is going to be *built* over a much shorter period, but still not at a stroke.

A Long and Complicated Transition Period

In a speech on 11 (24) January 1918 Lenin declared:

> We know very little about socialism . . . We are not in a position to give a description of socialism . . . The bricks of which socialism will be composed have not yet been made. We cannot say anything further.[10]

Socialism will have to be built by people who have been shaped by capitalism. As Lenin said in a speech on 27 November 1918:

> Things would not be so bad if we did not have to build socialism with people inherited from capitalism. But that is the whole trouble with socialist construction – we have to build socialism with people who have been thoroughly spoiled by capitalism. That is the whole trouble with the transition.[11]

Again, on 20 January 1919, in a speech to the Second Trade Union Congress, he said:

> The workers were never separated by a Great Wall of China from the old society. And they have preserved a good deal of the traditional mentality of capitalist society. The workers are building a new society without themselves having become new people, or cleansed of the filth of the old world; they are still standing up to their knees in that filth. We can only dream of clearing the filth away. It would be utterly Utopian to think this could be done all at once. It would be so Utopian that in practice it would only postpone socialism to kingdom come.[12]

Again, he wrote on 17 April 1919:

> The old Utopian socialists imagined that socialism could be built by men of a new type, that first they would train good, pure and splendidly educated people, and these would build socialism. We always laughed at this and said that this was playing with puppets, that it was socialism as an amusement for young ladies, but not serious politics.
>
> We want to build socialism with the aid of those men and women who grew up under capitalism, were depraved and corrupted by capitalism, but steeled for the struggle by capitalism. There are proletarians who have been so hardened that they can stand a thousand times more hardship than any army. There are tens of millions of oppressed peasants, ignorant and scattered, but capable of uniting around the proletariat in the struggle, if the proletariat adopts skilful tactics.[13]

The proletariat will have to change itself radically if it wants to lead in the establishment of a new society:

> The science which we, at best, possess, is the science of the agitator and propagandist, or the man who has been steeled by the hellishly hard lot of the factory worker, or starving peasant, a science which teaches us how to hold out for a long time and to persevere in the struggle, and this has saved us up to now. All this is necessary, but it is not enough. With this alone we cannot triumph. In order that our victory may be complete and final we must take all that is valuable from capitalism, take all its science and culture.[14]

The going will be very hard:

> we know perfectly well from our own experience that there is a difference between solving a problem theoretically and put-

ting the solution into practice . . . Thanks to a whole century of development, we know on which class we are relying. But we also know that the practical experience of that class is extremely inadequate.[15]

We were never Utopians and never imagined that we would build communist society with the immaculate hands of immaculate communists, born and educated in an immaculately communist society. That is a fairy-tale. We have to build communism out of the debris of capitalism, and only the class which has been steeled in the struggle against capitalism can do that. The proletariat, as you are very well aware, is not free from the shortcomings and weaknesses of capitalist society. It is fighting for socialism, but at the same time it is fighting against its own shortcomings.[16]

Though facing up to harsh reality, Lenin does not cease to be a revolutionary optimist: he sees salvation in the creative activity of the masses.

When the masses of the people themselves, with all their virgin primitiveness and simple, rough determination begin to make history, begin to put 'principles and theories' immediately and directly into practice, the bourgeois is terrified and howls that 'intellect is retreating into the background'. (Is not the contrary the case, heroes of philistinism? Is it not the intellect of the masses, and not of individuals, that invades the sphere of history at such moments? Does not mass intellect at such a time become a virile, effective, and not an armchair force?)

In the midst of the greatest hardships and tribulations – in October 1920 – Lenin quotes what he wrote in March 1906, long before the revolution.

The thing is that it is just the revolutionary periods which are distinguished by wider, richer, more deliberate, more methodical, more systematic, more courageous and more vivid making of history than periods of philistine, Cadet, reformist progress. But the Blanks turn the truth inside out! They palm off paltriness as magnificent making of history. They regard the inactivity of the oppressed or downtrodden masses as the triumph of 'system' in the work of bureaucrats and bourgeois. They shout about the disappearance of intellect and reason when, instead of the picking of draft laws to pieces by petty bureaucrats and liberal *penny-a-liner* journalists, there begins a period of direct political activity of the 'common people', who simply set to work without more ado to smash all the instruments for oppressing the people, seize power and take what was regarded as belonging to all kinds of robbers of the people – in short, when the intellect and reason of millions of downtrodden people awaken not only to read books, but for action, vital human action, to make history.[17]

With his usual realism, Lenin explains that the road ahead is not only difficult but bound to be very twisted and uneven, demanding continual adaptation and changes of gear.

The most difficult task in the sharp turns and changes of social life is that of taking due account of the peculiar features of each transition. How socialists should fight within a capitalist society is not a difficult problem and has long since been settled. Nor is it difficult to visualize advanced socialist society. This problem has also been settled. But the most difficult task of all is how, in practice, to effect the transition from the old, customary, familiar capitalism to the new socialism, as yet unborn and without any firm foundations. At best this transition will take many years, in the course of which our policy will be divided into a number of even smaller stages. And the whole difficulty of the task which falls to our lot, the whole difficulty of politics and the art of politics, lies in the ability to take into account the specific tasks of each of these transitions.[18]

We are bound to make many mistakes. What does it matter! This is the price which has to be paid for the advance of socialism.

For every hundred mistakes we commit, and which the bourgeoisie and their lackeys (including our own Mensheviks and Right Socialist-Revolutionaries) shout about to the whole world, 10,000 great and heroic deeds are performed, greater and more heroic because they are simple and inconspicuous amidst the everyday life of a factory district or a remote village, performed by people who are not accustomed (and have no opportunity) to shout to the whole world about their successes.

But even if the contrary were true – although I know such an assumption is wrong – even if we committed 10,000 mistakes for every 100 correct actions we performed, even in that case our revolution would be great and invincible, and so it will be in the eyes of world history, because, for the first time, not the minority, not the rich alone, and the educated alone, but the real people, the vast majority of the working people, are themselves building a new life, are by their own experience solving the most difficult problems of socialist organization.

Every mistake committed in the course of such work, in the course of this most conscientious and earnest work of tens of millions of simple workers and peasants in reorganizing their whole life, every such mistake is worth thousands and millions of 'flawless' successes achieved by the exploiting minority – successes in swindling and duping the working people. For only *through* such mistakes will the workers and peasants *learn* to build the new life, learn to do *without* capitalists; only in this way will they hack a path for themselves – through thousands of obstacles – to victorious socialism.[19]

Lenin had no illusions about the fact that the construction of socialism would take a very long time indeed. 'We know that we cannot establish a socialist order now – God grant that it may be established in our country in our children's time, or perhaps in our grandchildren's time.'[20] However, with courage and perseverance, the proletariat is bound to win.

Perseverance, persistence, willingness, determination and ability to test things a hundred times, to correct them a hundred times, but to achieve the goal come what may – these are qualities which the proletariat acquired in the course of the ten, fifteen or twenty years that preceded the October Revolution, and which it has acquired in the two years that have passed since this revolution, years of unprecedented privation, hunger, ruin and destitution. These qualities of the proletariat are a guarantee that the proletariat will conquer.[21]

6

'We Need State Capitalism'

In his mistaken expectation of a peaceful period after the Brest-Litovsk peace treaty, Lenin turned to the task of developing an economic strategy leading on from where his *The Threatening Catastrophe*, written six months earlier, left off. During the months of March-June 1918 he devoted himself to seeking ways of managing industry and achieving some measure of economic reconstruction.

The Chaotic Economic Situation

The whole of Russia was in a state of turmoil. A vivid description of the economic breakdown is given by an English observer, a reporter for the *Manchester Guardian*, travelling in Russia during 1917 and 1918:

> It is no exaggeration to say that during November, December, and the greater part of January something approaching anarchy reigned in the industries of Northern Russia . . . There was no common industrial plan. Factory Committees had no higher authority to which to look for direction. They acted entirely on their own and tried to solve those problems of production and distribution which seemed most pressing for the immediate future and for the locality. Machinery was sometimes sold in order to buy raw materials. The factories became like anarchistic Communes . . . anarcho-syndicalist tendencies began to run riot.[1]

War-damaged industry continued to run down. 'The bony hand of hunger', with which the capitalist Riabushinsky had threatened the revolution, gripped the whole population in the spring of 1918. Powerful evidence of the gravity of the situation was provided by a telegram which Lenin and the food Commissar, Tsiurupa, dispatched to all provincial Soviets and food committees on 11 May 1918:

> Petrograd is in an unprecedentedly catastrophic condition. There is no bread. The population is given the remaining potato flour and crusts. The Red capital is on the verge of perishing from famine. Counter-revolution is raising its head, directing the dissatisfaction of the hungry masses against the Soviet Government. In the name of the Soviet Socialist Republic, I demand immediate help for Petrograd. Telegraph to the Food Commissariat about the measures you have taken.[2]

Bread riots were widespread throughout the country.

> The famine was so acute [wrote Victor Serge] that at Tsarkoe Selo, not far from Petrograd, the people's bread ration was only 100 grams per day. Rioting results. Cries of 'Long live the Constituent Assembly!' and even 'Long live Nicholas II!' were heard (this on 6-7 April). On 19 April there were 'hunger riots' . . . at

Smolensk . . . In this period [writes one worker-militant] hardly any horses were to be seen in Petrograd; they were either dead, or eaten or requisitioned, or sent off into the countryside. Dogs and cats were no more visible either . . . People lived on tea and potato-cakes made with linseed oil. As a member of the EC of the Vyborg Soviet [in Petrograd] I know that there were *whole weeks* in which no issues of bread or potatoes were made to the workers; all they got was sunflower seeds and some nuts . . . Soviet power seemed to be in a desperate situation.[3]

Speaking in Moscow before a popular meeting, Trotsky displayed a sheaf of telegrams : 'Viksi, Nizhni-Novgorod province : the shops are empty, work is going badly, shortage of 30 per cent of the workers through starvation. Men collapsing with hunger at their benches.' From Serglev-Posada the telegram says : 'Bread, or we are finished!' From Bryansk, 30 May : 'Terrible mortality, especially of children, around the factories of Maltsov and Bryansk; typhus is raging.' From Klin, near Moscow : 'The town has had no bread for two weeks.' From Paslov-Posada : 'The population is hungry, no possibility of finding corn.' From Dorogobuzh : 'Famine, epidemics . . .'[4]

One of the causes of the famine was the breakdown of transport. The number of disabled locomotives increased from 5,100 on 1 January 1917 to 10,000 on 1 January 1918; so that by the latter date 48 per cent of the total were out of commission.[5]

Industry was in a state of complete collapse. Not only was there no food to feed the factory workers; there was no raw material or fuel for industry. The oilfields of the Baku, Grozny and Emba regions came to a standstill. The situation was the same in the coalfields. The production of raw materials was in no better a state. The cultivation of cotton in Turkestan fell to 10-15 per cent of the 1917 level.

The collapse of industry meant unemployment for the workers. In Petrograd 18,000 workers from the 'Treugolnik' plant were thrown out of work, when the establishment was closed because of lack of fuel. The Petrograd tube works were transferred to Penza : 20,000 Petrograd workers lost their jobs. At the works of Siemens and Halske, the numbers of men fell from 1,200 to 700, and later to 300. The Nevsky shipbuilding works also closed, 10,000 men being dismissed. The Obukhov works were shut down, due to lack of coal. Altogether, 14,000 men were dismissed. The same thing happened at the Putilov works, where more than 30,000 men were laid off.[6]

A similar collapse of industry and mass sackings of workers took place in other towns. Drastic measures had to be taken. And Lenin was not one to shirk responsibility, however unpleasant the task.

'We Need State Capitalism'

Lenin had earlier, in *The Threatening Catastrophe*, developed and elaborated the transitional programme of reforms which had been put forward by Marx and Engels in the *Communist Manifesto* to follow the proletarian conquest of power. Now, in March/April 1918, he produced an entirely new formulation: between capitalism and socialism one must have 'state capitalism', which for him was synonymous with the state regulation of private industry. The defence of state capitalism constituted the essence of his economic policy for this period. By it he meant an extended period of joint management with privately owned industry. He thought that future economic development would proceed chiefly by way of mixed companies, state and private, the attraction of foreign capital, the granting of concessions, etc., i.e. capitalist and semi-capitalist forms of production controlled and directed by the proletarian state. Under these conditions the cooperative organizations would take part in the distribution of goods produced by state capitalist industry, and consequently would become a constituent part of the state capitalist economic apparatus linking industry with the peasantry.*

---

* It should be noted that Lenin uses the term 'state capitalism' in a completely different context from that of many later Marxists, including the present writer,[7] when they describe Stalin's Russia as state capitalist. For Lenin state capitalism meant private capitalism under state control (whether the state were a capitalist or a proletarian state). When Stalin's Russia is called state capitalist, this means a regime under which the state is the repository of the means of production, and in which the proletariat is deprived of all political and economic power, while the bureaucracy carries out the functions of capitalism – the extortion of surplus value from the workers and the accumulation of capital.

State capitalism, of course, is not what we are aiming to achieve: 'We . . . must tell the workers: Yes, it is a step back, but we have to help ourselves to find a remedy.'[8]

Lenin did not stop at a declaration of intent. He took active steps towards achieving a partnership between private capital and the state. Accordingly negotiations were opened with Meshchersky, a prominent iron and steel magnate whose group owned the principal locomotive and wagon-building works in the country. In March 1918 Meshchersky put forward an ingenious proposal by which his group would hold half the shares in a new metallurgical trust, and the state the other half, the group undertaking the management of the trust on behalf of the partnership. By a narrow majority VSNKh, the Supreme Council of National Economy, decided to negotiate on this basis. About the same time Stakhaev, another industrialist, proposed a trust for the iron and steel industry of the Urals, 200 million rubles of the share capital to be subscribed by his group, 200 million by the state, and 100 million by unnamed American capitalists. An alternative proposal was for the state to put up all the capital, and for the Stakhaev group to manage the trust on behalf of the state.

Another group of financiers advanced a scheme for the formation of international trading companies – Russo-French, Russo-American, Russo-Japanese – to develop foreign trade on the basis of an exchange of goods. About this time a memorandum was prepared on Russian–American commercial relations, in which American capital was to be invited to participate in the exploitation of the fishing, mining, construction and agricultural resources of Siberia and northern Russia.[9]

In industry generally, Lenin tried to achieve a working compromise between the ruling proletariat and the still property-owning capitalists. Thus the decree on workers' control of 14(27) November gave the factory committees 'the right to supervise the management' and 'to determine a minimum of production' and the right of access to all correspondence and accounts; at the same time the general instructions appended to the decree expressly reserved to the proprietor the exclusive right of giving orders about the conduct of the enterprise, and forbade the factory committees to interfere in this or to countermand such orders.

Article 9 forbade committees 'to take possession of the enterprise or direct it', except with the sanction of the higher authorities.

Lenin was adamant on the need to make the compromise between the dictatorship of the proletariat and the capitalists.

> the present task could not be defined by the simple formula: continue the offensive against capital. Although we have certainly not finished off capital and although it is certainly necessary to continue the offensive against this enemy of the working people, such a formula would be inexact, would not be concrete, would not take into account the *peculiarity* of the present situation in which, in order to go on advancing successfully *in the future*, we must 'suspend' our offensive *now*.
>
> This can be explained by comparing our position in the war against capital with the position of a victorious army that has captured, say, a half or two-thirds of the enemy's territory and is compelled to halt in order to muster its forces, to replenish its supplies of munitions, repair and reinforce the lines of communication, build new storehouses, bring up new reserves, etc. To suspend the offensive of a victorious army under such conditions is necessary precisely in order to gain the rest of the enemy's territory, i.e. in order to achieve complete victory. Those who have failed to understand that the objective state of affairs at the present moment dictates to us precisely such a 'suspension' of the offensive against capital have failed to understand anything at all about the present political situation.[10]

'We Need the Bourgeois Specialists'

Lenin stated unambiguously that economic collapse could not be stopped without the correct use of the bourgeois technicians, the specialists. 'It is now an immediate, ripe and essential task to draw the bourgeois intelligentsia into our work.'[11]

> Without the guidance of experts in the various fields of knowledge, technology and experience, the transition to socialism will be impossible, because socialism calls for a conscious mass advance to greater productivity of labour compared with capitalism, and on the basis achieved by capitalism.

Lenin goes on to discuss the question in the most practical way.

> Let us assume that the Russian Soviet Republic requires one thousand first-class scientists and experts . . . Let us assume also that we shall have to pay these 'stars of the first magnitude' . . .

25,000 rubles per annum each. Let us assume that this sum (25,000,000 rubles) will have to be doubled (assuming that we have to pay bonuses for particularly successful and rapid fulfilment of the most important organization and technical tasks), or even quadrupled (assuming that we have to enlist several hundred foreign specialists, who are more demanding). The question is, would the annual expenditure of fifty or a hundred million rubles by the Soviet Republic for the purpose of reorganizing the labour of the people on modern scientific and technological lines be excessive or too heavy? Of course not. The overwhelming majority of the class-conscious workers and peasants will approve of this expenditure because they know from practical experience that our backwardness causes us to lose thousands of millions . . . The corrupting influence of high salaries – both upon the Soviet authorities . . . and upon the mass of the workers – is indisputable. Every thinking and honest worker and poor peasant, however, will agree with us, will admit, that we cannot immediately rid ourselves of the evil legacy of capitalism.[12]

The proletariat has no alternative. Having achieved power, it must turn to the experience gained under capitalism.

Only those are worthy of the name of communists who understand that it is *impossible* to create or introduce socialism *without learning* from the organizers of the trusts. For socialism is not a figment of the imagination, but the assimilation and application by the protelarian vanguard, which has seized power, of what has been created by the trusts. We, the party of the proletariat, have *no other way* of acquiring the ability to organize large-scale production on trust lines, as trusts are organized, except by acquiring it from first-class capitalist experts.

But Lenin does not hide the harsh truth : giving privileges to specialists is a violation of communist principles.

Now we have to resort to the old bourgeois method and to agree to pay a very high price for the 'services' of the top bourgeois experts . . . Clearly, this measure is a compromise, a departure from the principles of the Paris Commune and of every proletarian power, which calls for the reduction of all salaries to the level of the wages of the average worker, which urge that careerism be fought not merely in words, but in deeds.
Moreover, it is clear that this measure not only implies the cessation – in a certain field and to a certain degree – of the offensive against capital (for capital is not a sum of money, but a definite social relation); it is also *a step backward* on the part of

our socialist Soviet state power, which from the very outset proclaimed and pursued the policy of reducing high salaries to the level of the wages of the average worker.

Marxists never hide the truth from the working class. To conceal from the people the fact that the enlistment of bourgeois experts by means of extremely high salaries is a retreat from the principles of the Paris Commune would be sinking to the level of bourgeois politicians and deceiving the people.[13]

One-Man Management

There were more difficult decisions to be accepted. To save industry from complete collapse, Lenin argued for the need to impose one-man management.

> Given ideal class-consciousness and discipline on the part of those participating in the common work, this subordination would be something like the mild leadership of a conductor of an orchestra. It may assume the sharp forms of a dictatorship if ideal discipline and class-consciousness are lacking. But be that as it may, *unquestioning subordination* to a single will is absolutely necessary for the success of processes organized on the pattern of large-scale machine industry.[14]

The specialist-manager must, at the same time, be subjected to pressure both from below, i.e. from the workers, and from above, i.e. from the workers' government and workers' organizations – the Soviet and trade unions.

> The masses must have the right to choose responsible leaders for themselves. They must have the right to replace them, the right to know and check each smallest step of their activity.[15]

> when putting 'management' in the hands of capitalists Soviet power appoints workers' Commissars or workers' committees who watch the manager's every step, who learn from his management experience and who not only have the right to appeal against his orders, but can secure his removal through the organs of Soviet power . . . 'management' is entrusted to capitalists only for executive functions while at work, the conditions of which are determined by the Soviet power, by which they may be abolished or revised.[16]

One must learn to combine workers' democracy with one-man management.

We must learn to combine the 'public meeting' democracy of the working people – turbulent, surging, overflowing its banks like a spring flood – with *iron* discipline while at work, with *unquestioning obedience* to the will of a single person, the Soviet leader, while at work.

We have not yet learned to do this.

We shall learn it.[17]

Undoubtedly, the opinion is very widely held . . . that one-man dictatorial authority is incompatible with democracy, the Soviet type of state and collective management. Nothing could be more mistaken than this opinion.[18]

Lenin also grasped another nettle: the need to impose strict discipline in the factories. Breaking management discipline was a central motive of proletarian action during the weeks and months prior to the October revolution. Now the proletariat in power has to impose a new discipline, a proletarian kind of discipline. To start with, in a speech on 13 (26) January 1918, Lenin defined the necessary work discipline based on the collective will of the proletariat, as *radically* different from the discipline imposed under capitalism: 'The socialist revolution is on, and everything now depends on the establishment of a discipline of equals, the discipline of the working masses themselves, which must take the place of capitalist barrack-room discipline.'[19]

On 23 April 1918, Lenin repeated this point:

the most difficult, the gravest phase in the life of our revolution has now begun . . . only iron endurance and labour discipline will enable the revolutionary Russian proletariat, as yet so solitary in its gigantic revolutionary work, to hold out till the time of deliverance when the international proletariat will come to our aid.[20]

Again, on 5 July 1918, he said:

We say that every new social order demands new relations between man and man, a new discipline. There was a time when economic life was impossible without feudal discipline, when there was only one kind of discipline – the discipline of the lash; and there was a time of the rule of the capitalists, when the disciplinary force was starvation. But now, with the Soviet revolution, with the beginning of the socialist revolution, discipline must be built on entirely new principles; it must be a discipline of faith in the organizing power of the workers and poor peasants, a discipline of comradeship, a discipline of the utmost mutual respect, a discipline of independence and initiative in the struggle.[21]

To impose discipline, Lenin calls for the application of the methods of capitalism itself. With implacable logic he demands the utilization of methods developed in order to intensify the exploitation of the workers, in order to raise productivity.

> We must raise the question of piece-work and apply and test it in practice; we must raise the question of applying much of what is scientific and progressive in the Taylor system;* we must make wages correspond to the total amount of goods turned out, or to the amount of work done by the railways, the water transport system, etc., etc. . . . The task that the Soviet government must set the people in all its scope is – learn to work. The Taylor system, the last word of capitalism in this respect, like all capitalist progress, is a combination of the refined brutality of bourgeois exploitation and a number of the greatest scientific achievements in the field of analysing mechanical motions during work, the elimination of superfluous and awkward motions, the elaboration of correct methods of work, the introduction of the best system of accounting and control, etc. The Soviet Republic must at all costs adopt all that is valuable in the achievements of science and technology in this field. The possibility of building socialism depends exactly upon our success in combining the Soviet power and the Soviet organization of administration with the up-to-date achievements of capitalism. We must organize in Russia the study and teaching of the Taylor system and systematically try it out and adapt it to our own ends.[22]

Lenin does not in any way disguise the nature of Taylorism as a method of increasing the intensity of labour. He had, after all, in 1914 described Taylorism as 'man's enslavement by the machine'.[23]

---

* F. W. Taylor, the American industrial expert (author of *Principles of Scientific Management*, 1911), pioneered the use of the stop-watch in industry as a means of extracting intensified labour from workers.

The Petty Bourgeois Threat

All the capitalist measures Lenin argued for – state capitalism, the employment of bourgeois specialists, one-man management, Taylorism, etc. – were necessary, in his view, because of the enormous threat facing the proletarian dictatorship in the form of the mass petty bourgeois peasantry. The island of industry in the hands of the proletariat might be engulfed by the vast seas of the backward peasantry.

He enumerated the socio-economic elements co-existing in the country as follows:

1. patriarchal, i.e. to a considerable extent natural, peasant farming;
2. small commodity production (this includes the majority of those peasants who sell their grain);
3. private capitalism;
4. state capitalism;
5. socialism.

Russia is so vast and so varied that all these different types of socio-economic structures are intermingled. This is what constitutes the specific feature of the situation.[24]

The greatest threat to workers' power are the first two elements: in the transition from capitalism to socialism our chief enemy is the petty bourgeoisie, its habits and customs, its economic position. The petty proprietor . . . has only one desire – to grab, to get as much as possible for himself.[25]

Either we subordinate the petty bourgeoisie to *our* control and accounting . . . or they will overthrow our workers' power as surely and as inevitably as the revolution was overthrown by the Napoleons and Cavaignacs who sprang from this very soil of petty proprietorship.[26]

Compared with petty bourgeois production and exchange, state capitalism, Lenin argues, has great positive advantages.

State capitalism would be a gigantic step forward . . . because victory over disorder, economic ruin and laxity is the most important thing; because the continuation of the anarchy of small ownership is the greatest, the most serious danger, and it will *certainly* be our ruin (unless we overcome it) . . . state capitalism will lead us to socialism by the surest road. When the working class has learned how to defend the state system against the anarchy of small ownership, when it has learned to organize large-scale production on a national scale, along state capitalist lines, it will hold, if I may use the expression, all the trump cards, and the consolidation of socialism will be assured.

In the first place, *economically*, state capitalism is immeasurably superior to our present economic system.

In the second place, there is nothing terrible in it for Soviet power, for the Soviet state is a state in which the power of the workers and the poor is assured.[27]

State capitalism is the bridge over which the peasantry will go forward to socialism. 'If the petty bourgeois were subordinated to state capitalism, the class-conscious workers would be bound to greet that with open arms, for state capitalism under the Soviet government would be three-quarters of socialism.'[28]

'At present, petty-bourgeois capitalism prevails in Russia, and it is *one and the same road* that leads from it to *both* large-scale state capitalism and to socialism, *through one and the same* intermediary station called "national accounting and control of production and distribution".'[29]

We Have to Learn New Methods of Organizing the Millions

The situation after the revolution demanded a totally new method of organizing the masses, according to Lenin:

We organized thousands under the tsar and hundreds of thousands under Kerensky. That is nothing, it does not count in politics. It was preparatory work, it was a preparatory course. Until the leading workers have learnt to organize tens of millions, they will not be socialists or creators of a socialist society, they will not acquire the necessary knowledge of organization. The road of organization is a long road and the tasks of socialist construction demand stubborn, long-continued work and appropriate knowledge, of which we do not have enough.[30]

The organizing work must also be radically new in qualitative terms. It must be practical and businesslike.

The chief and urgent requirement now is precisely the slogan of practical ability and businesslike methods . . . One can say that no slogan has been less popular among [revolutionaries]. It is quite understandable that as long as the revolutionaries' task consisted in destroying the old capitalist order they were bound to reject and ridicule such a slogan. For at that time this slogan in practice concealed the endeavour in one form or another to come to terms with capitalism, or to weaken the proletariat's attack on the foundations of capitalism, to weaken the revolutionary struggle against capitalism. Quite clearly, things were bound to undergo a radical change after the proletariat had conquered and consolidated its power and work had begun on a wide scale for laying the foundations of a new, i.e. socialist, society.[81]

Strengthening the Dictatorship of the Proletariat

Of course the policy of concessions to capitalism – in the form of state partnership with private industry, the employment and granting of economic privileges to technicians and specialists, who were bourgeois elements inherited from the old regime, one-man management, Taylorism, etc. – put the proletarian regime at risk. Only fools would not see this. And Lenin as always calls a spade a spade : 'the strength of the working class has always been that it looks danger boldly, squarely and openly in the face, that it does not fear to admit danger and soberly weighs the forces in "our" camp and in "the other" camp, the camp of the exploiters'.[32]

To face up to the threats to the proletarian power inherent in state capitalism does not mean to run away. Only cowards, argued Lenin, are paralysed by threats. What was necessary was to compromise with capitalist elements in the economic field, while strengthening the political dictatorship of the proletariat over them.

Of course we should not trust the bourgeois specialists :

the Soviet government has no loyal intelligentsia at its service. The intelligentsia are using their experience and knowledge – the highest human achievement – in the service of the exploiters, and are doing all they can to prevent our gaining victory over the exploiters . . . We have no one to depend upon but the class with which we achieved the revolution and with which we shall overcome the greatest difficulties, cross the very difficult zone that lies ahead of us – and that is the factory workers, the urban and rural proletariat.[33]

Above all, the dictatorship of the proletariat must be strengthened. We must 'ensure that we have a revolutionary authority, which we all recognize in words when speaking of the dictatorship of the proletariat, but instead of which we often see around us something as amorphous as jelly'.[84]

In Conclusion

After coming to power Lenin had to face a very difficult theoretical and practical task: to give flesh and blood to the concept of the *transition period* between capitalism and socialism. Without attempting to evade the reality, Lenin made it clear that this period would be one in which contradictory elements from the past and the future would co-exist while struggling with each other.

Communist and capitalist economic organization have many common characteristics. The workers' state – a transition stage between capitalism and communism – must inevitably include features of the society from whose ruins it rises, and some of the nuclei of the society of the future. These antagonistic elements will, however, be bound together in the transition period, the former being subordinated to the latter, the past to the future.

Workers' power and workers' control over production will immediately become a bridge between mental and manual labour, and the point of departure for their future synthesis, the total abolition of classes.

Technicians constitute a necessary element in the process of production, an important part of the productive forces of society, whether capitalist or communist. Under capitalism they form a level in the hierarchy of production. They come into being as part and parcel of this hierarchy, which socialism will abolish. In the transition period it will continue to exist in one sense, but in another it will be done away with. Insofar as mental labour remains the privilege of the few, hierarchical relations will continue to exist in the factories, railways, etc., even after the proletarian revolution. But as the place of the capitalist in the hierarchy will be taken by the workers' state, i.e. by the workers as a collective, the technicians will be subordinated to the workers, and the mental hierarchy in this sense will be abolished. Workers' control over technicians means the subordination of capitalist elements to socialist ones. The more effective workers' power, and the higher the material and cultural level of the masses, the more will the monopolist position of mental workers be undermined; eventually it will be completely abolished and a full synthesis of mental and manual labour will be achieved.

The founders of marxism pointed out that, because of the dual role of technicians in their relation to workers in the process of production, their subordination to the interests of society as a whole would be one of the most difficult tasks faced by the new society. Thus Engels wrote:

> If . . . a war brings us to power prematurely, the technicians will be our chief enemies; they will deceive and betray us wherever they can and we shall have to use terror against them but shall get cheated all the same.[35]

The imposition of labour discipline would be very difficult. Every form of social production needs the co-ordination of the different people participating in it; in other words, every form of social production needs discipline. Under capitalism this discipline confronts the worker as an external coercive power, as the power which capital has over him. Under socialism discipline will be the result of consciousness, it will become the habit of a free people. In the transition period it has to be the outcome of a combination of the two elements – consciousness and coercion. The proletarian state institutions will constitute the organization of the masses as a conscious factor. Collective ownership of the means of production by the workers, i.e. the ownership by the workers' state of the means of production, will be the basis for the conscious element in labour discipline. At the same time the working class as a collective, through its institutions – soviets, trade unions, etc. – will act as a coercive power in disciplining the individual workers in production.

The technicians, supervisors, etc., have a special place in labour discipline. Under capitalism, the supervisor is the means by which capitalist coercion of the worker is transmitted and exercised. Under communism a supervisor will not fulfil any coercive function. His relations with the workers will be analogous to those between a conductor and his orchestra, as labour discipline will be based on consciousness and habit. In the transition period, whereas the workers will be both a disciplining and a disciplined factor, a subject and an object, the technicians will serve only as a transmission mechanism, this time for the workers' state, even though they formally retain the role of disciplining the workers.[36]

7
War Communism
(1918–1921)

As we saw in the last chapter, in March and April 1918 Lenin developed an economic policy aimed at achieving a long process of reform on the basis of the proletarian revolution. However, the intensification of the class struggle, and the outbreak of civil war in May 1918, totally shattered this policy.

Nationalization of Industry Replacing Workers' Control

The policy of the Bolsheviks after October – workers' control of industry and selective nationalization – was sabotaged initially by the capitalists. Still hoping for restoration of their former power, and unwilling to work under workers' control, they practised large-scale sabotage.

Thus the All-Russian Congress of Employers' Associations declared at the beginning of December 1917 that those 'factories in which the control is exercised by means of active interference in the administration will be closed'.[1]

The Société Internationale des Wagon-Lits and the Sergeev-Ugalenski mines were nationalized because of 'the refusal of the management to continue work in the workshops', and because of 'the refusal of the management to submit to the Decree on Workers' Control'; M.Helferich-Sade's business was nationalized in January because management 'had closed down its factory and abandoned its principal office at Kharkov'. Similarly, the aeroplane works of Andreev Lanski and Company were taken over because of the company's declared intention to dismiss its workers; the Sestronetsk metallurgical works for refusing to continue production; Rostkino dye works for 'the categorical refusal of its owner to continue production in spite of the reserves of material and fuel in stock'.[2]

The workers reacted spontaneously to capitalist sabotage. As Serge put it:

> The liquidation of the political defences of their capitalist exploiters launched a spontaneous movement among the workers to take over the means of production. Since they were perfectly able to take control of the factories and workshops, why should they abstain? If they could, they ought. The employers' sabotage of production entailed expropriation as an act of reprisal.[3]

Of individual firms that had been nationalized before July 1918, only about 100 were nationalized by decree from the centre, while over 400 were nationalized on the initiative of local organizations.[4]

With the outbreak of civil war, not only did the bourgeoisie's attitude to the regime harden, and any previous willingness to cooperate evaporate completely, but for the Soviet government military necessity immediately took precedence over all other considerations. Such big capitalists as had not previously done so packed their bags and passed through the White Army's lines. For the Soviet authorities direct control over production quickly became an urgent necessity, both to combat attempts at sabotage and to ensure priority for military supplies. Hence there was wholesale nationalization. Altogether it was estimated that 70 per cent of all nationalizations in this period took place because the employers refused to accept workers' control or abandoned their enterprises.[5]

Not until 2 May 1918 was a whole industry nationalized – the sugar industry; then on 17 June the petroleum industry; on 28 June a decree was made for the nationalization of the largest undertakings in the mining, metallurgical, textile, electro-technical, pottery, tanning and cement industries. This set off a vast process of confiscation which continued until all the large factories in Soviet territory had been taken over by the state.

In many cases the nationalization of industry was carried out *independently* of the Soviet government. Thus between July and December 1918, of 1,208 enterprises nationalized, only 345 were expropriated by state decree, while the rest – 863 enterprises – were taken over by local soviets, or local national economic councils.[6]

The process continued, until it covered not only large-scale and medium-sized industry, but even small factories. In November 1920 a decree announced the nationalization of all enterprises employing more than five workers where mechanical power was used, and more than ten workers in purely handicraft workshops; by the end of the year as many as 37,000 enterprises were listed as belonging to the state. This figure included many thousands of quite small workshops: 18,000 of the 37,000 enterprises did not use mechanical power, and more than 5,000 of them were employing only one worker.[7]

The Bolsheviks were forced to go far beyond what they thought economically rational, and to expropriate capitalists in industry and trade, large and small. As the distinguished economic historian of the period, Kritzman, put it:

> In the atmosphere of the kindling civil war every joint effort of capital and the proletarian dictatorship (workers' control, mixed joint-stock companies etc.) is seen to be a quickly evaporating Utopia.
> The intervention of world capital, which fanned the expiring counter-revolutionary resistance within Russia into a new blaze, forced its consequence onto the proletariat – the inexorable expropriation of large-scale capital and capital generally, the confiscation of the property of the ruling classes, the suppression of the market and the construction of an all-embracing proletarian organization of the political economy, which depended on overcoming the market, and its exploitation.[8]

Thus from June 1918 onwards the imperative measures were general nationalization of industry and confiscations. The economic policy which Lenin drew up, involving an indirect attack on capitalism while making use of the captains of industry and the bourgeois technicians, proved unworkable.

The Collapse of Industrial Production

The wholesale nationalization of industry was accompanied by a catastrophic decline of industrial production. The civil war tore apart the Russian economy. The main industrial regions of northern and central Russia remained under Soviet rule throughout the civil war. But the factories in these regions and the railway system, were dependent on sources of raw materials and fuel which were often cut off for long periods. The engineering industry of Petrograd, Briansk, Tula and other Soviet industrial towns needed coal from the Donets Basin and iron from the Urals and from the Ukraine. The Urals region was lost from the summer of 1918 until the summer of 1919, when Kolchak was driven back into Siberia. The Donets Basin was completely cut off from Russia from the time of the German occupation of the Ukraine in spring 1918 until the retreat of Denikin's army in the latter months of 1919 (with the exception of a brief period early in 1918, when part of it was held by the Soviets). Baku oil was lost from the time the Turks occupied Baku in summer 1918 until the Red Army entered it in spring 1920. The secondary oil source in Grozny in the North Caucasus was cut off by Denikin. The textile mills of Moscow and the ring of factory towns around it depended on cotton from Turkestan, but Turkestan was cut off from Soviet Russia, first as a result of the Czechoslovak troops' onslaught on the Volga in the summer of 1918, and later, until the latter part of 1919, by Kolchak's advance. By that time the peasants of Turkestan had largely given up planting cotton (and substituted crops which would yield something to eat).

Foreign blockade dealt another serious blow to Soviet Russia's industry:

	Import	Export
	(in million pud)*	
1913	936·6	1472·1
1917	178·0	59·6
1918	11·5	1·8
1919	0·5	0·0
1920	5·2	0·7[9]

* pud = 16·38 kg = 36·11 lb.

A shortage of raw materials, fuel and food combined to bring about a disastrous fall in industrial productivity. Starvation, or semi-starvation, gravely affected workers' efficiency. According to approximate calculations, the gross product per head of the Russian worker changed as follows:

	Productivity per worker (in stable rubles)	
1913	100	–
1917	85	100
1918	44	52
1919	22	25
1920	26	30[10]

Absenteeism reached unprecedented levels. It was sometimes as high as 60 per cent, and quite commonly exceeded 30 per cent.[11] The average rate of absenteeism before the war had been about 10 per cent. In 1920 absenteeism in the best 'shock' plants increased threefold. In the Sormovsky plant it reached 36 per cent in July; in August it dropped to 32 per cent. At the Briansk plant it was 40 per cent during the winter months and rose to 48.5 per cent in June and to 50 per cent in August. At the Tver plant it was 44 per cent during July and August.[12]

It is impossible, of course, to evaluate the precise weight of the various factors leading to the decline in labour productivity. However, an attempt at an estimate, which should be taken only as a rough guide, was made by a Soviet economist, S.G.Strumilin. His assessment was that the decline of productivity in industry was caused by the following factors:

	%
Physical exhaustion of workers	44
Slackening of work discipline	22
Move to time-wages	19
Defects in work organization	6
Shortage of raw materials	6
Wear and tear of machines	4

Even if Strumilin's calculation is taken only as an approximation, it still unmistakably underlines the fact that the physical exhaustion of workers, brought about by undernourishment, was the major cause of the decline in labour productivity.[13] Workers were so wretchedly fed that it was not uncommon for them to faint at the bench. It was an act of heroism to work at all. The labour front demanded no less fortitude than the military front.

The catastrophic decline of large-scale industry can be seen from the following (production in 1913 = 100):

for 1917	77
for 1918	35
for 1919	26
for 1920	18[14]

What happened in different branches of industry can be seen from the following table:

Production in 1920 (1913 = 100)

Petroleum	42.7	Electric bulbs	10.1
Tobacco	42.5	Sugar	6.7
Leather	38	Electrical engineering	
Linen yarn	38	machinery and power	
Salt	30	current apparatus	5.4
Wool yarn	27	Cotton yarn goods	5.1
Coal	27	Railway carriage	
Paper and pulp	25	construction	4.2
Hemp spun yarn	23	Vegetable oils	3.0
Locomotive		Cement	3.0
construction	14.8	Pig iron	2.4
Matches	14	Bricks	2.1
Ploughs	13.3	Iron ore	1.7
Accumulators	12.5	Copper	0.0[15]

Railway transport, central to all economic (as well as military) activities, was in a critical state. The picture here was:

Year	% of damaged locomotives
1913	17
1918	41
1919	52
1920	57[16]

The Compulsory Requisition of Grain

The civil war, as well as breaking up the national economy of Russia, also imposed on industry massive demands from the Red Army. In summer 1920 the army was taking the following proportions of the country's centralized supplies:

	%		%
Flour	25	Fats	40
Groats	50	Soap	40
Feedstuffs	40	Tobacco	100
Fish	60	Matches	20
Meat	60	Cotton material	40
Dried fruit	90	Other textiles	70-100
Sugar	60	Footwear	90[17]
Salt	15		

After the army took its share of the shrinking industrial output, very little remained for the peasantry, so that the economic connection between industry and agriculture, between town and country, was broken. The peasant got very few industrial goods in exchange for the grain he delivered, as can be seen from the following table:

	Supply of grain from peasantry (million pud)*	Supply of textiles to peasantry (million arshin)**	Ratio between the two (arshins of textiles per pud of grain)
1919	108	325	1:3·00
1920	212	180	1:0·85[18]

* pud = 16·38 kg = 36·11 lb.
** arshin = 28 inches.

The only way the army and the town population could be guaranteed food was by the compulsory requisitioning of grain from the peasant. The all-powerful Food Commissariat took from industry whatever it produced for distribution among the population, and took from agriculture whatever could be extracted from the peasants, for distribution to the army and the town population, through rationing.

The collapse of industry and the violent suppression of

commercial relations between town and country meant that the exchange of grain and industrial goods which took place was not a real exchange. While the better-off peasantry supplied the majority of the grain, the poor peasantry got the industrial goods. As Kritzman said: 'The state exchange of products was . . . not so much an exchange between industry and agriculture, as an exchange of industrial products against the services that the poor peasants gave in the extraction of products from the farms of the well-to-do layers of the village.'[19]

The attempt at centralized state control of grain supplies was repeatedly undermined by the activity of millions of peasants,* as well as that of hungry townspeople foraging for food. Thus in 1919 out of the 136·6 million pud of cereal which reached the consumers, 40 per cent (i.e. 54·4 million pud) were delivered by the state distribution bodies (the People's Commissariat for food distribution) and 60 per cent (82·2 million pud) by illegal 'free' trade.[20]

Food Rationing

A central characteristic of the economic system at the time of the civil war was distribution of grain by the state according to rigid class criteria.

In September 1918 the Moscow Soviet divided the population into four categories. The first consisted of manual workers engaged in harmful trades; the second, of workers who were obliged to perform heavy physical labour; the third, of workers in light tasks, employees, housewives; the fourth, of professional men and women and people living on unearned income or without employment. Such food supplies as were available were doled out to these four categories in the ratio 4:3:2:1. However, even the most favoured category got very meagre rations indeed. People in the first category in Petrograd during May 1919 received the following allotments: 15½ pounds of bread, one pound of sugar, half a pound of margarine, four pounds of herrings, two pounds of other fish, one pound of salt and a quarter of a pound of mustard.[21]

---

* See Chapter 10 for the peasants' massive resistance to requisitions.

At the worst period the meagre bread ration of 2 oz. for workers was issued on alternate days.[22]

A Soviet author calculates that the food-card system in Moscow gave the population about one-seventh of the calories which the Germans received on ration cards during the war and about one-tenth of the calories which the British obtained. Even if one makes allowance for the fact that the Russians may have been able to purchase extra food on the private market, it is evident that malnutrition and in some cases downright starvation were far more prevalent in Russia than in wartime Germany or Britain.[23]

Hunger, Epidemics and Cold

Hunger stalked the towns. One result was a massive flight of the population to the countryside. The urban population, and particularly the number of industrial workers, declined very sharply between 1917 and 1920. In the autumn of 1920 the population of 40 capitals of provinces had declined since 1917 by 33 per cent, from 6,400,000 to 4,300,000, and the population of 50 other large towns by 16 per cent, from 1,517,000 to 1,271,000. The larger the city, the greater the decline. The population of Petrograd fell from 2,400,000 in 1917 to 574,000 in August 1920.

In the footsteps of hunger came epidemics, above all typhus. The following is the number of typhus victims in European Russia (in thousands):

1914	83	1918	180
1915	90	1919	2105
1916	102	1920	3114
1917	88		

So in two years over *five million* people fell ill with typhus.[24]

Without exaggeration Lenin could declare to the Seventh Congress of Soviets on 5 December 1919:

A scourge is assailing us, *lice*, and the *typhus* that is mowing down our troops. Comrades, it is impossible to imagine the dreadful situation in the typhus regions, where the population is broken, weakened, without material resources, where all life, all public life ceases. To this we say, 'Comrades, we must concentrate everything on this problem. *Either the lice will defeat socialism, or socialism will defeat the lice!*[25]

Deaths from typhus alone in the years 1918-20 numbered 1·6 million, and typhoid, dysentery and cholera caused another 700,000.[26] All told, the number of premature deaths is estimated for the period from 1 January 1918 to 1 July 1920 at *seven million*, i.e. at 7 per cent of the total population.[27]

This estimate does not cover the peripheral areas of Russia such as Siberia and the South East. If these were included the number of premature deaths must have been more than nine million. This far surpasses the number of deaths in combat – estimated at about 350,000.

Cold added to the suffering of the population. As the most essential industries and the transport system were chronically short of fuel, practically nothing was allocated for domestic heating. So abandoned houses were torn down by the people who had strength for such activity, and the wood used for heating.

Suffering was indescribable. Numerous cases of cannibalism occurred. A quarter of Russia's population – 35 million – suffered from continuous acute hunger. Several million orphan waifs roamed roads, railway tracks and city streets, living on charity and crime. The weak suffered most. And nobody was weaker than the children. On 2 April 1920 Gorky wrote to Lenin: 'In Petrograd there are over 6,000 juvenile delinquents aged 9 to 15, all of them recidivists and with no few murderers amongst them. There are 12-year-olds who have as many as three murders to their name.'[28]

Victor Serge described the terrible affliction of children at the time:

Do you know what Tata is doing? She can't sleep with the commissars, not with a broken nose and a voice like an old worn-out shoe. But she found herself a racket. She undresses little kids. 'Here, little boy, come here. I've got something interesting to show you ...'

She takes the kid by the hand, all sweet and nice, and leads him into a hallway. Two slaps across his little face and Tata collects his coat, his hat, his gloves, a good day's work.

'That turns my stomach,' said Katka. 'Poor little kids.'

'They're gonna croak one way or another,' said Manya softly. 'These days.'

'And anyway,' ventures Dunya-the-Snake, 'if they're the kids of the bourgeois, too bad for them.'

'Shut up, you stupid little Agit-Prop. You know that big building they're putting up over on the canal? Well, a whole gang of kids is holed up in there, with Olenka-the-Runaway as their chief. What do you say to that? Ah, now there's a somebody for all her thirteen years. Looks like a little lamb; sweet, well-mannered and all that, but cunning. I'm sure she's the one who killed that little boy by the Oats Market. You know what they thought up? They catch cats, they eat them, and sell the skins to the Chinese . . . They also work poorboxes in the churches and ration cards in the food lines.'[29]

Egalitarianism

Strict egalitarianism was preached and practised by the Bolshevik party. 'Our salaries were linked to the "Communist Maximum",' Serge recalled, 'equal to the average wage of a skilled worker.' He went on to relate how the eldest son of Ionov, Zinoviev's brother-in-law, an executive member of the Soviet and director of the state Library, died of hunger before their very eyes.[30]

> In the Kremlin, he [Lenin] still occupied a small apartment built for a palace servant. In the second winter, he, like everyone else, had had no heating. When he went to the barber's he took his turn, thinking it unseemly for anyone to give way to him.[31]

Lenin was very angry when he found out that he had been paid too much, and on 23 May 1918 he rebuked V.D.Bonch-Bruevich, office manager of the Council of People's Commissars:

> In view of your failure to fulfil my insistent request to point out to me the justification for raising my salary as from 1 March 1918, from 500 to 800 rubles a month, and in view of the obvious illegality of this increase, I give you a severe reprimand.[32]

Krupskaya used to go to the Kremlin restaurant to fetch the family dinner. She was often seen walking along the icy Kremlin pavement with a big chunk of black bread under her arm, and carrying in front of her a pot of soup. But though her trip to the restaurant was timed for Lenin's return home, she rarely found him there. Maria, Lenin's sister, would phone his office. He promised to come right away. After ten or fifteen minutes she would phone again, pleading with him to come home as the food was getting cold. When at last he did come home, as punishment he would have to wait till the food was warmed again.

A high government official in the Kremlin could tell the *Manchester Guardian* correspondent Arthur Ransome:

> Today is the first day for two months that we have been able to warm this building. We have been working here in overcoats and fur hats in a temperature below freezing point . . . Many of my assistants have fallen ill. Two only yesterday had to be taken home in a condition something like that of a fit, the result of prolonged sedentary work in unheated rooms. I have lost the use of my right hand for the same reason.[33]

Super-Centralization of Management

War communism meant extreme centralization of economic management. But this did not mean rational planning of the economy. Disintegration of production, the substitution of compulsion for exchange between town and country, and compulsion in the labour field, did not aid rational calculation and planning. Orders from the centre were also often confused and contradictory, because of the sheer pressure of the civil war conditions and the inexperience of the administration. As Lenin put it: 'such is the sad fate of our decrees: they are signed, and then we ourselves forget about them and fail to carry them out'.[34]

Kritzman called the resultant confusion 'the most complete form of proletarian natural-anarchistic economy'. 'Anarchistic' because of conflicts between administrative departments and because of the lack of any coherent plan. Anarchistic too because of the 'shock' *(udarnii)* campaigning methods, by which the authorities rushed from bottleneck to bottleneck, creating new shortages while seeking feverishly to deal with others.

There was no unified economic plan. The war was given priority and improvisation was substituted for rational planning. As Maurice Dobb, an economic historian of the period, put it:

The administrative chaos and delays which resulted from the passing of so many decisions about matters of detail through a few central bottlenecks had their reaction in what came to be known as the 'shock' system . . . To by-pass the administrative congestion when its economic results became alarming, certain enterprises of special importance, usually from the immediate military point of view, were singled out as 'shock' enterprises. These were given top priority in the supply of fuel and materials and food rations for their workers, and the best organizers available were assigned to their administration. When applied only to a limited range of industry, it was, of course, a reasonable method of applying priorities and its effect was beneficial (for example, in improving the situation in transport). In the situation of civil war it is difficult to see what other method could have been quickly applied. But in the course of time, as soon as it had come to be applied to all widely, it tended in many cases to increase rather than to lessen the economic confusion.[35]

Has the Communist Millennium Arrived?

The desperate measures taken by the Bolsheviks seemed to many at the time to be an unexpectedly rapid realization of the Party programme for achieving Communism. Socialization of industry, the requisitions of food, the payment of wages in kind, the liquidation of money, the state's growing role in the distribution of resources throughout the national economy, the abolition of the market economy which was the breeding ground of capitalism – all looked like the achievement of full communism. After all, according to Marx, the future Communist economy was to be a natural economy in which socialist planned production and distribution would take the place of production for the market. The Bolshevik leaders were therefore naturally inclined to see the essential features of communism embodied in the war economy of the civil war period. The stern egalitarianism which the party preached and practised strengthened this belief.

In March 1919 Lenin wrote: 'In the sphere of distribution, the present task of Soviet power is to continue steadily replacing trade by the planned, organized and nation-wide distribution of goods . . . The Russian Communist Party will strive as speedily as possible to introduce the most radical measures to pave the way for the abolition of money.'[36]

On the second anniversary of the October revolution Lenin could define the economic system prevailing as communist.

> In Russia, labour is united communistically insofar as, first, private ownership of the means of production has been abolished, and, secondly, the proletarian state power is organizing large-scale production on state-owned land and in state-owned enterprises on a national scale, is distributing labour-power among the various branches of production and the various enterprises, and is distributing among the working people large quantities of articles of consumption belonging to the state.[87]

However, Lenin sometimes contradicted himself, saying that the prevailing system was very primitive, and far from real communism.

> We give the name of communism to the system under which people form the habit of performing their social duties without any special apparatus for coercion, and when unpaid work for the public good becomes a general phenomenon . . . The expropriation of the landowners and capitalists enabled us to organize only the most primitive forms of socialism, and there is not yet anything communist in it. If we take our present-day economy we see that the germs of socialism in it are still very weak and that the old economic forms dominate overwhelmingly; these are expressed either as the domination of petty proprietorship or as wild, uncontrolled profiteering.[88]

The Bolshevik leader who was most enthusiastic about War Communism as real communism was Bukharin. He saw the distribution of rations in kind instead of wages in money as the disappearance of wage labour. He thought that the monetary system, and with it the commodity system in general, would collapse during the period of transition, this being made manifest through the devaluation of the currency.[39]

Marx's concept of communist society, however, was based on highly developed productive forces with a superabundance of goods and services, and rational organization of the economy. Economic inequality was to be abolished by levelling up living standards. War Communism was, on the contrary, the result of the destruction and disintegration of production, of the unparalleled scarcity of goods and services.

As Marx stated repeatedly: 'Law can never be higher than the economic structure and the cultural level conditioned by it.' The Bolsheviks had no doubt that the material heritage they had acquired on taking power was very meagre, not only in comparison with contemporary developed capitalist countries, but even with these same countries at an early stage of their capitalist development.

The most complete and accurate calculation of the national income in different countries at different periods was undertaken by Colin Clark in his book *The Conditions of Economic Progress* (London, 1940). He estimates the real income per occupied person in Russia in 1913 to be 306 International Units (IUs).* As against this the real income per occupied person in some developed countries was:

Great Britain		France		Germany		USA	
Year	I.U.	Year	I.U.	Year	I.U.	Year	I.U.
1688	372	1850-59*	382	1850	420	1850	787
1860-69*	638	1860-69*	469	1877	632	1880	1,032
1904-10*	999	1911	786	1913	881	1900	1,388
1913	1,071					1917	1,562
						1929	1,636

* Annual average

Thus the average income per occupied person in Russia in 1913 was only 80·9 per cent of the corresponding figure for Britain in 1688.[40] The level of literacy in Russia at the time of the revolution was *below* that of France at the time of its revolution, in 1789!

The Utopian hopes of the Bolsheviks in the period of War Communism appear completely inexplicable at first glance. However, they were based on the hope of an early victory of the revolution in the West, which would have made possible a *direct* progression from War Communism to the systematic construction of socialism. In addition, the illusions prevailing were an integral part of the moral courage of the masses and were imposed by the harsh exigencies of the civil war.

---

* Clark defines the 'International Unit' as 'the amount of goods and services which one dollar would purchase in USA over the average of the period 1925-34'.

In Retrospect

After the civil war and the ending of War Communism, Lenin summed up the balance of experience of the period, admitting both the errors of the time, and their inevitability. Thus, in a speech on 17 October 1921, he said:

> Partly owing to the war problems that overwhelmed us and partly owing to the desperate position in which the Republic found itself owing to these circumstances, and a number of others, we made the mistake of deciding to go over directly to communist production and distribution. We thought that under the surplus-food appropriation system the peasants would provide us with the required quantity of grain, which we could distribute among the factories and thus achieve communist production and distribution.
>
> I cannot say that we pictured this plan as definitely and as clearly as that; but we acted approximately on those lines . . .
>
> that line was wrong . . . it ran counter to what we had previously written about the transition from capitalism to socialism . . . Ever since 1917, when the problem of taking power arose . . . our theoretical literature has been definitely stressing the necessity for a prolonged, complex transition, through socialist accounting and control, from capitalist society (and the less developed it is the longer the transition will take) to even one of the approach to communist society.[41]

The mistakes of the party were the result of overenthusiasm and euphoria, according to Lenin.

> Borne along on the crest of the wave of enthusiasm, rousing first the political enthusiasm and then the military enthusiasm of the people, we expected to accomplish economic tasks just as great as the political and military tasks we had accomplished by relying directly on this enthusiasm. We expected – or perhaps it would be truer to say that we presumed without having given it adequate consideration – to be able to organize the state production and the state distribution of products on communist lines in a small-peasant country directly as ordered by the proletarian state. Experience has proved that we were wrong. It appears that a number of transitional stages were necessary – state capitalism and socialism – in order to *prepare* – to prepare by many years of effort – for the transition to communism. Not directly relying on enthusiasm, but aided by the enthusiasm engendered by the great revolution, and on the basis of personal interest, personal incentive and business principles, we must

first set to work in this small-peasant country to build solid gangways to socialism by way of state capitalism.[42]

Nothing can be an excuse for hiding one's own mistakes. 'We are not afraid to admit our mistakes and shall examine them dispassionately in order to learn how to correct them.'[43]

The Soviet government had to probe the strength of the enemy, to gauge its own forces, to determine by experience the path actually open for systematic development of economic life; and these tasks could not have been achieved without resort to the methods of War Communism. As Lenin, looking back at the period, put it:

To explain my views and to indicate in what sense we can, and in my opinion should, say that our previous economic policy was mistaken, I would like to take for the purpose of analogy an episode from the Russo-Japanese War ... the capture of Port Arthur by the Japanese General Nogi. The main thing that interests me in this episode is that the capture of Port Arthur was accomplished in two entirely different stages. The first stage was that of furious assaults, which ended in failure and cost the celebrated Japanese commander extraordinarily heavy losses. The second stage was the extremely arduous, extremely difficult and slow method of siege, according to all the rules of the art. Eventually, it was by this method that the problem of capturing the fortress was solved. When we examine these facts we naturally ask in what way was the Japanese general's first mode of operation against the fortress a mistake? ...
At first sight, of course, the answer to this question would seem to be a simple one. If a series of assaults on Port Arthur proved to be ineffective – and that was the case – if the losses sustained by the assailants were extremely heavy – and that, too, was undeniably the case – it is evident that the tactics of immediate and direct assault upon the fortress of Port Arthur were mistaken ... On the other hand, however, it is easy to understand that in solving a problem in which there are very many unknown factors, it is difficult without the necessary practical experience to determine with absolute certainty the mode of operation to be adopted against the enemy fortress, or even to make a fair approximation of it. It was impossible to determine this without ascertaining in practice the strength of the fortress, the strength of its fortifications, the state of its garrison, etc. Without this it was impossible for even the best of commanders, such as General Nogi undoubtedly was, to decide what tactics to

adopt to capture the fortress . . . without . . . the practical
attempt to carry the fortress by assault . . . there would have
been no grounds for adopting the more prolonged and arduous
method of struggle . . . Taking the operations as a whole, we
cannot but regard the first stage, consisting of direct assaults
and attacks, as having been a necessary and useful stage, because
. . . without this experience the Japanese army could not have
learnt sufficiently the concrete conditions of the struggle.[44]

The direct, furious assault on capitalism represented by War
Communism was similarly a necessary stage in the development
of the dictatorship of the proletariat, an inevitable product of the
raging civil war.

The capitalist apparatus – the management of the factories,
the banks, etc. – was destroyed. There was no possibility of coming
to terms economically with the bourgeoisie, even in terms of
concessions or restricted workers' control. With the bourgeois
apparatus of economic management destroyed, there was no
alternative but to create a substitute, however crude. The policy
of compulsory grain requisition and centralized direction of labour
followed from the collapse of the market and the conditions of
siege economy. As Trotsky put it in retrospect:

This 'communism' was rightly called *War Communism* not only
because it replaced economic methods by military ones but also
because it served military purposes above all others. It was not
a question of assuring a systematic development of economic life
under the prevailing conditions, but of securing the indispensable food supply for the army at the fronts and of preventing
the working class from dying out altogether. War Communism
was the regime of a beleaguered fortress.[45]

In his Report to the Tenth Party Congress in March 1921,
introducing the New Economic Policy (NEP) Lenin reiterated that
War Communism had been unavoidable.

There was no other way out in the conditions of the unexampled
ruin in which we found ourselves, when after a big war we were
obliged to endure a number of civil wars. We must state quite
definitely that, in pursuing our policy, we may have made mistakes and gone to extremes in a number of cases. But in the wartime conditions then prevailing, the policy was in the main a
correct one. We had no alternative but to resort to wholesale
and instant monopoly, including the confiscation of all surplus

stocks, even without compensation. That was the only way we could tackle the task.[46]

And in a pamphlet, 'The Tax in Kind' explaining NEP, written on 21 April 1921, Lenin repeats:

It was the war and the ruin that forced us into War Communism. It was not, and could not be, a policy that corresponded to the economic tasks of the proletariat. It was a makeshift.[47]

Despite all the criticism of the policy of War Communism, there is no doubt that it was this policy that enabled Soviet Russia to emerge victorious, despite the breakdown of the economy and the excruciating suffering of the workers and peasants. It enabled the Soviet government to mobilize sufficient strength and concentrate the energy and heroism of the revolutionary masses on the most vital immediate task.

8
The Heroic and the Tragic Intertwine

The Wide Sweep of the Revolution

'Miracles of proletarian organization must be achieved.' This idea of Lenin's provides a key to the victory of the working class. In 1917 and the period following, the policy of the Bolsheviks consisted mainly in awakening – and at the same time guiding – the initiative of the masses. In three years of struggle the proletariat, first in the conquest of power, then in its consolidation and defence, showed exceptional collective heroism and self-sacrifice amidst unparalleled tortures of hunger, cold and constant peril. Every time there was a real threat to the regime thousands of proletarians volunteered for the war front and for voluntary labour behind the front. In fact, half of all trade unionists volunteered for the Red Army, and scattered along a front stretching for thousands of miles, they died and taught others how to die. The revolutionary idealism of the proletariat was unprecedented. Half-starved people in felt shoes and dirty linen showed supreme heroism in the struggle for freedom. Lenin could justifiably declare in March 1920:

> We overthrew the landowners and capitalists because the men of the Red Army, workers and peasants, knew they were fighting for their own vital interests.
> We won because the best people from the entire working class and from the entire peasantry displayed unparalleled heroism in the war against the exploiters, performed miracles of valour, withstood untold privations, made great sacrifices and got rid of scroungers and cowards.[1]

> The determination of the working class, its inflexible adherence to the watchword 'Death rather than surrender!' is not only a historical factor, it is the decisive, the winning factor.[2]

The victories wrested by the Red Army from armies which were infinitely better equipped were a product of the astonishing heroism displayed by the proletariat and its indomitable will to defend Soviet power. For all their miseries, squalor and cruelty, the years of the civil war were years not only of destruction, but also of a mighty sweep of creation, courage and soaring hope.

In the revolution and the period of consolidation of Soviet power, the party relied above all on the aspirations of the masses. Addressing the Second All-Russian Congress of Soviets, at the very moment of the Bolshevik seizure of power, Lenin declared: 'We must allow complete freedom to the creative faculties of the masses.' A few days later he said: 'Creative activity at the grass roots is the basic factor of the new public life . . . living, creative socialism is the product of the masses themselves.'[3] And in an appeal to the population published in *Pravda* of 6 (19) November 1917, he wrote:

> Comrades, working people! Remember that now *you yourselves* are at the helm of state. No one will help you if you yourselves do not unite and take into *your* hands *all affairs* of the state . . . Get on with the job yourselves; begin right at the bottom, do not wait for anyone.[4]

Never before had the working class become the ruling class of a great country, and never had the revolutionary class fought more tenaciously and heroically against a mighty coalition of domestic and foreign enemies. The first workers' republic in world history survived thanks to the most resolute measures carried out by the proletariat and its party. As Lenin stated in retrospect:

> The defence of the workers' and peasants' power was achieved by a miracle, not a divine miracle – it was not something that fell from the skies – but a miracle in the sense that, no matter how oppressed, humiliated, ruined and exhausted the workers and peasants were, precisely because the revolution went along with the workers, it mustered very much more strength than any rich, enlightened and advanced state could have mustered.[5]

Never before had such radical changes in social structure been carried out in so short a time. Semi-feudal relations of land ownership were swept away far more radically than even the French Revolution had done. Practically all the factories, mines and other valuable natural resources of the country were taken over by the workers' state.

The sweep of the revolution was no less wide in the field of what Marx called 'the ideological superstructure'. Above all, it brought about an insatiable appetite for culture in the mass of the workers. Thus Trotsky wrote: 'The greatest advantage, the greatest conquest that the revolution has offered up to this time . . . has been the awakening of a powerful thirst for culture among the working masses.'[6]

John Reed wrote:

> The thirst for education, so long thwarted, burst with the Revolution into a frenzy of expression. From Smolny Institute alone [during] the first six months, went out every day tons, car-loads, train-loads of literature, saturating the land. Russia absorbed reading matter like hot sand drinks water, insatiable. And it was not fables, falsified history, diluted religion, and the cheap fiction that corrupts – but social and economic theories, philosophy, the works of Tolstoy, Gogol, and Gorky . . .
> Then the talk, beside which Carlyle's 'flood of French speech' was a mere trickle. Lectures, debates, speeches – in theatres, circuses, school-houses, clubs, Soviet meeting-rooms, union headquarters, barracks . . . Meetings in the trenches at the front, in village squares, factories . . . What a marvellous sight to see Puti-

lovsky Zavod [the Putilov factory] pour out its forty thousand to listen to Social Democrats, Socialist Revolutionaries, Anarchists, anybody, whatever they had to say, as long as they would talk! For months in Petrograd, and all over Russia, every street-corner was a public tribune. In railway trains, streetcars, always the spurting up of impromptu debate everywhere.[7]

Serge remembers:

In spite of . . . grotesque misery, a prodigious impulse was given to public education. Such a thirst for knowledge sprang up all over the country that new schools, adult courses, universities and Workers' Faculties were formed everywhere. Innumerable fresh initiatives laid open the teaching of unheard of, totally unexplored domains of learning. Institutes for retarded children were founded; a network of institutions for pre-school infants was created; the Workers' Faculties and the special short courses placed secondary education within the grasp of the workers. Soon afterwards the conquest of the universities was to begin. In this period too, the museums were enriched by the confiscation of private collections – extraordinary honesty and care characterized this expropriation of artistic riches. Not one work of any significance was lost.[8]

New libraries were established; a large cheap edition of the works of the leading Russian classical authors in all fields was initiated; there was an effort to expand the primary school system.[9]

Thousands of workers crowded the theatres.

There is great activity in theatres, now set free from the thraldom of the box-office, and crowded nightly . . . It is the proletariat now, in half-sheepskin and home-spun and birch-bark, that fills the boxes and stalls . . . Moscow's workers feasted their imaginations till they passed out from the brightness and glamour of the theatre into the white night and the dust and the hunger outside.[10]

There was hectic activity on the part of painters and sculptors immediately after the Revolution, and for a time futurists and cubists held the centre of the scene and decorated blank walls, pavements and other available places with their creations. Trotsky wrote:

The popular masses were still quivering in every fibre, and were thinking aloud for the first time in a thousand years. All the best youthful forces of art were touched to the quick. During those first years, rich in hope and daring, there were created not only the most complete models of socialist legislation, but also the best productions of revolutionary literature. To the same times belong, it is worth remarking, the creation of those excellent Soviet films which, in spite of a poverty of technical means, caught the imagination of the whole world with the freshness and vigour of their approach to reality.[11]

Above all, the revolution meant the awakening of the personality of the workers. In 1845 Engels had found the essence of socialism to be to create 'for all *people* such a condition that everyone can freely develop his human nature and live in a human relationship with his neighbours.'[12] In the Russian revolution the souls of the oppressed yearned after a purer, better life. With incisiveness Trotsky defined the revolution thus:

> the revolution is in the first place an awakening of human personality in the masses – who were supposed to possess no personality. In spite of occasional cruelty and the sanguinary relentlessness of its methods, the revolution is, before and above all, the awakening of humanity, its onward march, and is marked with a growing respect for the personal dignity of every individual, with an ever-increasing concern for those who are weak.[13]

> Yesterday the man of the mass was still a nobody, a slave of the Tsar, of the gentry, of the bureaucracy, an appendage to the ... machine ... a beast of burden ... Having freed himself, he is now most acutely aware of his own identity and begins to think of himself as of ... the centre of the world.[14]

Lenin's Revolutionary Realism

The élan of the mass of the workers indicates the goal they are striving to reach. The legacy – material and cultural – of the old order determines their point of departure on the long march. Lenin, who always combined determined perseverance in fighting for revolutionary ideals with a sense of realism, who had his head in the clouds but his feet firmly on the ground, could not but be very conscious of the sharp contradiction between the grand aspirations of the workers and their actual poverty, material and cultural. Lenin knew well that the fate of the revolution lay in this contradiction and its development. Titanic struggles would decide how the contradiction would be solved.

In the period following the revolution, Lenin achieved the highest synthesis of daring in design and prudence in application. A clear understanding of the objective circumstances made it possible for the party and its leadership to retain their bearings and their confidence through the twists and turns of the struggle.

Lenin again and again repeated that the Bolsheviks were badly prepared to govern. Thus in a pamphlet entitled *The Achievements and Difficulties of the Soviet Government*, written in March-April 1919, he wrote:

> The science which we, at best, possess is the science of the agitator and propagandist, of the man who has been steeled by the hellishly hard lot of the factory worker, or starving peasant, a science which teaches us how to hold out for a long time and to persevere in the struggle, and this has saved us up to now. All this is necessary, but it is not enough. With this alone we cannot triumph.[15]

The Bolsheviks were by no means ready to face the problems of managing the economy. Lenin told the Party Congress on 18 March 1919:

> At first we regarded them in an entirely abstract way, like revolutionary preachers, who had absolutely no idea of how to set to work. There were lots of people, of course, who accused us – and all the socialists and Social-Democrats are accusing us today – of having undertaken this task without knowing how to finish it. But these accusations are ridiculous, made by people who lack the spark of life. As if one can set out to make a great revolution and know beforehand how it is to be completed! Such knowledge cannot be derived from books and our decision could spring only from the experience of the masses. And I say that it is to our credit that amidst incredible difficulties we undertook to solve a problem with which until then we were only half familiar, that we inspired the proletarian masses to display their own initiative.[16]

What was needed above all was perseverance, readiness to admit mistakes and correct them. Lenin and his friends showed these attributes in abundance.

> Perseverence, persistence, willingness, determination and ability to test things a hundred times, to correct them a hundred times,

but to achieve the goal come what may – these . . . qualities of the proletariat are a guarantee that the proletariat will conquer.[17]

What was needed for the inexperienced party leading the government of a large country was to confront reality directly.

It is precisely because we are not afraid to look danger in the face that we make the best use of our forces for the struggle – we weigh the chances more dispassionately, cautiously and prudently.[18]

Our strength lies in complete clarity and the sober consideration of *all* the existing class magnitudes, both Russian and international; and in the inexhaustible energy, iron resolve and devotion in struggle that arise from this.[19]

Neither the euphoria of optimism nor the morass of pessimism is useful. 'Pessimism or optimism? *Calculation of forces.* Sober approach and fervent dedication,'[20] wrote Lenin in late March-early April 1921.

The Harsh Circumstances
of Proletarian Dictatorship in Russia

The French Revolution took place in a country that had achieved the highest level of economic and cultural development in the world except for England. Russia was one of the most backward countries in Europe. And from the outset the Russian bourgeoisie resorted to harsh counter-revolutionary measures, relying on the support of world capitalism. The pressure of counter-revolution and the civil war forced the Bolsheviks to take the extremely harsh economic measures of War Communism, dealt with in the last chapter.

The proletarian dictatorship was forced, therefore, to direct its weapons not only against the big bourgeoisie, but also against the petty bourgeoisie and the mass of the peasantry. With the proletariat in a minority, especially as there were no sharp divisions between proletariat and peasantry, and with hunger and cold gnawing into the very nerves of the workers, the danger was, of course, that the dictatorship would be directed not only against the big bourgeoisie as well as the petty bourgeoisie and peasantry, but also against the proletariat itself. To run ahead of the story, the Central Committee thesis adopted on 22 January 1920 may be quoted:

> In a society which is in a transitional phase of its development and which is hardened with the inheritance of a distressing past, the passage to a planned organization of socialized labour is inconceivable without compulsory measures being applied to the parasitic elements, to the backward sections of the peasantry, and even to the working class itself.[21]

Thus in its weakness, the proletariat which was ripe for dictatorship over society is found to tolerate a dictatorship over itself. The collective, democratic base of the dictatorship of the proletariat was undermined still further by the fact that, as a result of the collapse of industry, the proletariat itself almost ceased to exist.

For Marx the revolution was a prerequisite for the maturing of the proletariat, for it to change itself so as to be able to change society: the 'revolution is necessary, therefore, not only because the ruling class cannot be overthrown in any other way, but also because the class *overthrowing* it can only in a revolution succeed in ridding itself of all the muck of ages and become fitted to found society anew'.[22]

What would happen if the 'old excrement' were too massive and the proletariat too small, and too much weakened in the process of the revolution, to revolutionize itself?

In the Russian proletariat during the civil war there were both collective heroism and paltriness, backwardness and bestiality intermingled; 'obtuse bestiality and the highest revolutionary idealism' intertwined, were Trotsky's words.[23] Novels and stories of the time reveal this duality everywhere. Isaac Babel's stories reveal this – revolutionary heroism mixed with passion, cruelty, fear and blind violence. In the stories in his collection *The Red Cavalry*, he describes his companions flashing their swords right and left to the war cry of 'All hail to the world revolution'. They die for this slogan, but they also die shouting obscenities, blasphemies or imbecile jokes. The appalling cruelty of the Cossacks is fitted in these stories into a heroic framework. Thus in a story called 'Berestechko' Babel describes how in a devastated village in Belorussia, among corpses of old men and pregnant women with their bellies split open by the retreating Poles, Babel's friend Kudrya, a Red Cossack, cuts the throat of a Jew accused of spying. Anti-semitic obscenities flow from the mouths of heroic soldiers. For instance: 'And what did we see in the town of Maykop? We saw there that the rear was not of the same mind as the front and that everywhere was treachery and full of dirty Yids like under the old regime.' In a story entitled 'Salt', a soldier murders a peasant woman because she deceived him in order to sneak into an overcrowded train. Telling the story he ends: 'So I took my faithful rifle off the wall and washed away that stain from the face of the workers' land and the republic.' These same soldiers turn into heroes ready to give up their lives for comrades and for the cause of the revolution. 'During weekdays . . . the conscious-ness of the class becomes absorbed and distracted by current cares and concerns; the differences in the interests and views among the various groupings within the working class come to the forefront. But the very next major events completely reveal the profound unity of the working class that has passed through the fiery school of the revolution,' Trotsky writes.[24]

One would not expect the masses emerging from capitalism to be free of the filth of this society, as Lenin said: 'the corpse of bourgeois society cannot be nailed in a coffin and buried. The corpse of capitalism is decaying and disintegrating in our midst, polluting the air and poisoning our lives, enmeshing that which is new, fresh, young and virile in thousands of threads and bonds of that which is old, moribund and decaying.'[25]

One may read the stories of Isaac Babel, the poetry of Demian Bedny, describing the less admirable side of the people, or Trotsky's articles about the need to clean one's boots and not to throw cigarette butts on the floor, or the need to avoid swearing and bad language, and say, 'See how inadequate the revolution was, how dull the masses were!' The reaction should be exactly the opposite: see how magnificently the masses behaved, despite famine and the closeness of death, while they still carried the barbarous inheritance of capitalism, and were emerging from the darkness and destitution of Tsarism without any tradition of commanding or wielding power.'

The heroic and tragic also intertwined in the fate of the

party. The fact that a revolutionary party is vital for the victory of the revolution demonstrated both the bond between the party and the class, and the disparity between the vanguard and the rest of the class in terms of the level of consciousness and organization. By organizing the vanguard, the party increased its weight within the working class as a whole. But the party is not omnipotent, and its power depends directly on the level of activity and strength of the proletariat. The process of decomposition of the proletariat must have a radical influence on the party. There are limits to the force of the will and nerves even of the toughest revolutionaries.

In the agony of terrible hunger, cold and death, with the assault of the international counter-revolutionary forces, with the decline in the size, economic and social weight of the Russian proletariat – what prospects could there be for the development, or even preservation, of proletarian democracy? How would the Soviet institutions, by which workers' freedom was brought about, be affected? What would be the fate of the party? What would happen if the international proletariat was late in coming to the rescue of the Russian revolution?

The great Soviet poet of the Russian revolution, Vladimir Mayakovsky, wrote these lines:

> We shall commit heroic deeds,
> three times harder
> than the deeds of God.
> He bestowed things upon emptiness,
> but we must not merely indulge in reveries,
> but must dynamite that which is old.

But what if the old survived the dynamite? What if the heritage of Tsarist barbarism were too heavy for the small young plant of socialism to bear?

The Dream and the Reality

Lenin was above all a revolutionary realist who combined the greatest vision with the urge to look reality in the face. His hero was neither the down-to-earth, commonsense Sancho Panza, nor the builder of castles in the air, Don Quixote. He knew how to distinguish clearly between the communist end and the immediate revolutionary need. For him, as for Marx, socialism was a classless, stateless, self-governing community based on an abundance of material goods in which 'the free development of each is the condition for the free development of all' *(Communist Manifesto)*. Dictatorship, state planning, economic growth and efficiency, iron discipline – all were means to the end, means from which Lenin did not shrink, but not ends in themselves. Lenin was well aware that the road to socialism would be very rough indeed.

He emphasized that the leap into the realm of freedom would happen only after a whole transitional period – and a very harsh period at that.

> it was not without reason that the teachers of socialism spoke of a whole period of transition from capitalism to socialism and emphasized the 'prolonged birth-pangs' of the new society. And this new society is again an abstraction which can come into being only by passing through a series of varied, imperfect concrete attempts to create this or that socialist state.[26]

He compares the birth of the new socialist society to childbirth.

> Consider the descriptions of childbirth given in literature, when the authors aim at presenting a truthful picture of the severity, pain and horror of the act of travail, as in Emile Zola's *La joie de vivre* (The Joy of Life), for instance, or in Veresayev's *Notes of a Doctor*. Human childbirth is an act which transforms the woman into an almost lifeless, bloodstained heap of flesh, tortured, tormented and driven frantic by pain. But can the 'individual' that sees *only* this in love and its sequel, in the transformation of the woman into a mother, be regarded as a human being? Who would renounce love and procreation for *this* reason?
> Travail may be light or severe. Marx and Engels, the founders of scientific socialism, always said that the transition from capitalism to socialism would be inevitably accompanied *by prolonged birth pangs*. Engels outlines simply and clearly the indisputable and obvious fact that a revolution that follows and is connected with a war (and still more – let us add for our part – a revolution which breaks out during a war, and which is obliged to grow and maintain itself in the midst of a world war) is a *particularly severe* case of childbirth.[27]

In Soviet Russia hopes turned into despair. With the proletariat decimated and the state and party largely bureaucratized, the *means* for victory – the dictatorship of the proletariat – negated itself.

Lenin knew, like Marx and Engels before him, that the means cannot perfectly *prefigure* the end, that there must be a contradiction between means and ends, between the dictatorship of the proletariat and fully fledged socialism, or communism. As the revolution is a product of a class society it necessarily bears the traits of this society. It reflects capitalism rather than socialism, the present and the past, not the future. As the proletarian dictatorship has to fight bourgeois counter-revolution, it inevitably has to be symmetrical with it, in order to inflict blows on it. However, with all the diversion of *means* from *ends*, unless there is a central core connecting them, the means *will not* lead to the supposed end. 'Seeds of wheat must be sown in order to yield an ear of wheat', to use Trotsky's words about the relation between means and ends in his pamphlet *Their Morals and Ours*. The plough breaking up the hard soil may help the seed of wheat to germinate and grow, but the plough does not prefigure the wheat; in the same way the Cheka may be necessary to smash capitalist counter-revolution, without this institution in any way prefiguring, having in it even the germ, of future socialism. Unfortunately the plough alone will not produce wheat. The liberation of the working class can be achieved only through the action of the working class. Hence one can have a revolution with more or less violence, with more or less suppression of civil rights of the bourgeoisie and its hangers-on, with more or less political freedom, but one *cannot* have a revolution, as the history of Russia conclusively demonstrates, without workers' democracy – even if restricted and distorted. Socialist advance must be gauged by workers' freedom, by their power to shape their own destiny, and by the material and cultural well-being achieved by the masses. Without workers' democracy the immediate means leads to a very different end, to an end that is prefigured in these same means.

In Part II of Goethe's *Faust*, Faust decides to reclaim a strip of land from the sea in order to settle it with 'many millions' of people of 'free toil', thus would 'a free people stand on a free soil'. But during the construction itself Faust deals with the builders as though they were dull-witted slaves.

> To speed the greatest enterprises
> One mind for thousand hands suffices.

With both carrot and stick, the workers are driven on to accomplish the mightiest achievements. Mephistopheles, the fore-man, is encouraged by Faust:

> Workmen throng on throng address
> Thyself to get. Put forth all vigour.
> Now with indulgence, now with rigour
> Encourage. Pay, entice, impress!
> Let every day bring news of our successes,
> How this new trench, this mighty groove progresses.

Thus the future community of 'free people' is the Faustian aim, while the serfdom of the toilers is the Mephistophelean means. The link between them is Faust's belief in enlightened despotism: 'One mind for thousand hands suffices.' Will the means not swallow up the aim, the 'groove' become a 'grave'?

Lenin certainly did not call for a dictatorship of the party over the proletariat, even less for that of a bureaucratized party over a decimated proletariat. But fate – the desperate condition of a revolution in a backward country besieged by world capitalism – led to precisely this.

The question of means and ends – not in abstract form, but in all its reality – tortured Lenin repeatedly in the last few months of his life, when after each further stroke he came back as if from the dead to watch over what he was going to leave behind him. In the statements, speeches and notes he made in his last active period, expressions such as 'the fault is mine', 'I must correct another mistake of mine', 'I am to blame',[28] occur re-peatedly until they culminate in the statement of 30 December 1922 – the last notes he dictated to his secretary – 'I suppose I have been very remiss with respect to the workers of Russia.'[29]

The machine of state and party was moving in a direction which Lenin certainly did not wish or expect, as he told the 11th Party Congress, in March 1922, the last congress he attended:

The machine refused to obey the hand that guided it. It was like a car that was going not in the direction the driver desired, but in the direction someone else desired; as if it were being driven by some mysterious, lawless hand, God knows whose . . . Be that as it may, the car is not going quite in the direction the man at the wheel imagines, and often it goes in an altogether different direction.[30]

Lenin never shirked looking reality in the face. At the end of the civil war he stated: 'Russia emerged from the war in a state that can most of all be likened to that of a man beaten to within an inch of his life; the beating had gone on for seven years, and it's a mercy she can hobble about on crutches! That is the situation we are in.'[31]

He saw the collapse of the economy, the decomposition of the proletariat, the changes in state institutions and the party, but he could not be certain until the end whether the climax would be a fatal catastrophe in the tradition of Greek tragedies, or whether, as with Goethe, vision and hope would avert disaster and triumph would be achieved over all the odds by the timely arrival of the international working class army to the rescue. The international revolution, was however, very belated. Towards the end of his life we find Lenin facing tragic disappointments

That keep the word of promise to our ear,
And break it to our hope.[32]

9
The Proletariat
Under War Communism

The Proletariat Burns Itself Out in the Struggle

The collapse of industry led to a drastic reduction in the number of workers. This was severely accentuated by the massacre of the civil war, the exodus to the countryside from the towns, and the fact that many of the politically most advanced took up positions in the new state administration, the Soviets, the army, the Cheka and other public bodies, or in industrial management. The number of industrial workers fell from 3,024,000 in 1917 to 1,243,000 in 1921-2, a decrease of 58·7 per cent.[1]

The drop in the number of industrial workers was particularly sharp in Petrograd. While at the time of the October revolution there were 400,000 factory workers there, this fell to 120,495 on 1 April 1918; of these 48,910 were unemployed. So the total number of workers employed in industry was only 71,575.[2]

This shattering decline alarmed the Bolshevik leaders. A warning note was sounded by Y.E.Rudzutak, the leading Bolshevik trade unionist, at the Second All-Russian Congress of Trade Unions in January 1919: 'We observe that in many industrial centres the workers, thanks to the curtailment of production in the factories, are being dissolved into the peasant mass, and instead of a population of workers, we are getting a semi-peasant or sometimes purely peasant population.'[3]

Similarly Lenin, with heavy heart, said to the Eighth Congress of the party on 18 March 1919: 'The top layer of workers who actually administered Russia during the past year, who bore the brunt of the work in carrying out our policy, and who were our mainstay – this layer in Russia is an extremely thin one.'[4] And some time after the end of the civil war he said, in retrospect: 'The creation of a military and state machine capable of successfully withstanding the trials of 1917-21 was a great effort, which engaged, absorbed and exhausted real "forces of the working class".'[5]

The decline of the proletariat was not only quantitative, but also qualitative. The number of industrial workers, as we have said, declined from some 3 million to 1¼ million, but the number of people who stopped being industrial workers was far larger than 1¾ million, for, as Lenin explained, 'Since the war, the industrial workers of Russia have become much less proletarian than they were before, because during the war all those who desired to evade military service went into the factories. This is common knowledge.'[6] Thus many of the workers of 1921-2 were actually former students, shopkeepers and their children, etc. The group that was most reduced was the metal workers, the mainstay of the Bolsheviks in 1917.

Members of the working class were forced by the scarcity of food to act like small individualistic traders, rather than as a collective, or a united class. It has been calculated that in 1919-20 the state supplied only 42 per cent of the grain consumed by the towns, and an even smaller percentage of other foodstuffs, all the rest being bought on the black market.[7] Workers' wages were not enough to pay for the miserable food they and their families had to live on. Thus, while in 1917 an unskilled worker earned 26.75 rubles per month and spent, with his family, 11.57 rubles on food, in 1918 his earnings were 280 rubles per month, but food alone cost him 902.25 rubles per month.[8]

In March-April 1919, 75 per cent of the Petrograd workers bought bread on the black market.[9] It was common for workers to stay away from work in order to forage in the countryside.

During the civil war factories paid part of wages in kind. The workers used a portion themselves and sold the rest on the black market. A speaker at the First All-Russian Congress of Councils of National Economy in May 1918 drew attention to this practice, which acquired the nickname 'piece-selling'.

'Bagging [foraging for food by townspeople] is a terrible evil, piece-selling is a terrible evil; but it is an even greater evil when you begin to pay the workers in kind, in their own products . . . and when they themselves turn piece-sellers.'[10] But the practice persisted, and the Second All-Russian Congress of Councils of National Economy in December 1918 had little option but to turn a blind eye to the practice, passing yet another resolution in favour of payment of wages to factory workers in kind. Two years later the scandal had grown much worse.

At the Fourth Congress of Trade Unions in May 1921 the disorganization of industry and the demoralization of the proletariat were illustrated by a statement that workers in factories were stealing 50 per cent of the goods produced and that the average worker's wage covered only one-fifth of his cost of living, so that he was compelled to earn the rest by illicit trading.[11]

Many workers took to petty thieving and peddling (which,

according to one prominent Soviet economist, brought in up to two-fifths of their income at the time).[12] Under these circumstances they inevitably became middlemen, parasitic on the economy and increasingly inclined to look after their own interests.

On 24 August 1919 Lenin wrote: 'industry is at a standstill. There is no food, no fuel, no industry.'[13] And he summed up the disintegration of the proletariat in these words:

> The industrial proletariat . . . owing to the war and to the desperate poverty and ruin, has become declassed, i.e. dislodged from its class groove, and has ceased to exist as a proletariat. The proletariat is the class which is engaged in the production of material values in large-scale capitalist industry. Since large-scale capitalist industry has been destroyed, since the factories are at a standstill, the proletariat has disappeared. It has sometimes figured in statistics, but it has not been held together economically.[14]

> our proletariat has been largely declassed; the terrible crises and the closing down of the factories have compelled people to flee from starvation. The workers have simply abandoned their factories; they have had to settle down in the country and have ceased to be workers . . . the disruption of proper relations between town and country and the cessation of grain deliveries have given rise to a trade in small articles made at the big factories – such as cigarette lighters – which are exchanged for cereals, because the workers are starving, and no grain is being delivered . . . That is the economic source of the proletariat's declassing and . . . bourgeois, anarchist trends.[15]

> Owing to our present deplorable conditions, proletarians are obliged to earn a living by methods which are not proletarian and are not connected with large-scale industry. They are obliged to procure goods by petty-bourgeois profiteering methods, either by stealing, or by making them for themselves in a publicly-owned factory, in order to barter them for agricultural produce . . .[16] And the proletariat is declassed, i.e. dislodged from its class groove. The factories and mills are idle – the proletariat is weak, scattered, enfeebled.[17]

Workers' Control Over Production

With an enfeebled proletariat, how could the Bolshevik slogan of workers' control over production in fact be applied? Would not the weakness of the agent of control lead inevitably to its distortion, or even its demise? These questions had to be answered by harsh reality.

In Bolshevik propaganda before October the concept of workers' control was that of a half-way house, a *limitation* by workers of management power, the surveillance and even the obstruction by workers of the decisions taken by the capitalist management, which still retained ultimate sovereignty. The situation in which workers themselves possessed sovereignty and collectively initiated all decisions in respect of production was called 'workers' management'. Now, after October, the question was posed sharply: would workers' control remain as such, or would it develop into workers' management?

As we have seen in Chapter 7, the capitalists for their part did all they could to sabotage workers' control. They destroyed the capitalist apparatus of economic management. As this happened on a national scale, as well as in each individual enterprise, the Bolsheviks had to create a substitute apparatus.

Could workers' control be replaced by workers' management of industry? Unfortunately, the weakness of the proletariat, given that workers had not been trained by capitalism to manage, and that the economic collapse strengthened centrifugal tendencies among them, undermined not only workers' control, but also the possibility of workers' management.

Centrifugal forces split the working class. Workers in different factories took over individual enterprises, as if they were their own property. The journal of the People's Commissariat of Labour described the situation thus:

> the factory committees often, and even in the majority of cases, adhered to the narrow interests of a particular enterprise. For the committee it was important that its factory functioned normally, that it was supplied with orders and funds. Individual members often acted in the capacity of expediters to satisfy these needs of the enterprise . . . The factory committees adhering to their 'factory interests' developed their own parochial patriotism and local pride . . . A competition began among the workers of individual factories to assure 'their own factories' of deliveries of coal or metal. The factory committees delegated their emissaries to the provinces, for example, to the Donets Basin, where they exerted pressure to obtain coal or steel, trying

to assure 'their own' factories of it. For example, the Obukhov-
skii factory . . . delegated about 50 worker-expediters who tried
to obtain coal for their own factory.[18]

One Soviet historian summed up the situation thus: 'Com-
petition and the effort to guarantee for themselves scarce raw
materials needed for production led the factory committees to
oppose each other; the factories were converted into autonomous
federations of a semi-anarchist character.'[19]

An article in *Izvestiia* asked:

> What has workers' control given us up to the present? We must
> have the courage to admit that its results are not always satis-
> factory. Often – it may be observed in many enterprises – in
> place of the former owner of the business, another proprietor
> came who was just as individualistic and anti-social as the pre-
> vious one. The name of this proprietor is the 'Control Commis-
> sion'.[20]

Workers' control on the railways was described in stark
words by Shliapnikov, People's Commissar of Labour, in his speech
to VTsIK on 20 March 1918:

> What is happening on the railways can only be described as com-
> plete disorganization which is getting worse every day . . . The
> trains are often operating without lights, there is no signalling,
> the cars are never cleaned, etc. The usual excuse is that no kero-
> sene or candles are available. However, I found out that both
> these items were available but were being pilfered in the most
> shameless manner.
>
> Train crews, being not at all interested in the exploitation of
> the railways, frequently refuse to take charge of the trains.
> Because of this, both cars and locomotives may be available, but
> there are no engineers and no conductors. They either pretend
> illness or simply refuse to go. It sometimes happens that on cer-
> tain trains which require a certain number of persons, a substi-
> tute has to be found [for someone] who is really ill, but the
> station-master is unable to exercise his authority, for as soon as
> he puts someone in place of the sick man the substitute tells him
> that he will not go without the consent of the Committee. Since
> it is impossible to get the Committee together on the spot, the
> train cannot be dispatched . . .
>
> By present-day rules the workers are guaranteed their pay. The
> worker turns up at his job and spends some time at his bench.
> Whether he does anything or not, no one can say anything to
> him because the shop committee is powerless. If the shop com-

mittee attempts to control the shops, it is immediately dis-
banded and another committee is elected. In a word, things are
in the hands of a crowd that, due to its ignorance and lack of
interest in production, is literally putting a brake on all work.[21]

It was this chaos which led the Soviet government to abolish
workers' control in industry, starting with the railways on 26
March 1918. Towards the end of 1918 workers' control councils
were abolished in a number of leading branches of industry, such
as machine and metal-working plants (18 October 1918) and
leather and shoe factories (13 November 1918).[22]

Factory Committees, the Trade Unions and the State

With the drastic weakening of the industrial proletariat, and
with the anarchic centrifugal forces pulling it apart, Lenin and
the Bolsheviks had no alternative but to put an end to the autonomy of the factory committees which had played such a central
role in October. One of the first problems they faced after the
revolution was that of the relationship between the factory committees and the trade unions.

At the first All-Russian Conference of Factory Committees,
which was held a few days before the October revolution, the
Bolshevik Schmidt, the future Commissar of Labour, stated: 'At
the moment when the factory committees were formed the trade
unions actually did not yet exist, and the factory committees
filled the vacuum.'[23] The trade unions that arose in 1917 were
Menshevik-dominated and their efforts to bring the factory committees under their control were naturally rebuffed. But now,
after the revolution, at the First All-Russian Congress of Trade
Unions in January 1918 the Bolsheviks found themselves the
dominant force in the trade unions, as they had already been for
some time in the factory committees. At the Congress, out of 428
delegates with voting rights, 281 were Bolsheviks, 67 Mensheviks,
32 non-party, 21 Left Socialist Revolutionaries, 10 Right Socialist
Revolutionaries, 6 Maximalists and 6 Anarcho-Syndicalists.

The main report on the subject of the relations between the
factory committees and the trade unions was given by the Bolshevik Riazanov, who was chairman of the Petrograd Council of
Trade Unions, a member of the All-Russian Central Council of

Trade Unions, and on its executive committee. The workers' government, he argued, should exert control over the factory committees.

> Before us . . . stands the question of control by the workers' government, by the whole working class over the workers in individual factory enterprises . . . Without such control on the part of all the working class, on the part of the proletariat – and for this we need a whole network of organs which control the activity of each such individual cell in each factory, in each enterprise – without such a network of organs we will have only a pillage of the people's economy, a pillage of the economy which we want to socialize and organize into a whole out of many parts. We will have a mass of atomized cells.[24]

The Bolshevik Veinberg stated: 'the trade unions – or, more correctly, the industrial unions – espouse the point of view not of the individual factory, not even of the workers of a particular city, but the point of view of the working class of all industry. [Therefore] the factory committees must be subordinated to the trade unions.'[25] By an overwhelming majority the Congress decided that the factory committees should be incorporated into the unions.

In order that workers' control may produce the maximum benefit for the proletariat, it is necessary to reject completely any idea of undermining that control by giving the workers of an individual enterprise the right to make final decisions on questions affecting the very existence of the enterprise.

> The workers of every enterprise and their elected organization – factory-shop committees – will be in a better position to carry on the work [of control] if they operate on the basis of a general plan formulated by the higher organs of workers' control and the regulatory organs of the economy.
>
> In this colossal work which the organs of workers' control have assumed, the trade unions should take the most active part by championing the interests of the workers as a whole as opposed to the sectional and group interests of the workers of a given trade or enterprise.
>
> The trade unions which are organized by industries should take part in the local and central organs of workers' control and should assume the role of ideological and organizational leadership.

The trade unions must go over each decree of the factory committees in the sphere of control, explain through their delegates at the factories and shops that control over production does not mean the transfer of the enterprise into the hands of the workers of a given enterprise, that workers' control does not equal the socialization of production and exchange but is only a preparatory step towards it.[26]

Factory and workshop committees should become local organs of the corresponding trade unions.[27]

The factory committees, as well as the trade unions, also had to relate to another newly established institution. On 2 (15) December 1917 the VSNKh was established. The relevant decree described its function thus:

The task of the Supreme Economic Council is organization of the national economy and state finance. With this aim in view the Supreme Economic Council works out guidelines and plans for regulating the country's economy; coordinates and unifies the activity of central and local regulating institutions (conferences on fuel, metal, transport, the Central Food Committee, etc.), the corresponding people's commissariats (of trade and industry, food supplies, agriculture, finance, army and navy, etc.), the All-Russia Workers' Control Council, as well as the relevant activity of working-class organizations.[28]

The VSNKh was to be the central planning and directing organ of the economic life of the country. Its close relationship with the trade unions is clear from the weight granted to their representatives in its composition:

The All-Russian Central Executive Committee – 10 representatives.
The All-Russian Council of Trade Unions – 30 representatives.
The Regional Councils of National Economy – 20 representatives.
The All-Russian Council of Workers' Cooperatives – 2 representatives.
The People's Commissariat of Food – 2 representatives.
The People's Commissariat of Ways and Communication – 1 representative.
The People's Commissariat of Labour – 1 representative.
The People's Commissariat of Agriculture – 1 representative.
The People's Commissariat of Finance – 1 representative.
The People's Commissariat of Commerce – 1 representative.
The People's Commissariat of the Interior – 1 representative.[29]

In the administration of individual branches of the economy the trade unions and VSNKh again worked very closely together. While accepting complete subordination to VSNKh in administrative measures, the trade unions insisted on having a majority of representatives (two thirds) on the administrative bodies. And so at the First All-Russian Congress of the Councils of the National Economy in May 1918, Tomsky, appearing as a delegate of the All-Russian Central Council of Trade Unions, could declare: 'VSNKh and the trade unions are organizations so completely akin, so closely interwoven with each other, that independent tactics on the part of these two organizations are impossible.'[80]

The trade unions also obtained significant powers in relation to the People's Commissariat of Labour. At the Fourth Conference of Trade Unions (12-17 March 1918), the Bolshevik resolution on the relations between the trade unions and the People's Commissariat of Labour stated:

> all decisions of principle of the higher organs of the trade unions (congresses, conferences, etc.) are binding upon the Commissariat of Labour. All legislative proposals and special binding decisions concerning the conditions of labour and production, must be preliminarily approved by the appropriate organs of the trade unions (i.e. the All-Russian and local Soviets of Trade Unions).[81]

The People's Commissar of Labour, V.Schmidt, was proposed for the post by the trade unions, and was himself an active trade unionist. Most of the officials of the People's Commissariat of Labour as well as its regional and local representatives, were from now on nominated by the trade unions. The Commissariat of Labour was to be bound by the principal decisions of the higher bodies of the trade unions, and the unions had to give prior approval to all decisions of the Commissariat.

The Trade Unions and the State

The experience of the first months of the Bolshevik government showed that conflicts were bound to arise between the factory committees, the trade unions and the state.

The factory committees, by definition, had centrifugal tendencies. The trade unions, as mass organizations, consisted of diverse elements with varying levels of class consciousness, and were therefore divided by sectional interests, with various groups of workers trying to further their own interests, at times possibly *against* the interests of the working class as a whole. According to Lenin, it was only the revolutionary party, the vanguard of the class, that represented the total, historical, interests of the proletariat, to which sectional and temporary interests were subordinated. The Soviet government, composed as it was of Bolsheviks, was bound to come into conflict with the trade unions, which represented sectional interests.

Of course the party had to persuade the working class to make the revolution. It had to convince the majority of the proletariat to prepare and organize for it. After the revolution it still had to fight in order to lead the proletariat in the factory committees, in the trade unions, in the Soviet.

But this could not be done *mechanically*, by imposition of the party will. Only through a long struggle to overcome the vacillation of the masses could the party win this leadership. It had to battle again and again to win the confidence of the proletariat, above all of that section of it which was organized in the trade unions.

If the trade unions were autonomous, i.e. self-administering, the revolutionaries could win their confidence only by persuasion. They could not impose a line of conduct with which the majority of the union members did not agree.

The process of conflict and the development of unity between party, state, trade unions and factory committees would have taken a long time to achieve the Marxist goal of the withering away of the state and complete merging of state and trade unions. For this to take place, a situation of increasing economic plenty would be needed, which would also result in the withering away of the trade unions. For if the standard of living of the workers is high and rising, their need to defend it becomes less and less imperative, until a stage is reached when every person 'gets according to his needs' and trade unions as organs for the defence of workers' interests become superfluous. At the same time, incentives for higher production and the use of the unions as a means of urging the workers to greater effort would become unnecessary. The tension in society would decrease and so the state, as well as the unions, would begin to wither away.

Until the complete achievement of communism, the trade unions must be able to defend the workers against their employers, even if this is the state. At the same time as workers' organizations, the unions have to defend the workers' state. They should be both independent of the state and symbiotic with it.

After the revolution in Russia, under the harsh conditions of the civil war, these relationships could not exist: the trade unions could not be independent of the state. Industry was turned into a supply organization for the Red Army, and industrial policy became a branch of military strategy. As industry relied on the state to supply necessary products to the workers, the trade unions were in fact part of the state administration of industry and distribution.

In particular, the trade unions' participation in fixing wage rates lost all significance, since payment in kind to all intents and purposes replaced money wages.*

The Trade Unions,
the Military Front and the Labour Front

With the outbreak of civil war, thousands of trade union members went into the army. It was mainly through the unions that the government mobilized men both for the Red Army and for industry. As the civil war dragged on, the trade unions called up 50 per cent of their members into the Red Army. At the same time there was an enormous increase in the number of union members, mainly made up of workers in the new civil service:

(thousands)	
Mid 1917	693
Mid 1918	1,946
Mid 1919	3,707
Mid 1920	5,222[32]

* The fact that the proportion of wages in kind was very large, made the difference between price rises and wage rises, referred to above, far less significant. If workers' wages had not been largely paid in kind, their lives, harsh as they were, would have been completely unbearable.

The Bolsheviks quickly came to the conclusion that the unions must play a central role in mobilizing workers on the labour front as well. Accordingly the newly adopted party programme (March 1919) stated:

> it is essential to utilize to the utmost all the labour power at the disposal of the state. Its correct assignment and reassignment as between the various territorial areas and as between the various branches of economic life is the main task of the economic policy of the Soviet power. It can be fulfilled in no other way than by an intimate association between the Soviet power and the trade unions. The general mobilization by the Soviet power of all members of the population who are physically and mentally fit for work (a mobilization to be effected through the instrumentality of the trade unions), for the discharge of definite social duties, must be achieved far more widely and systematically than has hitherto been the case.[33]

And the government imposed a very strict control over the labour of every citizen. For instance, on 7 April 1919, a decree forbade any miner to leave his job.[34] On 12 April another decree prohibited all persons employed in a Soviet institution from transferring on their own initiative to another institution.[35]

In addition compulsory mobilization of labour took place. In 1920 some twenty mobilization orders were decreed, affecting the most important trades:

Former railway workers	30 January
Skilled railway personnel	15 March
Sugar industry workers	24 March
Water transport workers	7 April
Miners	16 April
Skilled water transport personnel	27 April
Construction workers	5 May
Statistical workers	25 June
Medical personnel	14 July
Workers formerly employed in fish industries	6 August
Workers in shipbuilding	8 August
Wool industry workers	13 August
Former metal workers	20 August
Tanning industry workers	15 September
Electro-technical workers	8 October
Former aviation industry workers	20 October

Women for sewing underwear for Red Army	30 October
Tailors and shoemakers who worked in Great	
Britain and the United States	October[36]

Labour Armies

It was a short step from the mobilization of workers to building labour armies. In January 1920 a decree on general labour service provided for: (a) call-up of the entire able-bodied population (men between 16 and 50, women between 16 and 40) for occasional or regular work, to be performed in addition to normal employment; (b) the use of unoccupied army and navy units for civilian work; (c) the transfer of skilled workers engaged in the forces or in agriculture to state enterprises; (d) the distribution of labour according to the needs of the country's economy. On 15 January 1920 a decree of the Workers' and Peasants' Council of Defence, at the suggestion of the leading army personnel, authorized the temporary use for civil work of the Third Army Corps operating in the Urals. When fighting there ceased, practically all the combatant units were sent to the southern and western fronts; but an enormous administrative apparatus was left behind, which it was not thought advisable to demobilize, and which was therefore used for industrial reconstruction work. This unit adopted the name of First Revolutionary Labour Army Corps and was used chiefly for the repair of railway lines and procurement of timber and coal.

With the further temporary easing of the military situation, a second labour army corps was created in March 1920 in the area of the Donbas and parts of the Caucasus. A third was formed in Petrograd, but the war with Poland soon forced both to revert to military duties. A Ukrainian labour army corps was formed in January 1920 in the area of the south-western front. At that time, too, the Workers' and Peasants' Council of Defence decreed the use of the 'Reserve Army of the Republic for the reconstruction of the Moscow–Kazan railway line and the repair of its rolling stock'.[37]

Stalinist legend has it that Trotsky was chiefly responsible for the militarization of labour. Nothing could be further from the truth. It was true that Trotsky was enthusiastic about the policy.

But so was Lenin. Thus, for instance, Lenin told the Third All-Russian Congress of Economic Councils on 27 January 1920:

> in order to utilize our apparatus with the greatest possible dispatch, we must create a labour army . . . In launching this slogan we declare that we must strain all the live forces of the workers and peasants to the utmost and demand that they give us every help in this matter. And then, by creating a labour army, by the harnessing all the forces of the workers and peasants, we shall accomplish our main task.[38]

In a speech on 2 February 1920 he reiterated:

> we must at all costs create labour armies, organize ourselves like an army, reduce, even close down a whole number of institutions . . . in the next few months . . . When the All-Russia Central Executive Committee endorses all the measures connected with labour conscription and the labour armies, when it has succeeded in instilling these ideas in the broad mass of the population and demands that they be put into practice by local officials – we are absolutely convinced that then we shall be able to cope with [the] most difficult of tasks.[39]

Thus we see that for Lenin, during the civil war, and especially in the latter part of it, the mobilization of labour and, in general, the incorporation of the trade unions, their subordination to the state, were of vital and immediate importance.

Under the conditions of civil war the factory committees, which played a crucial role in winning the proletariat to Bolshevism in 1917, completely lost their autonomy, becoming local organs of the trade unions. The trade unions lost their power to dictate wages and conditions and became integrated into the state as organs for mobilizing on the military and labour fronts.*

Subbotniks

The merging of state and unions under War Communism did not preclude the emergence of a new phenomenon, *subbotniks*, i.e. unpaid voluntary Saturday labour. The fact that enthusiastically supported unpaid voluntary labour could exist side by side with state compulsion in the form of the militarization of labour,

---

* On relations between trade unions and state, see further Volume 4, Chapter 9.

resulted from the prevailing egalitarianism and the deep devotion of the proletariat to the revolution. These blurred the boundaries between compulsion and voluntarism.

On 10 May 1919 the first *subbotnik* was carried out by the Moscow railway workers. It was argued for and led by party members. The resolution of the General Council of Communists of the *Subraion* of the Moscow–Kazan Railway, introducing *subbotniks*, stated that

> in order to overcome the class enemy . . . the communists and their sympathizers again must spur themselves on and extract from their time off still another hour of work, i.e. they must increase their working day by an hour, add it up and on Saturday devote six hours at a stretch to physical labour thereby producing immediately a real value. Considering that communists should not spare their health and lives for the victory of the revolution, the work is conducted without pay.[40]

Lenin was full of praise for the whole concept of the *subbotnik*. On 28 June 1919, in a pamphlet entitled *A Great Beginning*, he wrote:

> Communist *subbotniks* are of . . . enormous significance precisely because they demonstrate the conscious and voluntary initiative of the workers in developing the productivity of labour, in adopting a new labour discipline, in creating socialist conditions of economy and life . . . The communist *subbotnik* organized by the workers of the Moscow–Kazan Railway is one of the cells of the new, socialist society . . . these starving workers . . . are organizing 'communist *subbotniks*', working overtime *without any pay*, and achieving *an enormous increase in the productivity of labour* in spite of the fact that they are weary, tormented and exhausted by malnutrition. Is this not supreme heroism? Is this not the beginning of a change of momentous significance?[41]

In Petrograd the first *subbotnik* on a mass scale took place in August 1919. Again during the fuel crisis of November and December there seems to have been an upsurge of revolutionary élan. Yet it appears from the material available the movement did not reach its short-lived apogee until the spring of 1920. On 11 April 1920 a one-day issue of a newspaper called *Kommunisticheskii Subbotnik* was published, itself a *subbotnik* achievement of the staff of three Moscow papers and the printers of VTsIK publishing house. It contained an article by Lenin on the practical value and moral significance of this voluntary effort.

By decision of the Ninth Party Congress of March-April 1920, May Day, which happened to fall on a Saturday, was to be a gigantic all-Russian *subbotnik*. In Moscow alone 425,000 workers were said to have taken part in it.[42]

The Decomposition of the Proletariat and the Dictatorship of the Proletariat

Paradoxically, the proletariat was economically the most deprived class under the dictatorship of the proletariat. As Lenin put it in a speech to the First All-Russian Congress of Mineworkers in April 1920: 'the dictatorship entailed the greatest sacrifice and starvation on the part of the workers who were exercising it.'

> Nobody during these two years went as hungry as the workers of Petrograd, Moscow and Ivanovo-Voznessensk. It has now been computed that during these two years they received not more than seven pud of bread a year, whereas the peasants of the grain-producing guberniias consumed no less than seventeen pud. The workers have made great sacrifices, they have suffered epidemics, and mortality among them has increased.[43]

There was a dictatorship of the proletariat, even though the proletariat had disintegrated. As Lenin put it to the Tenth Conference of the Party, on 26 May 1921: 'even though the proletariat has to go through a period when it is declassed ... it can nevertheless fulfil its task of winning and holding political power'.[44]

With some cynicism, Shliapnikov, spokesman of the newly formed Workers' Opposition, could say to the Eleventh Party Congress: 'Vladimir Ilyich said yesterday that the proletariat as a class, in the Marxian sense, did not exist. Permit me to congratulate you on being the vanguard of a non-existing class.'[45]

Of course, to a vulgar materialist it sounds impossible to have a dictatorship of the proletariat without the proletariat, like the smile of the Cheshire cat without the cat itself. But one must remember that the ideological as well as the political superstructure never reflect the material base *directly and immediately*. Ideas have their own momentum. Usually in 'normal' times they are a source of conservatism: long after people's material circumstances change, they are still dominated by old ideas. This interrelation of the ideological superstructure with the economic base became a source of strength to Bolshevism during the civil war. As Lenin put it in a speech of 3 November 1920:

> the habits, usages and convictions acquired by the working class in the course of many decades of struggle for political liberty – the sum total of these habits, usages and ideas – should serve as an instrument for the education of all working people . . . The dictatorship of the proletariat would have been out of the question if, in the struggle against the bourgeoisie, the proletariat had not developed a keen class-consciousness, strict discipline and profound devotion, in other words, all the qualities required to assure the proletariat's complete victory over its old eemy.[46]

Marx has taught us that the class in itself and the class for itself are not one and the same, i.e. that the class can be powerful in its position in production and yet not be conscious of this. The other side of the same coin is that the class which loses three-quarters of its economic power can still maintain its political dominance through its experience, its traditional position in society and the state.

But in the long run, the enfeeblement of the proletariat must in practice lead to a catastrophic decline in morale and consciousness of the people who are supposed to form the ruling class of the new state.

10
War Communism and the Peasantry

Collectivism and Individualism

The October revolution was a fusion of two revolutions – that of the proletariat, and that of the peasantry. We have seen that the civil war led to a catastrophic decline in the relative weight of the proletariat. What was the impact of the revolution on that of the peasantry?

As has been pointed out earlier, Lenin always insisted that the peasantry was fundamentally different from the proletariat. Throughout the development of the party's agrarian policy there are two central points in Lenin's thinking: (i) the working class must lead the peasantry; (ii) the workers' party has to maintain its independence and clearly distinguish itself from the peasantry.[1]

'We stand by the peasant movement to the end,' Lenin said, 'but we have to remember that it is the movement of another class, *not the one* which can and will bring about the socialist revolution.'[2]

Now, after the revolution, Lenin again emphasized the clear distinction between the proletariat and the peasantry.

> Marx and Engels sharply challenged those who tended to forget class distinctions and spoke about producers, the people, or working people in general . . . There are no working people or workers in general; there are either small proprietors who own the means of production, and whose mentality and habits are capitalistic – and they cannot be anything else – or wage-workers with an altogether different cast of mind, wage-workers in large-scale industry, who stand in antagonistic contradiction to the capitalists and are ranged in struggle against them . . .[3]

> our aim is to abolish classes. As long as workers and peasants remain, socialism has not been achieved . . .[4]

> Their social conditions, production, living and economic conditions make the peasant half worker and half huckster . . .[5]

> We have one extremely dangerous secret enemy, more dangerous than many open counter-revolutionaries; this enemy is the anarchy of the petty proprietor . . . whose life is guided by one thought: 'I grab all I can – the rest can go hang.' This enemy is more powerful than all the Kornilovs, Dutovs and Kaledins put together.[6]

To fight against the anarchy of the petty proprietor in the countryside, Lenin in his *April Theses* suggested two measures: (1) forming large model farms, and (2) organizing the rural poor in Soviets of their own:

The weight of emphasis in the agrarian programme to be shifted to the Soviets of Agricultural Labourers' Deputies.

Confiscation of all landed estates.

Nationalization of *all* lands in the country, the land to be disposed of by the local Soviets of Agricultural Labourers' and Peasants' Deputies. The organization of separate Soviets of Deputies of Poor Peasants. The setting up of a model farm on each of the large estates (ranging in size from 100 to 300 *desiatins*,* according to local and other conditions, and to the decisions of the local bodies) under the control of the Soviets of Agricultural Labourers' Deputies and for the public account.[7]

The April Conference of the Bolsheviks again advised the 'proletarians and semi-proletarians of the countryside' to seek 'the formation out of every landlord's estate of a sufficiently large model farm which would be run for the public account by Soviets of Deputies of agricultural workers'.[8]

As it turned out, the agrarian revolution following the Bolshevik seizure of power in no way aided the formation of large model farms. It is estimated that of all the land confiscated throughout Russia, 93.7 per cent was distributed to the peasants, 1.7 per cent was turned over to collective farms, and only 4.6 per cent remained in the hands of the state.[9]

Lenin did not stop urging collectivization of agriculture. In a speech at a meeting of delegates from the Poor Peasants' Committees of the Central *gubernias* on 8 November 1918, he argued: 'Division of the land was all very well as a beginning. Its purpose was to show that the land was being taken from the landowners and handed over to the peasants. But that is not enough. The solution lies only in socialized farming.' He announced:

> The Soviet government has decided to assign one thousand million rubles to a special fund for improving farming. All existing and newly formed communes will receive monetary and technical assistance . . . the transition to the new form of agriculture may perhaps proceed slowly, but the beginnings of communal farming must be carried into practice unswervingly.[10]

In a speech on 11 December 1918 to the First All-Russian Congress of Land Departments, Poor Peasants' Committees and

---

* *Desiatin* = 1.09 hectares = 2.7 acres.

Communes, Lenin's theme was the coming of socialism in the countryside. What was now necessary was 'the transition from small individual peasant farms to the socialized working of the land'. But of course this was a very arduous task.

> We fully realize that such tremendous changes in the lives of tens of millions of people as the transition from small individual peasant farming to collective farming, affecting as they do the most deep-going roots of the peasants' way of life and their mores, can only be accomplished by long effort, and only when necessity compels people to reshape their lives.[11]

Following Lenin's report, the Congress passed a resolution that the chief aim of agrarian policy must be 'the consistent and unswerving pursuit of the organization of agricultural communes, Soviet communist farms and the socialized working of the land'.

On 14 February 1919 VTsIK issued a new decree on collectivization of agriculture. It proclaimed 'the transition from individual to collective forms of the utilization of land', and declared that 'all forms of individual utilization of land could be regarded as transitory and obsolete'. Its 138 clauses included elaborate provisions for the constitution, prerogatives and obligations of Soviet farms and agricultural communes.[12]

In practice very little came of the mountains of formulations, decrees and resolutions. It is estimated that by the end of 1918 there may have been nearly 3,000 agricultural cooperatives of all types, embracing some 0.15 per cent of the rural population.[13]

In 1920 the total population of the kolkhozes was 717,545, and their land area 700,464 *desiatins*.[14]

The sovkhozes, the state farms, covered a slightly larger area – 1,918,214 *desiatins* in 1919.[15] Altogether less than 1 per cent of all the cultivated land in 1920 was on state, collective and commune farms.

The Agricultural Proletariat

In 1905, in his *Two Tasks of Social-Democracy in the Democratic Revolution*, Lenin argued that while in the first stage of the revolution the proletariat has to march with the peasantry as a whole against the landlord, in the second stage the proletariat would split the peasantry in two, and march with the 'semi-proletarian' poor peasants against the rich peasants.

In May 1918 he again emphasized that the petty bourgeois elements in the countryside could be held in check only 'if we organize the poor, that is, the majority of the population or semi-proletarians, around the politically conscious proletarian vanguard'.[16]

However, the Bolshevik policy of splitting the peasantry and relying on the proletarian elements in the villages could not succeed. First of all the Bolsheviks were very weak in the countryside. At the end of 1917 the party's rural cadres numbered a mere 2,400, grouped in 203 organizations; a year later the figures were 97,000 and 7,370 respectively.[17] At the end of 1919 the number of Bolsheviks in village cells was no more than 60,000.[18] Many of the members were not peasants, but workers and officials living in rural areas. The weakness of the party showed in the fact that as late as 1922 the communists made up only 6·1 per cent of the rural Soviets.[19]

But more important than this, the agrarian revolution weakened, instead of strengthening, the agricultural proletariat. It weakened the class differentiation of the peasantry, leading to a striking equalization of the size of farms. The following table shows this:

(per cent of farms)

Year	No arable land	Arable land up to 2 desiatins	2–4 desiatins	4–10 desiatins	10 desiatins and over
1917	10·6	30·4	30·1	25·2	3·7
1920	4·7	47·9	31·6	15·3	0·5

Year	No horse	1 horse	2 horses	3 horses	4 horses	5 horses and over
1917	29·0	49·2	17·0	3·4	0·9	0·5
1920	27·6	63·6	7·9	0·7	0·2	— [20]

According to one Soviet statistician, the number of agricultural workers in European Russia fell from 2,100,000 in 1917 to a mere 34,000 in 1919.[21]

Looking back, Lenin said on 27 March 1921:

You know that there has been a levelling off in the Russian countryside in this period. The number of peasants with large areas under crop and without any at all has decreased, while the number of medium farms has increased. The countryside has become more petty bourgeois.[22]

Again on 21 April he wrote: 'In a very large number of cases the peasant "poor" (proletarians and semi-proletarians) have become middle peasants. This has caused an increase in the small-proprietor, petty-bourgeois "element".'[23]

Poor Peasants' Committees

In May 1918 the Bolsheviks decided to organize committees of poor peasants, *Kombedy*. This policy was forced on them by the imperative need to get food for the townspeople and the new-born Red Army.

At a conference of the Petrograd Soviet with delegates from the food supply organizations on (14) 27 January 1918, Lenin advocated the following:

> All soldiers and workers must be recruited to form several thousand groups (consisting of 10-15 men, and possibly more) who shall be bound to devote a certain number of hours (say, 3-4) daily to the food supply service.[24]

> The most reliable and best armed groups of the mass of revolutionary contingents organized to take extreme measures to overcome the famine shall be detailed for despatch to all stations and *uezds* [counties] of the principal grain supplying *guberniias*. These groups, with the participation of railwaymen delegated by local railway committees, shall be authorized, firstly, to control the movement of grain freights; secondly, take charge of the collection and storage of grain; thirdly, adopt the most extreme revolutionary measures to fight speculators and to requisition grain stocks.[25]

Under the threat of impending famine, Lenin looked for a way of obtaining support in the villages for the food requisitioning detachments. On 9 May VTsIK issued a 'decree to confer on the People's Commissariat of Supply extraordinary powers for the struggle with the rural bourgeoisie which conceals grain stocks and speculates in them'.

To reaffirm its stand in favour of the grain monopoly and fixed prices, as well as to recognize the necessity of continuing a merciless fight against the bread speculators and bagmen and of compelling every possessor of surplus grain to declare within a week from the promulgation of this resolution in the *volost* [small rural district] that he is ready to hand over all in excess of what he needs . . .

To call on all the toilers and propertyless peasants to unite at once and begin a merciless fight against the kulaks . . .

To confiscate without compensation any surplus grain which has not been reported in accordance with Article 1. One half of the value of the confiscated grain, determined on the basis of fixed prices and after it has actually reached the railway station, shall go to the person who gave the information about the concealed surplus; the other half shall go to the village community. Information about concealed surpluses shall be given to the local food organizations.

The decree did not disguise the fact that only force would achieve what was proposed. Anyone hoarding surplus grain

shall be handed over to the Revolutionary Court to be sentenced to prison for a term of not less than ten years, and shall be expelled for ever from their communes and suffer confiscation of their property . . .

To use armed force in cases of resistance to the requisition of grain and other food products.[26]

This decree was christened by its opponents the 'Food Dictatorship Decree' and was later commonly referred to by this name. To aid the implementation of the decrees, VTsIK issued a resolution on 20 May calling for the organization of the rural poor.

The All-Russian Central Executive Committee, having discussed the question of the tasks of the soviets in the village, considers it imperative to point out the urgent necessity of uniting the toiling peasantry against the village bourgeoisie. Local Soviets must undertake immediately the task of explaining to the poor that their interests are opposed to those of the kulaks, and of arming the poor with the purpose of establishing their dictatorship in the village.[27]

Two days later Lenin wrote a long open letter to the workers of Petrograd entitled 'On the Famine', in which he called on them to join the food detachments organized by the Commissariat of Supply in thousands.

We need a mass 'crusade' of the advanced workers to every centre of production of grain and fuel, to every important centre of supply and distribution – a mass 'crusade' to increase the intensity of work tenfold, to assist the local organs of Soviet power in the matter of accounting and control, and to eradicate profiteering, graft, and slovenliness by armed force.[28]

On 4 June 1918, at a meeting of VTsIK, Lenin declared that what was needed was unity of the workers . . . for the purpose of carrying on agitation in the villages and of waging a war for grain against the kulaks . . . A new form of struggle against the kulaks is emerging, namely, an alliance of the poor peasants . . . We are willing to make . . . awards to the poor peasants, and we have already begun to do so . . . We shall encourage and give every possible inducement to the poor peasants and shall help them if they help us to organize the collection of grain, to secure grain from the kulaks.[29]

On 11 June VTsIK formulated a decree about Committees of Poor Peasants. These were to be instruments for the 'requisitioning of surplus grain from the kulaks and the rich', for the distribution of food and articles of necessity, and in general for the execution on the spot of the agricultural policies of the government. The poor peasants were to be rewarded for their services by obtaining allocations of grain from the quantities seized, free till 15 July, at a discount of 50 per cent on the fixed prices till 15 August, and thereafter at 20 per cent discount.[30]

The organizing of the food detachments took an almost military form. According to an ordinance of the Commissariat of Food of 20 August 1918, 'Every food detachment is to consist of not less than twenty-five men and two or three machine guns.' They were assisted by a Food Army Administration.

Lenin saw in the organization of the Poor Peasants' Committees the transition from the bourgeois revolution to the socialist revolution in the countryside. In a report to the Eighth Party Congress on 18 March 1918 he said:

In a country where the proletariat could only assume power with the aid of the peasantry, where the proletariat had to serve as the agent of a petty-bourgeois revolution, our revolution was largely a *bourgeois* revolution until the Poor Peasants' Committees were set up, i.e. until the summer and even the autumn of 1918 . . . only when the October Revolution began to spread to the rural districts and was consummated, in the summer of 1918, did we acquire a real proletarian base; only then did our revolution *become a proletarian revolution in fact*, and not merely in our proclamations, promises and declarations.[31]

Thus the impact of hunger and civil war pushed the Soviet regime along a path of expediency which also seemed to be the path of socialism. But if a socialist agricultural policy means a policy directed towards collective farming, there was nothing socialist in the food requisition policy of the *Kombedy*. Furthermore, experience proved: (1) that the poor peasants were less numerous than the Bolshevik leaders assumed, and (2) that they were less independent of the middle peasants, and even the kulaks.

So quite early, on 2 December 1918, VTsIK issued a decree disbanding the Poor Peasants' Committees. The party had to come to terms with the fact that, in Lenin's words, the poor peasants 'have become middle peasants'.

Peasant Resistance to Compulsory Requisitions

The mass of the peasantry quite naturally resisted the requisitioning of food. They began by concealing their harvests. It was estimated that in 1920 more than a third of the total harvest was successfully hidden from the government's collection teams.[32] The peasants also began to till only enough land to meet their own needs, so that by the end of 1920 the acreage sown in European Russia was only three-fifths of the 1913 area.[33]

Grain output in 1920 was less than 35 million metric tons, compared with an annual output of 72.5 million in the period 1909-13; the peasants' own consumption was less than 17 million metric tons, a catastrophic reduction of about 40 per cent compared with pre-war levels.[34]

However, the peasants' attitude to the Bolshevik government during the civil war was not one of simple antagonism. While resenting the food requisitions, they did welcome the protection the Bolsheviks gave them against the threat of the landlords returning in the wake of the White Armies.

The ambivalent attitude of the peasantry to the new rulers,

a combination of submissiveness and hatred, was well described by Boris Pilnyak in his story 'Mother Earth'. The Communist Nikulev says: if you ask the fisherman Vassil Ivanov Starkov

> 'How many Communists have we in Viazovy?' he will answer, 'We don't have many Communists, what we have around here is mostly common folk, there's only two families of the Communists.' And if you press him further as to who exactly these common folk are, he will say, 'Common folk, like everyone knows, is common folk. Common folk is something like what you might call Bolsheviks.'[35]

It seemed that the Bolsheviks were acceptable – the party which gave the land to the peasants in 1917 was called Bolshevik; but the communists were few in number and very unpopular: the party changed its name to 'Communist' in 1918, and it was the communists who carried out the grain requisitions. The ambivalent attitude of the peasants, according to Lenin, expressed itself in the slogan: 'For Soviet power. For the Bolsheviks. Down with the *communia*.'[36]

An even clearer expression of the double-edged attitude to Bolshevism was given by a village delegate to the Third All-Russian Congress of Soviets: 'The land belongs to us: the bread to you: the water to us: the fish to you: the forest to us: the timber to you.'[37]

It had been one thing for the peasant to support a government which distributed land, but it was quite another matter when the same government began to requisition his produce to feed the hungry populations of the cities. This dual attitude towards Soviet power was expressed in either passive resistance or open rebellion.

Yet so long as the White Armies were threatening to bring about the return of the landlords, peasant opposition to Soviet state requisitions was limited.

The Peasants' Resistance Shapes the State

There was a close similarity between the attitude of the French peasantry to the state under Robespierre and that of the Russian peasantry to the state under Lenin. In both France and

Russia, at the time of their revolutions, the peasantry made up an overwhelming majority of the population, and the attitude of the peasantry to the state very largely shaped its physiognomy.

The attitude of the French peasantry to the Jacobin government was described by Engels as follows:

> In the first French revolution the peasants acted in a revolutionary manner just so long as was required by their most immediate, most tangible private interests; until they had secured the right of ownership to their land which had hitherto been farmed on a feudal basis, until feudal relations were irrevocably abolished and the foreign armies ejected from their district. Once this was achieved, they turned with all the fury of blind avarice against the movement of the big towns which they failed to understand, and especially against the movement in Paris. Countless proclamations by the Committee of Public Safety, countless decrees by the Convention, above all those concerning the maximum and the profiteers, mobile columns and travelling guillotines had to be directed against the obdurate peasants. And yet no class benefited more from the Terror which drove out the foreign armies and put down the civil war than these same peasants.[38]

One of the best descriptions of the Russian experience, which was so similar to the French, is in a report written by Antonov Ovseenko, head of the Cheka of Tambov province. This report was sent to Lenin on 20 July 1921, and a copy of it was found in Trotsky's archives in Harvard. The report is some 40 pages long, and we shall have to restrict ourselves to excerpts.

It starts by describing a mass protest rising in Tambov province. In this province of 3½ million people, tens of thousands of peasants were actively involved in the rising.

> By the middle of January the organization of the uprising had taken on definite shape:
> In five *uezds* as many as 900 village committees had been set up, elected by meetings and interlinked by *volost* and then *reion* [district], *uezd* and, finally, *guberniia* committees . . .
> In February the fighting men numbered as many as 40,000 . . .
> Besides the 'field' troops there were also internal guard units, some 10,000 in number, in operation.
> The availability of organized collaboration from the local population made the bands less vulnerable, exceptionally mobile and,

so to speak, ubiquitous. Their tactics were confined to sudden attacks on our small, careless units by means of wide, complete encirclements with dense lines of cavalry ... The Soviet authorities from the villages in five of the *uezds* had almost entirely fled into the towns; the party organization in the countryside had been destroyed; it had not been able systematically and in good time to carry out the concentration and withdrawal of its forces from the villages that had risen up in arms, and up to a thousand communists were slaughtered.

The Red Army and the Cheka took extremely harsh measures against the peasant rebels. For instance:

pro-bandit villages are singled out, and in relation to these massive terrorism is applied: a special 'sentence' is pronounced on these villages, in which their crimes against the labouring people are enumerated, the entire male population is declared to be committed for trial before a Revolutionary Military Tribunal, all the families of bandits are removed to a concentration camp as *hostages* in respect of that member of the family who is a participant in a band, a term of two weeks is given for the bandit to give himself up, at the end of which the family is deported from the *guberniia* and its property (which earlier had been conditionally sequestrated) is confiscated for good. Simultaneously house-to-house searches are carried out, and, in the event of the discovery of weapons, the senior working member of the household is liable to shooting on the spot ...

As a model of the correct execution of these orders [one can point to] the example of the 1st Sector, where the stubbornly pro-bandit Parevskaia *volost* was crushed by the firm application of the hostage system and the public shooting of them in batches until this secured the surrender of arms and of active members of bands. The effective conduct of this campaign was helped by the successes of our Cheka and of our military ...

Of the 21,000 fighting men established by our intelligence as serving in the ranks of the gangs at the beginning of May only a few hundred remained by the middle of July; the remainder either had fallen casualty (up to 2,000 bandits were killed in June and July) or had given themselves up or been captured, or had fled ...

According to reports from the Political Commissions for the period 1 June till 2 July, 1,748 bandits have been taken and 2,452 deserters; 1,449 bandits have surrendered voluntarily ... and so have 6,672 deserters. In all 12,301 have been accounted for. 3,430 individual hostages have been taken and 913 families. 157

holdings have been confiscated and 85 houses have been burnt down or pulled down. During the last week the number of bandit deserters taken has risen to 16,000, of families to 1,500, of holdings confiscated to 500 and of houses burnt down or pulled down to 250. More than 300 bandit families were allowed to go free after the bandits had given themselves up ... the harshest measures were applied in the Belomestnaia and Dvoinia *volosts*, where those peasants who had persisted in concealing arms and bandits gave in only after the shooting of two batches of kulak hostages. In all 154 bandit hostages were shot here. 227 families of bandits were taken, 17 houses were burnt down and 24 pulled down, and 22 houses handed over to the village poor. In the Estalsk *volost* 75 hostages and bandits were shot, 12 houses were burnt down and 21 pulled down; in both *volosts* the peasants denounced up to 300 bandits, some of whom they brought in, and handed in 118 rifles, 25 sawn-off shotguns, 10 revolvers, etc. ...

In the village of Krivopoliane, after the shooting of 13 hostages, a store of spare parts for machine-guns was pointed out; several bandits were denounced and the refuge of the remnants of Selianskyi's band was pointed out. Altogether in the Tambov *uezd*, from 1 June up to 10 July, 59 bandits voluntarily gave themselves up with their arms and 906 without, and 1,445 deserters; 1,455 bandits and 1,504 deserters were eliminated. 549 families were taken as hostages; 295 outright confiscations of property were carried out; 80 houses were pulled down and 60 burnt down; 591 bandits and 70 hostages were shot and two persons for giving them shelter ...

About 5,000 hostages have been accumulated in the concentration camps.

Why did the mass of peasants take up arms against the regime? The Cheka report candidly explains:

The peasant uprisings develop because of widespread *dissatisfaction, on the part of small property-owners in the countryside with the dictatorship of the proletariat, which directs at them its cutting edge of implacable compulsion, which cares little for the economic peculiarities of the peasantry* and does the countryside no service that is at all perceptible ...

In general the Soviet regime was, in the eyes of the majority of the peasants, identified with flying visits by commissars or plenipotentiaries who were valiant at giving orders to the *volost* Executive Committees and village Soviets and went around imprisoning the representatives of these local organs of authority

for the non-fulfilment of frequently quite absurd requirements. It was identified also with the food-requisitioning units . . . The peasantry, in their majority, have become accustomed to regarding the Soviet regime as something extraneous in relation to themselves, something that issues only commands, that gives orders most zealously but quite improvidently.
The Soviet regime had the restrictiveness characteristic of a military administration.

In conclusion the report states:

in the countryside the Soviet regime is still predominantly military-administrative rather than economic in character; it is a force which issues instructions from the outside and not the acknowledged guide of the peasant farmer; in the eyes of the peasants it is tyrannical and not a system that, before all else, organizes and ministers to the countryside itself.[89]

The massive, stubborn opposition of the peasantry to the state inevitably distorted it away from the norm, the ideal, of the proletarian dictatorship as visualized by Lenin in *State and Revolution*. Following Marx and Engels, he argued there that the workers' state would impose a dictatorship on the minority – the bourgeoisie – while it represented total democracy for the majority. But the exigencies of a civil war in a backward country with its economy in ruins, and the international revolution belated, brought about impositions on the peasantry by the state so harsh as to make democracy for the majority – in this case the peasantry – impossible.

There was another factor which deformed the state even further. The peasantry inevitably influenced the mood of the young proletariat, who had only recently left the countryside. Thus the report of the Cheka in Tambov has this to say about the railwaymen of the province:

The railway-men continue to serve as a pivot for the counter-revolutionary organization . . .
For the protection of the railways a system of taking hostages from the adjacent settlements was applied as early as the end of April; in June this system was extended to the protection of the telegraph network and of the bridges on country roads; in July it was decided not to take hostages in these cases but to leave them in their villages, merely announcing that certain

families would be the first to answer for the destruction of rail-ways, etc.

Even the party was not immune from the mood of the peasantry in the province:

> the party organization was going through a grave crisis in the winter of 1920-1921: discipline fell, demoralizing influences gained strength ... and about half its members left
> The party organization has become weakened and overstrained; among the workers a mood of opposition is increasing ... The party organization numbers up to 5,000 members, instead of the 14,000 of last year.[40]

Thus the peasants' attitude to Communism was one of the main influences that shaped the state, giving it a Jacobin character, i.e. an extremely centralistic dictatorship by a revolutionary minority imposing its will on the great majority.

In Conclusion

We saw in the last chapter that the relative weight of the industrial proletariat declined. In this chapter we have seen that the weight of the agricultural proletariat was also reduced. In contrast, that of the petty bourgeois peasantry continued to rise. One graphic expression of the change in the relative power of the two classes is the change in their size. While the number of industrial workers, as we have seen, fell from 3,000,000 in 1917 to 1,240,000 in 1921-22 (a decline of 58.7 per cent), and the number of agricultural workers from 2,100,000 in 1917 to 34,000 in 1919 (a decline of 98.5 per cent), the number of peasant house-holds rose from 16.5 million on 1 January 1918 to over 24 million by 1920, an increase of about 50 per cent.[41]*

In an article entitled 'Economics and Politics in the Era of the Dictatorship of the Proletariat', published in *Pravda* on the third anniversary of the October revolution, Lenin quite rightly stated: 'it was the peasantry as a whole who were the first to gain, who gained most, and gained immediately from the dictatorship of the proletariat.'[42]

---

* Note that the figure for industrial workers gives the number of individuals, not households, i.e. the number of industrial workers' households was much smaller.

The situation and attitudes of the peasantry affected the whole structure of political organization – the state, the soviets, the state officialdom, the party – during the civil war, and even more after it.*

11
The Withering Away of the State?

During the civil war the Bolshevik government found itself under siege not only from world imperialism, but also among its own people, who were often indifferent, sometimes clearly hostile. These circumstances inevitably affected the functioning of the state.

The Dream

Let us deal first with the expectation. In his book *State and Revolution*, Lenin made it clear that the withering away of the state would begin immediately after the establishment of the dictatorship of the proletariat: 'according to Marx, the proletariat needs only a state which is withering away, i.e. a state so con-

---

*The class conflict between proletariat and peasantry explains why the Soviet electoral law under Lenin did not give even formal equality to the two: the All-Russian Congress of Soviets was made up of one deputy for every 25,000 city electors as against 125,000 rural inhabitants. (Since 51 per cent of the population were adults over 20, the urban population was overrepresented by something like 2·5 : 1 compared with the rural population.)

Lenin explained: 'Yes, we have violated equality between the workers and peasants . . . The vote of one worker is equal to several peasant votes. Is that unfair?

'No, in the period when it is necessary to overthrow capital it is quite fair'.[48]

stituted that it begins to wither away immediately, and cannot but wither away'.[1] However long the process, Lenin expected it to be progressive and continuing.

The state would have to be strong and ruthless in crushing the bourgeoisie. At the same time it would have to be democratic, as it would be a dictatorship exercised by a majority over a minority. This would give it a clearly democratic character, and enormously simplify its working. The period after the overthrow of capitalist rule

> is a period of unprecedented violent class struggle in unprecedented acute forms, and, consequently, during this period the state must inevitably be a state that is democratic *in a new way* (for the proletariat and the propertyless in general) and dictatorial *in a new way* (against the bourgeoisie) . . .
>
> the suppression of the minority of exploiters by the majority of the wage slaves of *yesterday* is comparatively so easy, simple and natural a task that it will entail far less bloodshed than the suppression of the risings of slaves, serfs or wage-labourers, and it will cost mankind far less. And it is compatible with the extension of democracy to such an overwhelming majority of the population that the need for a *special machine* of suppression will begin to disappear. Naturally, the exploiters are unable to suppress the people without a complex machine for performing this task, but *the people* can suppress the exploiters even with a very simple 'machine', almost without a 'machine', without a special apparatus, by the simple *organization of the armed people* (such as the Soviets of Workers' and Soldiers' Deputies).[2]

Lenin invokes the example of ancient democracy where the citizens themselves were administrators.

> Under socialism much of 'primitive' democracy will inevitably be revived, since, for the first time in the history of civilized society, the *mass* of the population will rise to taking an *independent* part . . . *in the everyday administration of the state.*[3]

The proletariat will be able

> to crush, smash to atoms, wipe off the face of the earth the bourgeois, even the republican-bourgeois, state machine, the standing army, the police and the bureaucracy and to substitute for them a *more* democratic state machine, but a state machine nevertheless, in the shape of armed workers who proceed to form a militia involving the entire population.[4]

And so 'the armed proletariat itself' will 'become the government'.[5]

The proletarian state will be a centralist one, but democratic, based on local autonomy of the communes, and the *voluntary* joining together: 'the proletariat and the poor peasants [will] take state power into their own hands, organize themselves quite freely in communes'.[6] And Lenin quotes approvingly the words of Engels: 'Complete self-government for the provinces (*guberniias* and regions), districts and communes through officials elected by universal suffrage. The abolition of all local and provincial authorities appointed by the state.'[7]

The first decrees and laws issued after the October revolution were full of repetitions of the word 'democracy': a 'democratic peace', 'democratization of the army'. 'As a democratic government', said Lenin introducing the land decree, 'we cannot evade the decision of the popular masses, even if we were not in agreement with it.' Tens and hundreds of similar statements were made. However, faced with the sullen opposition of the peasants, and with the proletariat a small and declining minority, the dictatorship of the proletariat in Russia was not to be that of the 'vast majority' but of a determined minority.

Let us now turn from the ideal to the reality, and see what deviations the situation made necessary from the norm described by Lenin on the eve of the October revolution.

State Administration

The first constitution of the Russian Socialist Federated Soviet (RSFSR), adopted by the Fifth All-Russian Congress of Soviets on 10 July 1918, declared: 'The All-Russian Congress of Soviets is the supreme authority of the Russian Socialist Federated Soviet Republic.'[8]

To start with the Congress of Soviets met frequently. Thus in the seven months between 7 November 1917, when power was declared to be in the hands of the Soviet, and the adoption of the constitution of 10 July 1918, there were four congresses. This frequency fell with the onset of the civil war. The constitution stated that the Congress of Soviets would convene 'at least twice a year'. This was changed to once a year in 1921.[9]

In fact the Congress met only annually during the period November 1918 to December 1922. A simple reason for the declining frequency of the Congresses of Soviets was the massive size of the assembly, which was not at all appropriate for the conditions of civil war: the number of delegates rose from 649 in November 1917 to 1,296 a year later and 2,214 in December 1922.[10]

The power of the Congress of Soviets shifted to its Central Executive Committee (VTsIK). In the constitution VTsIK was subordinate to the Congress. Article 29 states: 'The All-Russia Central Executive Committee is fully accountable to the All-Russia Congress of Soviets.' Nevertheless, the VTsIK was to be a powerful body. The constitution stated:

> In the intervals between Congresses the All-Russia Central Executive Committee is the supreme authority of the Republic.
>
> The All-Russia Central Executive Committee is the highest legislative, administrative and supervisory body of the Russian Socialist Federative Soviet Republic.
>
> The All-Russia Central Executive Committee gives general directives for the activity of the workers' and peasants' government and all organs of Soviet power in the country . . .
>
> The All-Russia Central Executive Committee examines and approves draft decrees and other proposals submitted by the Council of People's Commissars or by separate departments, and issues its own decrees and ordinances.
>
> The All-Russia Central Executive Committee convenes the All-Russia Congress of Soviets, to which it submits an account of its activity and reports on general policy and particular matters.
>
> The All-Russia Central Executive Committee appoints the Council of People's Commissars and . . . People's Commissariats.
>
> The All-Russia Central Executive Committee has the right to cancel or suspend any order or decision of the Council of People's Commissars.[11]

Thus VTsIK, according to the constitution, was a higher and more powerful body than the Council of People's Commissars, the Sovnarkom.

In practice, however, the power of VTsIK was whittled away by its own presidium (and by Sovnarkom). One reason, as in the case of the Congress of Soviets, was the sheer size of VTsIK, which in practice made it inflexible as an administrative leadership. The constitution called for a VTsIK of not more than 200 members. But this provision was altered to allow for an increase to 300 and later to 386 members by the Eighth (December 1920) and Ninth (December 1921) Congresses of Soviets.

The VTsIK met less and less frequently. At first it was required to meet at least once every two months. This was reduced to 'not less than three times a year' by provision of the Ninth Congress of Soviets.

At the Seventh Congress of Soviets (December 1919), Lenin justified the infrequency of the meetings of VTsIK by the requirements of the war against the Whites. 'It is said that the Soviets meet rarely and are not re-elected often enough.' The representative of the Bund complained, 'it is really a terrible crime if your Central Executive Committee has not met'. Lenin, quoting these words, replied:

> We are fighting against Kolchak, Denikin and the others . . . We are conducting a difficult and victorious war. You know that with every invasion we had to send all the members of the Central Executive Committee to the front . . . workers who have been tempered by several years of struggle and who have acquired the necessary experience to be able to lead are fewer in our country than in any other.[12]

The VTsIK was replaced, in practice, by its presidium. There was no such presidium in the system of organs originally established on 7 November 1917. An unofficial body, a presidium of 7 or 8 people was soon set up by VTsIK, however, to prepare material for the sessions, and provide continuous supervision over the existing VTsIK departments. In the succeeding months, it became the practice for VTsIK to entrust certain work to this presidium. But the first Soviet constitution still did not include the presidium among the organs of power.

Official recognition of the existing gap in the formal structure of power came a year and a half later, when the Seventh Congress of Soviets adopted the following specific decisions concerning the presidium of VTsIK on 9 December 1919:

> The presidium of VTsIK conducts the sessions of VTsIK.
> Prepares the materials for the sessions of VTsIK.

Introduces drafts of decrees for examination by the plenum of VTsIK.

Supervises the observance of decisions of VTsIK ...

Has the right, between sessions of VTsIK, to confirm decisions of Sovnarkom, as well as to suspend decisions of the latter, transferring them to the nearest plenum of VTsIK for decision.[18]

The expected frequency of the sessions of the presidium is not indicated. However, in a report on its activity between 19 March and 30 May 1921, Kalinin stated that during that period there were 19 meetings of the presidium. This would make an average of more than 3 meetings a week.[14]

In practice, however, neither the Congress of Soviets, nor VTsIK, nor even its presidium, retained any real power over the Council of People's Commissars, the Sovnarkom. With Sovnarkom staffed with the highest party members, it very early became clear that its subordination to the Congress of Soviets or VTsIK was only formal. The outstanding development of the years of the civil war was the concentration of central authority in the hands of Sovnarkom at the expense of the All-Russian Congress of Soviets and VTsIK.

The provisions of the constitution of 1918 that 'urgent measures can be taken by the Council of People's Commissars directly' was used more and more during the period of civil war and national emergency. Under such conditions, indeed, all decisions are likely to be measures of extreme urgency.

Sovnarkom not only enjoyed full executive authority, but also unlimited power of legislation by decree. In its first year it passed 480 decrees, of which only 68 were submitted to VTsIK for confirmation. Between 1917 and 1921 Sovnarkom issued 1,615 decrees, VTsIK only 375.[15]

Decline of the Power of Local Soviets

After the October revolution the People's Commissariat of Internal Affairs defined the role of local soviets thus:

Locally the Soviets are the organs of administration, the organs of local power: they must bring under their control all institutions of an administrative, economic, financial and cultural-educational character ...

Each of these organizations, down to the smallest, is fully autonomous in questions of a local character, but makes its activity conform to the general decrees and resolutions of the central power and to the resolutions of the larger Soviet organizations into the composition of which it enters.[16]

At the same time as the All-Russian Congress of Soviets was being deprived of its power by Sovnarkom, a process of concentration of authority at the centre at the expense of local soviets was taking place.

The civil war undermined the operation of the local soviets. The borough soviets in major cities disappeared. The administration of numerous city soviets was combined with those of the provinces and districts, while the regional organizations established by the constitution ceased to exist altogether. A major role at this time was played by the so-called Revkoms or Revolutionary Committees. These were set up in regions affected by the war, by a decree of Sovnarkom of 24 October 1919, and all local soviet organizations were instructed to obey them.[17] The Revkoms were frequently identical with the Bolshevik party committee.

At the Seventh All-Russian Soviet Congress in December 1919, Kamenev painted the following dark picture of the soviets during the civil war:

> We know that because of the war the best workers were withdrawn in large numbers from the cities, and that therefore at times it becomes difficult in one or another provincial or district capital to form a soviet and make it function . . . The soviet plenary sessions as political organizations often waste away, the people busy themselves with purely mechanical chores . . . General soviet sessions are seldom called, and when the deputies meet, it is only to accept a report, listen to a speech and the like.[18]

Much of the influence of the local soviets was taken over by the party. One reason was that the local soviet administrations were backward and corrupt. In reporting on the collapse of the eastern front in December 1918, Stalin argued that the local soviets bore the decisive responsibility for the defeat. He had found that most of the staff of this institution had been active in the Zemstva, the old Tsarist local government institutions, e.g. in Viatka 4,467 out of a total of 4,766 of the staff of the soviet authorities.[19] For this reason he called for a strengthening of the local party organization, in order to be able to supervise the unreliable soviets.

The Role of the Cheka

Another important development undermining the soviet, and directly associated with the harsh conditions of the civil war, was the rise of the secret police, the Cheka. Elsewhere we have referred to the rise of the Red Terror, and its instrument, the Cheka, as a response to the White Terror.* To start with the Cheka had a very small staff. But it expanded very quickly. In February 1918 the central Cheka had 120 employees. By the end of the year the entire organization was said by Latsis to have a staff of no less than 31,000.[20]

During the civil war the Cheka invaded every department of state administration, central and local. By August 1918 it had formed sub-committees in 38 *guberniias* and 365 districts, which in practice covered the whole of Russia under Soviet rule at the time. In an instruction from the Central Cheka to the local commissions of 28 August 1918 it was pointed out that in no circumstances should the Cheka be subordinated to any division or soviet executive committee, but that it had on the contrary to exercise the function of leadership.

One historian described the position of the Cheka at the time thus:

> The power of the Cheka was unlimited and nothing could be done without its local commissions in autumn 1918 in the field of supply and military defence, when Soviet Russia was under dire threat from the civil war and foreign intervention. The Cheka had its eyes everywhere. If the constant changing of the fronts caused the collapse of some Soviets, the Cheka, which disposed its own troops, represented the state authority in the areas affected by the war.[21]

At the end of November 1918 the Cheka was given the task of forming subdivisions for railways, water navigation, posts and telegraph. It also took over from the armed units of the Commissariat of Supply.

Since the Cheka had succeeded in building a chain of auth-

---

* See pp. 17-19.

ority right up to the district administration, by setting up local Extraordinary Commissions, and thus in principle represented a genuine central organ, it was not surprising that it came into conflict with the People's Commissariat of the Interior.

When in March 1918 the Cheka began to build up its local branches, the Commissariat for the Interior assumed that these commissions would become part of the soviet organizations and not interfere with the uniformity of the system. But, in fact, the subordination of the Extraordinary Commissions to the local soviets was not put into effect. In the following months the representatives of the soviets and the leaders of the security organs arrested each other from time to time in the fight for domination.[22]

A member of the People's Commissariat of the Interior complained that the slogan 'All power to the Cheka' would supersede the old slogan 'All power to the soviets'.

The tensions between local soviets and Extraordinary Commissions were made clear in an inquiry published by the Commissariat of the Interior on 20 November 1918. According to this, 119 soviets were in favour of the subordination of the Cheka to the Executive Committees of the soviets, 99 wanted to incorporate them into the 'administration divisions' of the soviets, and only 19 advocated an independent position.[23]

The threat that the Cheka might rise above the party was clear. At the turn of the year 1918-19 a press campaign was launched against the Cheka in *Pravda* and *Izvestiia*. Under the pressure of such great mistrust the Extraordinary Commissions were dissolved at district level by VTsIK on 24 January 1919.[24]

However, at the height of Kolchak's and Denikin's offensive in summer and autumn 1919, when the Soviet Republic for a time resembled a beleaguered fortress in an area with a radius of 600 km round Moscow, all criticism of the Cheka, as well as other extraordinary organs, was suppressed.

Although the Cheka was necessary for victory in the civil war, Lenin was aware of the danger that it could develop into a completely independent instrument. At the first opportunity which arose – immediately after the end of the civil war – he moved to curb the power of the Cheka.

In a speech on 23 December 1921 – one of the last speeches of his life – to the Ninth Congress of the Soviets, Lenin stated: 'It is essential to reform the Cheka, define its functions and powers, and limit its work to political problems . . . [It is essential] to put forward the firm slogan of greater revolutionary legality.'[25]

Accordingly the Ninth Congress of Soviets resolved:

> The Congress considers that the present strengthening of soviet power within and without makes it possible to narrow the extent of the activity of the Cheka and its organs, reserving for the judicial organs the struggle against violations of the laws of the soviet republics.
>
> Therefore the Congress of Soviets charges the presidium of VTsIK to review at the earliest date the statute of the Cheka and its organs in the sense of reorganizing them, of restricting their competence and of strengthening the principles of revolutionary legality.[26]

The Red Army

The main arm of the state is the army. In Lenin's words, the state 'consists of special bodies of armed men, having prisons, etc. at their command'.[27]

A few days after coming to power, he wrote: 'The wholesale arming of the people and the abolition of the regular army is a task which we must not lose sight of for a single minute.'[28]

In April 1917, Lenin posed the question: 'Should officers be elected by the soldiers?' And he answered unequivocally: 'Not only must they be elected, but every step of every officer and general must be supervised by persons especially elected for the purpose by the soldiers.'

Then he asked: 'Is it desirable for the soldiers, on their own decision, to displace their superiors?' And answered: 'It is desirable and essential in every way. The soldiers will obey and respect only elected authority.'[29]

Initially, the Bolshevik government introduced extreme measures of democratization for the army. Thus, on 16 (29) December 1917, Sovnarkom issued a decree stating:

> The full power within any army unit or combination of units is to be in the hands of its soldiers' committees and Soviets . . .
>
> The [soldiers'] committees are to exercise control over those

spheres of [the army's] activity which the committees do not handle directly.

The elective principle for army officers is hereby introduced. All commanders up to the regimental commander are to be elected by a general vote of the [different units] . . . Commanders higher than regimental commanders and including the supreme commander-in-chief are to be elected by a congress . . . of committees of the army units [for which the commander is being elected] . . .

Positions of a technical nature which require special training . . . such as physicians, engineers, aviators . . are to be appointed by the committees . . . from among persons having the required special knowledge.

Chiefs of staff are elected . . . from among persons with special training.

Next day Sovnarkom decided by decree

1. To do away with all ranks and titles from the rank of corporal to that of general, inclusive. The army of the Russian Republic is henceforth to be composed of free and equal citizens bearing the honorable title of 'soldier of the revolutionary army';
2. To do away with all privileges and the external marks formerly connected with the different ranks and titles;
3. To do away with saluting;
4. To do away with all decorations and other signs of distinction;
5. To do away with all officers' organizations . . .
6. To abolish the institution of orderlies in the army.[30]

However, the Bolsheviks were very quickly forced to retreat from the ideal of a democratically structured army. On 13 March 1918 Trotsky was appointed People's Commissar of War and President of the Supreme War Council. And he set about organizing the armed forces of the Republic.

The first soldiers of the revolution consisted of Red Guards. Any attempt to carry out conscription in the first months of the revolution would have been condemned to failure. The country was sick of war, and the main appeal of Bolshevism had been its search for peace. So it was decided to create Red forces of volunteers. More than 100,000 volunteers joined the Red Army up to April 1918.

But the exigencies of the civil war made it impossible for the Soviet government to rely on volunteers alone. With 16 armies defending a front of 8,000 kilometres, conscription had to be undertaken to raise the Red Army first to one, then two, then three and eventually to five million.

Trotsky started to build the Red Army by calling for volunteers from among the proletariat. Only when the proletarian core of the army had been firmly established did he begin to conscript the peasants, first the poor and then the middle peasants. These often deserted *en masse*, their morale oscillating violently with the ups and downs of the civil war.

It was estimated that the number of such deserters in the period from 1 January 1919 to 1 January 1920 was 2,846,000 in round figures. During the year 1919, 1,753,000 deserters were brought back to the army.

By February 1919 there were about a million men in the Red Army. The number rose by 1 January 1920 to about three million.[31] Over 90 per cent of the deserters were men who failed to comply with call-up orders. The total number of deserters for the second half of 1919 was about 1,500,000. The counter-measures ranged from threats of dire punishment to promises of pardon to those who reported for duty immediately. A Central Commission for Combating Desertion, with regional branches, was set up in December 1918 and reorganized in May 1919 with a wider network of local branches. Nearly one million deserters reported for duty voluntarily during the second half of 1919. At times there were new formations consisting almost entirely of this category of deserters.[32]

The combat efficiency of the soldiers had a great deal to do with their class origin. An article analysing the percentage of workers in the Red Army in 1920 stated:

In the divisions that had distinguished themselves in action, the percentage of workers ranged from 26.4 (8th Red Cavalry Division) to 19.6 (28th Rifle Division). In Budenny's famous First Cavalry Army the percentage of workers was 21.7. On the other hand, in the 9th Rifle Division, regarded as one of low combat value, the workers were only 10.5 per cent of the total number. In penal detachments, workers were 9.7 per cent of the total, in the detachments from apprehended deserters, 3·8 per cent. For the Red Army as a whole the percentage of workers at the time was 14·9; in the field units at the front it amounted to 16·5, while in the rear it fell to 11·13.[33]

The role of the Bolsheviks in the Red Army was clearly formulated by an order in May 1920 from Trotsky to the Commissar and commanding personnel of the western front.

> It is necessary that in each platoon, section and squad there should be a communist, even if a young one – but devoted to the cause. He should observe the morale of the nearest fellow-fighters, explain to them the problems and the aims of the war, and, in case he is himself perplexed, approach the commissar of his unit or some other responsible political worker for elucidation. Without such internal, unofficial, personal, day-by-day and hour-by-hour agitation under all conditions of the combat situation, the official agitation through articles and speeches will not give the required results ...
>
> *The conduct of communists* in the Red Army has a decisive significance for the morale and the battle efficacy of units. It is necessary, therefore, to distribute communists in an organized way, to guide them attentively and to keep careful check of their work . . . Revolutionary military councils and political departments of the armies, commissars and political departments of divisions, commissars of brigades and regiments should carefully check up on the behaviour of all communists subordinated to them with respect to combat functions after each new battle ordeal, ruthlessly casting out those lacking in decisiveness and meting out stern punishment to cowardly egotists.[34]

The Soviet military historian, F.Nikonov, suggests that during the civil war Red Army units were classified for combat efficiency according to the percentage of communists in their ranks. He estimates that those with less than 4 to 5 per cent of communists among their personnel were regarded as ineffective. Detachments with 6 to 8 per cent were looked upon as satisfactory, with an average combat efficacy. Units with 12 to 15 per cent communists were considered shock troops.[35]

The mass of communists were fanatically devoted to the cause. They were well aware that if they fell into the hands of the Whites and were recognized as party members they would be tortured and killed. So they fought with desperate courage and instilled something of their spirit into the mass of non-party soldiers.

The greatest obstacles to building the Red Army were moral and political. The whole of their recent vivid experience, including Bolshevik activities, encouraged soldiers to rebel against discipline and against authority. When Trotsky came to the conclusion that soldiers' committees could not lead regiments into battle successfully, and that the army needed centralization and formal discipline, this contradicted everything that the Bolsheviks had previously propagated. The tsar's officers who had been driven out of the army now had to be re-enrolled as specialists in the Red Army. Soldiers' committees, the embodiment of the revolution, were not now to be tolerated. The old discipline was still fresh in the memory when a new discipline had to be introduced.

In matters of defence, Trotsky argued, courage and revolutionary enthusiasm are not enough. 'As industry needs engineers, as farming needs qualified agronomists, so military specialists are indispensable to defence.'[36]

The first general call-up of military specialists took place on 29 July 1918; by the end of the year 36,971 such people had been mobilized, of whom 22,295 were officers.[37] By 15 August 1920, 48,409 former Tsarist officers had been called up, about 30,000 of whom saw active service. (The total number of 'commander' personnel towards the end of the civil war was about 130,000.)[38]

To control the ex-Tsarist officers Trotsky relied on the political commissars, who played a very important role. The commissar was supposed to watch over the political loyalty of the officers, to take charge of party work in the unit, and to carry on political propaganda and education work. According to the rules, the signature of the commissar was necessary on an operations order – to ensure that it did not have any hidden counter-revolutionary significance. Military responsibility for any such order, however, remained with the specialists.

From the beginning Trotsky made it clear that the commissar, who was entrusted with great power, would be severely punished if he neglected his duty. Thus on 14 August 1918 he declared: 'I hereby give warning that if any part of the army retreats of its own will the first to be shot will be the commissar, and the second the commander. The soldiers who show courage will be rewarded and promoted to positions of command. Cowards and traitors will not escape the bullets.'[39]

The commissars were an indispensable instrument of proletarian control. At the Seventh Congress of Soviets in December 1919 Trotsky eulogized the commissars: 'In our commissars . . . we have a new communist order of Samurais, the members of which have enjoyed no caste privileges and could die and teach others to die for the cause of the working class.'[40]

But despite the revolutionary spirit of the proletarian core of the Red Army and the heroic devotion of the communists, the Red Army was undeniably as far from Lenin's ideal of a workers' militia, as described in State and Revolution, as chalk from cheese.

The Bureaucratic Leviathan

There was a massive increase in the number of officials. There were 5,880,000 state officials by the end of 1920 – five times as many as the number of industrial workers.[41]

This state apparatus was mostly composed of people with bourgeois origins. It is true that hundreds of thousands of workers were mobilized by the party to strengthen it, but they were a minority, and their weight was further weakened by the dominance which technical superiority and higher cultural standards gave the old officials. As Lenin said on 12 June 1920: 'The soviet government employs hundreds of thousands of office workers, who are either bourgeois or semi-bourgeois . . . they have absolutely no confidence in our soviet government.'[42]

A confidential inquiry in the summer of 1922 among 270 engineers and technicians in responsible positions in Moscow, probably a fairly representative sample, confirmed Lenin's opinion. These engineers were divided into two categories, the first comprising those who belonged to the higher ranks of the administration before the revolution, and the second those who had been 'ordinary engineers' under the old regime. Three main questions were put to them: Were they sympathetic to the soviet government? Did they consider their work to be of social value? Did they consider the taking of bribes to be inadmissible? Those in the first group who answered the three questions affirmatively were 9, 30 and 25 per cent respectively; among the second group, 13, 75 and 30 per cent.[43]

If there was one person who was always aware of the danger of bureaucracy, who repeatedly used the strongest expressions to denounce it and demand a struggle against it, it was Lenin. Thus at the 11th session of the Petrograd Soviet on 12 March 1919 he spoke

> about the mouldiness, moss and red tape that has grown in the localities and about the need to fight it . . . We threw out the old bureaucrats, but they have come back . . . they wear a red ribbon in their buttonholes and creep into warm corners. What to do about it? We must fight this scum again and again and if the scum has crawled back we must again and again clean it up, chase it out, keep it under the surveillance of communist workers and peasants whom we have known for more than a month and for more than a year.[44]

At the Eighth Congress of the Party, in March 1919, Lenin said:

> The Tsarist bureaucrats began to join the soviet institutions and practise their bureaucratic methods, they began to assume the colouring of communists and, to succeed better in their careers, to procure membership cards of the Russian Communist Party . . . What makes itself felt here most is the lack of cultured forces.[45]

From 1921 onwards his denunciations of bureaucracy became more and more vehement. In a speech on 17 October 1921 to a conference of representatives of the Political Education Departments, Lenin said:

> At present bribery surrounds us on all sides . . . In my opinion, three chief enemies now confront one, . . . the first is communist conceit; the second – illiteracy, and the third – bribery.[46]

On 23 December 1921 he wrote to P.A.Bogdanov of VSNKh: 'We don't know how to conduct a public trial for rotten bureaucracy: for this all of us, and particularly the People's Commissariat for Justice, should be hung on stinking ropes. And I have not yet lost all hope that one day we shall be hung for this, *and deservedly so.*'[47]

On 21 February 1922 Lenin wrote to A.D.Tsiurupa, Deputy Chairman of Public Works Committee: 'The departments are shit; decrees are shit. To find men and check up on their work – that is the whole point.'[48]

With the same frankness and plainness, in his last speech to the Comintern Congress, on 13 November 1922, he indicted the bourgeois-conservative nature of the existing state machine:

> We took over the old machinery of state, and that was our mis-fortune. Very often this machinery operates against us. In 1917, after we seized power, the government officials sabotaged us. This frightened us very much and we pleaded: 'Please come back.' They all came back, but that was our misfortune. We now have a vast army of government employees, but lack sufficiently educated forces to exercise real control over them. In practice it often happens that here at the top, where we exercise political power, the machine functions somehow; but down below govern-ment employees have arbitrary control and they often exercise it in such a way as to counteract our measures. At the top, we have, I don't know how many, but at all events, I think, no more than a few thousand, at the outside several tens of thousands of our own people. Down below, however, there are hundreds of thousands of old officials whom we got from the tsar and from bourgeois society and who, partly deliberately and partly unwit-tingly, work against us.[49]

In Conclusion

The civil war shaped all the state institutions. In the words of Bukharin and Preobrazhensky, 'Today, when a fierce civil war is still raging, all our organizations have to be on a war footing. The instruments of the soviet power have had to be constructed on militarist lines . . . What exists today in Russia is not simply the dictatorship of the proletariat; it is a militarist-proletarian dictatorship.'[50]

The siege of the revolutionary state by foreign and Russian White armies, together with the sullen if not actively hostile attitude of millions of peasants, and the weakness of the industrial proletariat, were at the root of the bureaucratic centralism of all the state institutions.

The message of *State and Revolution*, which elsewhere I have called 'Lenin's real testament', and which was the guide for the first victorious proletarian revolution, was violated again and again during the civil war. But it was also invoked again and again against bureaucratic degeneration.

12
The Establishment of the Bolsheviks' Political Monopoly

Days of Innocence

To start with Lenin spoke of the *proletariat*, the *class* – not the Bolshevik Party – assuming state power. Thus on 11 (24) March 1917, in his *Letters from Afar*, he wrote: 'the proletariat must organize and arm *all* the poor, exploited sections of the population in order that they *themselves* should take the organs of state power directly into their own hands, in order that *they themselves should constitute* these organs of state power'.[1]

He did not visualize one-party rule. In *State and Revolution* the party receives very little attention. There are three references to it, two of which have no direct bearing on the issue of the dictatorship of the proletariat. One of these is an incidental remark concerning the need for the party to engage in the struggle 'against religion which stupefies the people';[2] the second, equally incidental, notes that 'in revising the programme of our party, we must by all means take the advice of Engels and Marx into consideration, in order to come nearer the truth, to restore marxism by ridding it of its distortions, in order to come nearer the truth, guide the struggle of the working class for its emancipation more correctly.'[3] The third and most relevant reference reads:

> By educating the workers' party, Marxism educates the vanguard of the proletariat capable of assuming power and *leading*

the whole people to socialism, of directing and organizing the new system, of being the teacher, the guide, the leader of all the working and exploited people, in organizing their social life without the bourgeoisie and against the bourgeoisie.[4]

It is not entirely clear from this passage whether it is the *proletariat* which is capable of assuming power or the *vanguard* of the proletariat, i.e. the workers' party which is so designated.

In general, Lenin distinguished clearly between the soviet state and the party: the former was the creation of the working class as a whole and involved the class as a whole in its operation: 'Under socialism . . . the *mass* of the population will rise to taking an *independent* part, not only in voting and elections, *but also in the everyday administration of the state*.'[5]

In Lenin's concept, the soviet state is the highest expression of the self-activity of the proletariat; the party is that section of the class which is most conscious of the historical role of this self-activity. Because the party and the state are not *identical*, in the same way as the vanguard and the class are not identical, more than one party can contend for influence and power within the framework of the institution of the workers' state.

All revolutionaries took it for granted before the October revolution that more than one workers' party would exist. Thus Trotsky, on being elected President of the Petrograd Soviet on 9 (22) September 1917, said:

> We are all party people, and we shall have to cross swords more than once. But we shall guide the work of the Petersburg soviet in a spirit of justice and complete independence for all fractions; the hand of the praesidium will never oppress the minority.

Sukhanov, quoting these words a few years later, commented:

> Heavens! What liberal views! What self-mockery! But the point is that about three years later, while exchanging reminiscences with me, Trotsky, thinking back to this moment, exclaimed dreamily:
> 'What a happy time!'
> Yes, wonderful! Perhaps not one person in the world, not excluding himself, will ever recall Trotsky's rule with *such* feelings.[6]

However, under the iron pressure of the civil war the Bolshevik leaders were forced to move, as the price of survival, to *a one-party system.*

The fate of the different parties was closely bound up with the development of the civil war. That the openly capitalist parties, above all the Cadets, would be ready to fight to the end against Bolshevik power was obvious. They wanted an open capitalist class dictatorship. The petty bourgeois parties – the Socialist-Revolutionaries and Mensheviks – were less clear in their position. On the one hand the petty bourgeois leaders rallied again and again to the counter-revolution. On the other they were repulsed by the extremism of the White terror, which did not spare even them. The result was vacillation in the SR and Menshevik camps. This was combined with serious fragmentation within the two parties. In each one section joined the Cadets, another moved cautiously and gradually towards the Bolsheviks, and another remained neutral. The positions of the different sections depended very much on the situation on the civil war front. A few Red Army reverses were enough to push the petty bourgeoisie, perpetually hesitant, in the direction of the right.

In suppressing the extreme right, the Bolshevik government faced a dilemma. What were they to do about the petty bourgeois who protested against the 'suppression of freedom'? This dilemma became increasingly difficult to solve by moderate measures: the Right Socialist Revolutionaries were practically indistinguishable from the 'Left' Cadets, and protested strongly when the latter were suppressed; the Right Mensheviks protested against the suppression of the Right SR; then again there was no clear boundary between the Right SR and the moderate SR, and between these and the Left SR, etc. The gradation was continuous. And as long as the final outcome of the civil war was not certain, i.e. for nearly three years, the level of tolerance of both the Bolsheviks and their opponents was very low. As E.H.Carr put it: 'If it was true that the Bolshevik regime was not prepared after the first few months to tolerate an organized opposition, it was equally true that no opposition was prepared to remain within legal limits. The premise of dictatorship was common to both sides of the argument.'[7]

The Cadets

On 28 November (11 December) 1917, Sovnarkom issued a decree banning the Cadet leaders because of their association with the Kornilov-Kaledin White forces. 'Leaders of the Cadet Party, the party of the enemy of the people, are to be arrested and handed over to the revolutionary tribunal. Local Soviets are ordered to keep a careful watch on the Cadet Party because of its connections with the Kornilov-Kaledin civil war against the revolution.'[8]

At a meeting of VTsIK the Left Socialist Revolutionaries and Menshevik Internationalists protested against this decree.[9]

At first, the measures the Bolshevik government took against the Cadets were seen as merely temporary. Thus, Sovnarkom's decree of 27 October (9 November), banning the Cadet press, stated:

> Those organs of the press will be closed which (a) call for open opposition or disobedience to the Workers' and Peasants' Government;
> (b) sow sedition by a frankly slanderous perversion of facts;
> (c) encourage deeds of a manifestly criminal character ...
> The above regulations are of a temporary nature and will be removed by a special decree just as soon as normal conditions are re-established.[10]

The Bolsheviks were even more lenient than the law allowed. Thus, in spite of the decrees, the Cadet newspaper, *Svoboda Rossii*, was still being published in Moscow in the summer of 1918. But this leniency evaporated when the civil war raged more fiercely.

Right Socialist Revolutionaries and Right Mensheviks

There was no clear line of demarcation between the Cadets and the Right SRs. O.H.Radkey, the historian of the SR party, describing its members in the Constituent Assembly, said:

> many of these people had developed a Cadet mentality, and were Cadets in everything but name.[11]
> All of these public welfare people, these functionaries, state employees, agronomists, cooperative officials, and others might, indeed, have contributed to the coming of revolution, but after it came, a few months of observing the people in action sufficed to convert them into one of the most conservative elements in

Russian society; the war did the rest by inflaming their latent nationalism. By any rational test, these right-wing populist intellectuals should have been in one camp with the Constitutional Democrats.

Why were they not? Why did they dissemble their convictions under the flag of Socialist Revolutionism? Sentiment might be one reason ... If not sentiment, then inertia helped to hold them where they were. Personal interest also may have had some influence. They may have realized that they would never achieve the position of power in the Cadet Party that they held in their own. There they would merely be foot soldiers, whereas here they were generals.[12]

After the October revolution the Right SRs quite naturally joined forces with the Cadets. In March 1918 they set up a common organization with the Mensheviks, called the 'League for Renewal' (*Soiuz Vozrozhdeniia*).

'The "League"', one of the Socialist Revolutionary leaders wrote, 'entered into regular relations with the representatives of the Allied missions at Moscow and Vologda.'[13]

In Moscow the Oktobrists, who traditionally stood to the right of the Cadets, joined the League for Renewal. The Military Commission of the Socialist Revolutionary Party organized the League's 'combat groups', whose command was entrusted to a general. The local committee of the League in Petrograd was made up of two Popular Socialists, one SR (A.R.Gotz, the leader of the party), one Cadet, Pepeliaev, who was to be one of Kolchak's ministers, and two Mensheviks, Potresov and Rozanov.

Another counter-revolutionary organization was created by the former SR terrorist, Boris Savinkov (one of the key participants in the abortive Kornilov coup) – the Fatherland and Freedom Defence League. Its chief of staff was a monarchist, while the majority of participants were Right SRs. This organization led a number of insurrections in the summer of 1918 in Iaroslav, Rybinsk, Murom, Kazan, Kaluga and Vladimirov.

When the Czechoslovak Legion rose in arms against the Bolsheviks in May 1918, it received the wholehearted support of the Right SR. When the Czechoslovaks occupied Samara, an SR committee of members of the Constituent Assembly proclaimed itself the government of the region, under its protection. A similar government was established at Omsk. At Archangel, under Allied protection, a mixed government of Populist Socialists and SRs was set up, headed by the old Narodnik, Peter Chaikovsky. In the Urals, at the end of July, after its capture by the Czechs and Russian White forces, a coalition government of Cadets, Right SRs, Populist Socialists and Right Mensheviks was formed. In Ufa a coalition government of monarchists, Cadets, Right SRs and Right Mensheviks was established under the leadership of Admiral Kolchak, and with the blessing of the French and British diplomatic representatives. By the spring of 1919 Kolchak had such a strong army as to represent a real threat to the survival of the Soviet regime.

The Soviet government had no alternative but to take severe measures against the Socialist Revolutionaries and Mensheviks. By a decree of 14 June 1918 VTsIK excluded both Right SR and Mensheviks from its ranks, because of their association with the Czech counter-revolutionaries seeking to 'organize armed attacks against the workers and peasants', and recommended all Soviets to exclude them.[14]

On 20 June 1918 the Bolshevik leader Volodarsky was assassinated by a Right SR – the first successful political assassination by the counter-revolution. On 30 August a Right SR, Dora Kaplan, made an attempt on Lenin's life and on the same day another Bolshevik leader, Uritsky, was assassinated by a Right SR.

Although he resorted to harsh measures against the counter-revolutionary acts of the Right SR, Lenin was always looking for a way of relaxing these measures. Thus when a professor of the University of Petrograd, Pitirim Sorokin, a former Right SR deputy to the Constituent Assembly, announced in November 1918, in a brief but sensational letter to the press, that he was giving up politics, this was seen by Lenin as:

> a symptom of a change of front on the part of a whole class, the petty-bourgeois democrats. A split among them is inevitable: one section will come over to our side, another section will remain neutral, while a third will deliberately join forces with the monarchist Constitutional-Democrats, who are selling Russia to Anglo-American capital and seeking to crush the revolution with the aid of foreign bayonets.

This development should be encouraged.

> One of the most urgent tasks of the present day is to take into account and make use of the turn among the Menshevik and Socialist-Revolutionary democrats from hostility to Bolshevism first to neutrality and then to support of Bolshevism ... A revolutionary proletarian must know whom to suppress and with whom – and when and how – to conclude an agreement ... But it would be ... foolish and ridiculous ... to insist only on tactics of suppression and terror in relation to the petty-bourgeois democrats when the course of events is compelling them to turn in our direction.[15]

On 8 February 1919 a conference of the Socialist Revolutionary organization in Petrograd 'decisively rejected any attempt to overthrow the soviet power by way of armed struggle' and denounced the Russian bourgeois parties and 'the imperialist countries of the Entente'. This demonstration of goodwill evoked a VTsIK resolution on 25 February 1919 legalizing the SR Party. But the Right SRs were not consistent in this line of benevolent neutrality towards the soviet government. With changing fortunes on the battlefields they repeatedly resorted to openly counter-revolutionary actions.

The Mensheviks

Despite their strong opposition to the Bolshevik government, for some time – i.e. until the armed uprising of the Czechoslovak Legion – the Mensheviks were not much hampered in their propaganda work. Thus the Left Menshevik paper, *Novaia Zhizn*, published a series of highly inflammatory articles between October 1917 and its suppression in July 1918, which did not bring down upon it the heavy hand of the state. Maxim Gorky, in the issue of 7 (20) November 1917, described the Bolsheviks thus:

> Blind fanatics and dishonest adventurers rushing madly, supposedly along the road of the 'social revolution'; in reality this is the road to anarchy, to the destruction of the proletariat and of the revolution. On this road Lenin and his associates consider it possible to commit all kinds of crimes, such as ... the abolition of freedom of speech, and senseless arrests – all the abomination which Plehve and Stolypin once perpetrated.

Gorky said about Lenin: 'Lenin is not an omnipotent magician but a cold-blooded trickster who spares neither the honour nor the life of the proletariat . . . Lenin's . . . madness . . . his Nechaev and Bakunin brand of anarchism . . .'[16] Three days later he wrote: 'Imagining themselves to be Napoleons of socialism, the Leninists rant and rave, completing the destruction of Russia. The Russian people will pay for this with lakes of blood.'[17] These statements were published in the legal press.

The outbreak of the civil war put the Mensheviks in an embarrassing position, since, for all their hostility to the Bolsheviks, they had still less to hope for from a restoration of the old regime.

A meeting of the Central Committee of the Mensheviks in Moscow on 17-21 October 1918 decided to give support – if critical – to the soviet government.

> The Bolshevik revolution of October 1917 was a historical necessity, since, by breaking the links between the labouring masses and the capitalist classes, it expressed the desire of the labouring masses to subordinate the trend of the revolution wholly to their own interests, without which the deliverance of Russia from the clutches of Allied imperialism, the pursuance of a consistent peace policy, the introduction of radical agrarian reform, and the regulation by the state of the entire economic life in the interests of the masses would have been inconceivable, and since this stage of the revolution has had the tendency to enlarge also the scope of the influence which the Russian revolution had on the course of world developments.[18]

The meeting renounced 'all political cooperation with classes hostile to democracy'; at the same time, while promising 'direct support of the military actions of the soviet government against foreign intervention', it demanded 'the abrogation of the extraordinary organs of police repression and the extraordinary tribunals' and 'the cessation of the political and economic terror'.[19]

This public declaration by the Mensheviks was followed by a very conciliatory speech by Lenin, declaring that no more was asked of the Mensheviks and SRs than 'good neighbourly relations': 'But we shall not forget there are still "activists" in your party, and for them our methods of struggle will remain the same, for they are friends of the Czechs and until the Czechs are driven out of Russia, you are our enemies too. We reserve state power for ourselves, *and for ourselves alone.*'[20]

The compromise with the SRs and Mensheviks could not last. When the military situation worsened in spring 1919, Lenin used much harsher language:

> We shall have to change our line of conduct very often, and this may appear strange and incomprehensible to the casual observer. 'How is that?' he will say. 'Yesterday you were making promises to the petty bourgeoisie, while today Dzerzhinsky announced that the Left Socialist Revolutionaries and the Mensheviks will be stood against the wall. What a contradiction!' Yes, it is a contradiction. But the conduct of the petty-bourgeois democrats themselves is contradictory: they do not know where to sit, and try to sit between two stools, jump from one to the other and fall now to the right and now to the left. We have changed our tactics towards them, and whenever they turn towards us we say 'Welcome' to them . . . we certainly do not want to use force against the petty-bourgeois democrats. We say to them, 'You are not a serious enemy. Our enemy is the bourgeoisie. But if you join forces with them, we shall be obliged to apply the measures of the proletarian dictatorship to you, too.'[21]

The Mensheviks, above all Martov, were searching for a 'third force'. Their (and the SR's) tragedy was that a 'third force' was not possible. As Martov wrote in a pathetic letter to Axelrod on 23 January 1920:

> We found a sympathetic audience but it invariably stood far to the right of us. By a healthy instinct, all who have been crushed down by Bolshevism supported us gladly as the most courageous fighters against it. But from our preaching they took only what they felt in need of, only our criticism and indictment of Bolshevism. As long as we exposed it, they applauded; the moment we began to say that another regime was necessary in order to conduct a successful struggle against Denikin, etc., to carry through the real liquidation of speculation and to assist the victory of the international proletariat over reaction, our audience turned cold and even hostile.[22]

In the spring of 1919 the outbreak of kulak uprisings in a number of provinces, and the successful advance of Kolchak, induced the majority of the SRs and Mensheviks to return to their extreme opposition to Bolshevism. In view of this, the Central Committee of the Bolsheviks in May 1919 issued a directive 'concerning the arrest of all prominent Mensheviks and SRs about whom it was not personally known that they were ready actively to support the soviet government in its struggle against Kolchak'.

The Left SRs

After seizing power, the Bolsheviks invited the Left SRs who supported the October revolution to join the Council of People's Commissars. After some hesitation the Left SR leaders reached an agreement with the Bolsheviks on 18 November (1 December) 1917, as a result of which representatives of the Left SR entered the government. They received seven Commissariats as against eleven for the Bolsheviks. The most important was the People's Commissariat of Agriculture.

For three months the Left SRs remained in the government. However, on 19 March 1918 they resigned in protest against the signing of the Brest-Litovsk Peace Treaty. They wanted to tear up the treaty and resume war with Germany. They also disagreed fundamentally with the agrarian policy of the Bolsheviks. They opposed the setting up of 'Committees of Poor Peasants' and the despatch of workers' detachments into the countryside for the purpose of requisitioning grain. These measures aroused strong opposition not only among the kulaks, but also among the middle peasants who were the main supporters of the Left SRs.

On 6 July the Left SRs assassinated Count Mirbach, the German Ambassador, in the hope of restarting the war between Russia and Germany, and at the same time launched a revolt against their previous allies in the streets of the capital.

The Left SR uprising was ruthlessly suppressed by the Bolsheviks. However, no overall banning of the Left SRs took place. On 15 July VTsIK passed a resolution that permitted as representatives of this body those members of the party who 'categorically renounce their solidarity with the assassination and with the revolt which followed it'. Legally, therefore, those Left SRs, and there were very many, who repudiated the action of their Central Committee were after July still entitled to sit in the soviets. The July revolt of the Left SRs caused a break-up of the party. The majority repudiated von Mirbach's assassination and attempted to preserve peace with the Bolsheviks.[23]*

The Bolshevik Party's Political Monopoly

The severity of civil war conditions, the weakness of the proletariat and the sullen animosity of the peasantry forced Lenin to greater and greater restriction of the freedom of action of the Mensheviks and SRs, of whatever variety. Had it been possible to isolate the Whites as the sole targets for attack, the situation would have been very different. Unfortunately, in order to wrench political support away from Kornilov, Denikin and Kolchak, the Bolsheviks had to suppress the Cadet Party. The majority of the Mensheviks and SRs were of course not prepared to defend the White generals, but they were not indifferent to the suppression of the Cadets. On the whole, Left Mensheviks would not defend the Cadets, but could not ignore the suppression of the Right Mensheviks and Right SRs who sided with the Cadets.

The Bolshevik Party programme adopted in March 1919 made it clear that the restriction of the rights of other parties was only temporary. Thus it stated: 'the forfeiture of political rights, and whatever limitations may be imposed upon freedom, are necessary only as temporary measures'.[25] However, circumstances conspired to demonstrate that sometimes there is nothing more permanent than what is intended to be temporary.

---

* The anarchists faced a dilemma in that they opposed both the dictatorship of the proletariat and Bolshevism, in particular, on the one hand, and the Whites on the other. Paul Avrich, the historian of Russian anarchism, writes:
'Ardent libertarians, the anarchists found the repressive policies of the Soviet government utterly reprehensible; yet the prospect of a White victory seemed even worse. Any opposition to Lenin's regime at this time might tip the balance in favour of the counter-revolutionaries; on the other hand, active support, or even benevolent neutrality, might enable the Bolsheviks to entrench themselves too deeply, to be ousted later.
'The acrimonious debates provoked by this dilemma served to widen the fissures in the anarchist camp . . . In the end, a large majority gave varying degrees of support to the beleaguered regime.'[24]

The need to fight a civil war with a weakened proletariat forced the Bolsheviks to suppress one opposition party after another, from Cadets to SRs to Mensheviks. The Fifth All-Russian Congress of Soviets in July 1918 was the last at which the opposition was present in strength. At the next Congress, held four months later, with 950 delegates, there were 933 Communists, 8 Revolutionary-Communists, 4 SRs, 2 Narodnik Communists, 1 Maximalist, 1 Anarchist and 1 non-party delegate.[26]

The Party and the Soviets

Thus it was about a year after the October revolution before an actual monopoly of political power was held by one party. How did this monopoly affect the working of the soviet and political life in general?

The Eighth Congress of the party in March 1919 defined the relations between the party and the soviet thus:

> The Communist Party poses as its task the conquest of a most decisive influence and complete direction in all the organizations of toilers: trade unions, cooperatives, village communes, etc. The Communist Party seeks especially the realization of its programme by the achievement of its complete dominance in the existing state organizations – the soviets . . . By practical, daily self-sacrificing work in the soviets, by putting forth its most stable and devoted members for all soviet posts, the Russian Communist Party must achieve for itself undivided political dominance in the soviets and actual control over all their work. But the functions of the party fractions must on no account be confused with the functions of the state organs – the soviets. Such confusion would produce fatal results . . . The party must carry out its decision through the soviet organs, *within the framework of the soviet constitution*. The party should endeavour to guide the activity of the soviets, not to supplant them.[27]

Again and again party congresses repeated that the party should not substitute itself for the soviet, but only try to guide it. Thus the Eleventh Party Congress (March 1922) resolved:

> Keeping for itself the general guidance and direction of the entire politics of the soviet state, the party must carry out a much more precise demarcation between its own current work and the work of the soviet organs, between its own apparatus and that of the soviets. Such a systematically executed demar-

cation should secure more systematic consideration and decision of . . . questions by the soviet organs, at the same time raising the responsibility of every soviet official for the work entrusted to him, and on the other hand, making it possible for the party to concentrate properly on the basic party work of general guidance of the work of all State organs.[28]

A most important task now is to establish the correct division of labour between party and soviet institutions and to delineate clearly the rights and duties of the one and the other.[29]

But with the party monopoly of power, the separation of party and state was necessarily only formal, especially as party members were bound by discipline to act as one. Thus, for instance, the Eighth Party Conference of December 1919 passed a statute which included the following:

At the general meeting of the non-party organization in which the fraction is working all fraction members must vote unanimously on matters which have been decided within the fraction. Persons violating this rule are subject to the usual disciplinary procedures.[30]

In fact the party and the soviets became increasingly fused. This fusion permeated all levels of the administration. Data from some 60 per cent of local soviets in the second half of 1919 showed that party members and candidates made up 89 per cent of the membership of executive committees of *guberniia* congresses of soviets, 86 per cent of executive committees of *uezd* congresses of soviets, 93 per cent of executive committees of city soviets in *guberniia* administrative centres and 71 per cent of executive committees of town soviets in *uezd* administrative centres.

'It was only at the lowest levels of the rural administration that party saturation of the government executive hierarchy remained incomplete.'[31] This saturation was greatest in units at the higher levels. In 1921, 42 per cent of the delegates to *uezd* congresses were communists compared with 75 per cent of delegates to *guberniia* conferences. Again, party membership levels were higher in the executive committees than in the congresses of soviets. In 1921, for instance, the respective averages were 72 per cent and 42 per cent at the *uezd* level and 88 per cent and 75 per cent at the *guberniia* level.[32]

The Decline of Democracy in State Institutions

Throughout 1917 and at the beginning of 1918 Lenin spoke of the dictatorship of the proletariat as implemented by the *proletariat*. Thus, to choose one statement out of many, at the Seventh Congress of the party in March 1918 he said: 'It is important for us to draw literally all working people into the government of the state. It is a task of tremendous difficulty . . . It can be implemented only by tens of millions when they have learned to do it themselves.'[33]

'As a democratic government', said Lenin, introducing the decree on land on 26 October (8 November) 1917, 'we cannot ignore the decision of the masses of the people, even though we may disagree with it.'[34]

As a result of changes in state–party relations during the civil war, Lenin now argued very differently. Thus he told the Eighth Congress of the Party in March 1919: 'the soviets, which by virtue of their programme are organs of government *by the working people*, are in fact organs of government *for the working people* by the advanced section of the proletariat but not by the working people as a whole'.[35]

Lenin mocked those who treated 'the dictatorship of one party as a bugbear', and added, 'The dictatorship of the working class is being implemented by the Bolshevik Party, the party which as far back as 1905 and even earlier merged with the entire revolutionary proletariat.'[36]

In a letter of 20 February 1922 to D.I.Kursky, the People's Commissar of Justice, he wrote, 'we conscious workers, we communists – who are the state'.[37]

At the Twelfth Party Congress in April 1923, which Lenin did not attend, Zinoviev poked fun at 'comrades who think that the dictatorship of the party is a thing to be realized in practice but not spoken about', and proceeded to develop the doctrine of the dictatorship of the party as a dictatorship of the Central Committee:

> We need a *single* strong, powerful Central Committee which is leader of everything . . . The Central Committee is the Central Committee because it is the same Central Committee for the soviets, and for the trade unions, and for the cooperatives, and

for the provincial executive committees and for the whole working class. In this consists the role of leadership, in this is expressed the dictatorship of the party.

The congress resolution declared that 'the dictatorship of the working class cannot be assured otherwise than in the form of dictatorship of its leading vanguard, i.e. the Communist Party'.[38]

In March 1921, arguing against the Workers' Opposition, Trotsky went to extremes in defending the rights of the party vis-à-vis the working class.

> The Workers' Opposition came out with dangerous slogans, in that they have made a fetish of democratic principles. They have placed the workers' rights to elect representatives for workers' organizations above the party, as though the party had no right to assert its dictatorship even in cases when that dictatorship clashes temporarily with the passing mood of the workers' democracy.
>
> It is essential that we should become aware of the revolutionary-historical birthright of the party, which is in duty bound to retain its dictatorship, regardless of the temporary vacillations of the amorphous masses, regardless of the temporary vacillations even of the working class.[39]

The almost complete fusion of party and state was clear to everyone. Thus Zinoviev told the Eighth Congress of the Party in March 1919:

> Fundamental questions of policy, international and domestic, must be decided by the Central Committee of our Party, i.e. the Communist Party, which thus carries these decisions through the soviet organs. It carries them, of course, cleverly and tactfully, not in such a way as to tread on the toes of Sovnarkom and other Soviet institutions.[40]

Kamenev told the Ninth Party Congress in 1920: 'The Communist Party is the government of Russia. The country is ruled by the 600,000 party members.'[41]

The same point was emphasized again by Trotsky in a speech to the Second Congress of the Comintern in July 1920:

> Today we have received a proposal from the Polish Government to conclude peace. Who decides such questions? We have the Council of People's Commissars but it too must be subject to certain control. Whose control? The control of the working class as a formless, chaotic mass? No. The Central Committee of the

party is convened in order to discuss the proposal and to decide whether it ought to be answered.[42]

Whether the party took over the state, or vice versa, is immaterial: the process of fusion went ahead and strengthened centralistic tendencies in both.*

Could democracy survive under a one-party monopoly? This question was posed clearly and prophetically by Rosa Luxemburg in her pamphlet *The Russian Revolution*, written during September and October 1918 in Breslau prison. She wrote that the proletarian

> dictatorship must be the work of the *class* and not of a little leading minority in the name of the class – that is, it must proceed step by step out of the active participation of the masses; it must be under their direct influence, subjected to the control of complete public activity; it must arise out of the growing political training of the mass of the people.[43]

What will be the result of limiting freedom to one party, or one trend? asks Rosa Luxemburg.

> Freedom only for the supporters of the government, only for the members of one party – however numerous they may be – is no freedom at all. Freedom is always and exclusively freedom for the one who thinks differently. Not because of any fanatical concept of 'justice' but because all that is instructive, wholesome and purifying in political freedom depends on this essential characteristic, and its effectiveness vanishes when 'freedom' becomes a special privilege.[44]

Rosa Luxemburg goes on to describe the effect on society of one-party monopoly:

> with the repression of political life in the land as a whole, life in the soviets must also become more and more crippled. Without general elections, without unrestricted freedom of press and assembly, without a free struggle of opinion, life dies out in every public institution, becomes a mere semblance of life, in which only the bureaucracy remains as the active element. Public life gradually falls asleep, a few dozen party leaders of inexhaustible energy and boundless experience direct and rule. Among them, in reality only a dozen outstanding heads do the leading and an elite of the working class is invited from time to

---

* On the party, see Chapter 13.

time to meetings where they are to applaud the speeches of the leaders, and to approve proposed resolutions unanimously – at bottom, then, a clique affair – a dictatorship, to be sure, not the dictatorship of the proletariat, however, but only the dictatorship of a handful of politicians, that is a dictatorship in the bourgeois sense, in the sense of the rule of the Jacobins.[45]

One must remember that these words were written by an enthusiastic supporter of the October revolution and the Bolsheviks:

Whatever a party could offer of courage, revolutionary far-sightedness and consistency in a historic hour, Lenin, Trotsky and the other comrades have given in good measure. All the revolutionary honour and capacity which western social democracy lacked were represented by the Bolsheviks. Their October uprising was not only the actual salvation of the Russian revolution; it was also the salvation of the honour of international socialism.[46]

She also saw clearly that it was the isolation of the Russian revolution that impelled the Bolsheviks to restrict the democratic rights of the masses. Without international revolutionary support, Rosa Luxemburg wrote, 'even the greatest energy and the greatest sacrifices of the proletariat in a single country must inevitably become tangled in a maze of contradictions and blunders'.[47]

After pointing out the contradictions and blunders in Bolshevik policy, Rosa Luxemburg unearths their causes:

Everything that happens in Russia is comprehensible and represents an inevitable chain of causes and effects, the starting point and end term of which are: the failure of the German proletariat and the occupation of Russia by German imperialism. It would be demanding something superhuman from Lenin and his comrades if we should expect of them that under such circumstances they should conjure forth the finest democracy, the most exemplary dictatorship of the proletariat and a flourishing socialist economy. By their determined revolutionary stand, their exemplary strength in action, and their unbreakable loyalty to international socialism, they have contributed whatever could possibly be contributed under such devilishly hard conditions.[48]

However, to explain the reasons for the Bolsheviks' circumscribing of workers' democracy is not to justify it. Rosa Luxemburg above all criticized the Bolshevik leaders for not admitting openly that their deviation from their original policies of workers' democracy was forced on them: 'The danger begins only when they [the Bolshevik leaders] make a virtue of necessity and want to freeze into a complete theoretical system all the tactics forced upon them by these fatal circumstances.'[49]

Undeniably Lenin, with his 'stick-bending', was inclined to do just this. Although he would deal with a particular situation very *concretely*, he always inclined to generalize too far from the immediate task in hand.

Experience showed Lenin the cul-de-sac which a government got into without workers' democracy. When during the trade union debate* he argued 'We now have a state under which it is the business of the massively organized proletariat to protect itself, while we, for our part, must use these workers' organizations to protect the workers from their state, and to get them to protect our state,'[50] the implications for the question of proletarian democracy were far-reaching. If the unions are to defend themselves against the state, they must have the right freely to discuss views different from those of their employer-state, and to select freely the leaders who are to voice these views. If the leaders of both the state and the trade unions are nominated, in practice, by one and the same central body – the Central Committee of the party, its Politbureau or its Secretariat – then the trade unions cannot defend the workers from the state. With party fractions under the same discipline as the other institutions – soviets, trade unions, etc. – the separation of function between them must be largely formal.

As we shall see, Lenin became more and more alarmed by the merging of state and party. Speaking in 1922 at the Eleventh Party Congress (the last he attended), he said: 'The relations between the party and the soviet government bodies are not what they ought to be'; 'the party machinery must be separated from the soviet government machinery'; 'we must raise the prestige of the Council of People's Commissars',[51] in other words of the state, *vis-à-vis* the party.

---

* See Volume 4, Chapter 9.

The establishment of Bolshevik Party monopoly led to a deterioration of political life in general, and a decline of the soviets in particular, which was summed up by Victor Serge:

> With the disappearance of political debates between parties representing different social interests through the various shades of their opinion, soviet institutions, beginning with the local soviets and ending with the VTsIK and the Council of People's Commissars, manned solely by communists, now function in a vacuum: since all the decisions are taken by the party, all they can do is give them the official rubber-stamp.[52]

In conclusion: to assert that the banning of all parties, except for the Bolshevik Party, must have had deleterious consequences, is one thing. To assert that the Bolsheviks could have acted differently, and could have allowed freedom of parties, is altogether different. In essence the dictatorship of the proletariat *does not* represent a combination of abstract, immutable elements like democracy and centralism, independent of time and place. The actual level of democracy, as well as of centralism, depends on three basic factors: (1) the strength of the proletariat; (2) the material and cultural legacy left to it by the old regime; and (3) the strength of capitalist resistance. The level of democracy feasible must be in direct proportion to the first two factors, and in inverse proportion to the third. The captain of an ocean liner can allow football to be played on his vessel; on a tiny raft in a stormy sea the level of tolerance is far lower.

13
Transformation of the Party

Changes in the Social Composition of the Party
In 1917 the Bolshevik Party was overwhelmingly proletarian in composition. There were hardly any intellectuals in local party

committees, or in the party as a whole.[1] During the civil war, further hundreds of thousands of workers joined the party. But the effects of the struggle radically changed it social composition.

With the primary task the need to run the administration, tens of thousands of worker party members became state officials. A substantial proportion of party members went into the Red Army during the civil war; in 1920 it reached about 300,000, i.e. every second communist.[2] Over half a million communists saw service with the Red Army during the civil war, of whom roughly half were sent into the army by civilian party organizations and half recruited by the party while on army service. Some 200,000 communists lost their lives.

Lenin could declare in April 1920:

> every time a difficult situation arose during the war, the party mobilized communists, and it was they who were the first to perish in the front ranks; they perished in thousands on the Iudenich and Kolchak fronts. The finest members of the working class perished; they sacrificed themselves.[3]

One inevitable result was a catastrophic decline in the proportion of party members working at the factory bench. Thus statistics for 1919 show that only 11 per cent of party members were then working in factories; 53 per cent were working as government officials; 8 per cent were party and trade union officials, and 27 per cent were in the army.[4]

At the Tenth Congress in March 1921, Shliapnikov deplored the fact that among the metal workers of Petrograd, who before the revolution were a mainstay of Bolshevism, no more than 2 per cent were party members. The corresponding figure for Moscow was 4 per cent.[5]

At the Eleventh Party Congress in March-April 1922, the secretary of the Moscow committee stated that, while 22 per cent of the communists in the capital were members of factory cells, 'a good half' of these were employed in administrative posts, and that in other industrial centres the proportion of workers at the bench was even lower.[6]

At the same Congress, Zinoviev complained: 'It is a fact that there are big districts, mines, etc., where there are from 10,000 to 12.000 workers, where we have a party nucleus of only six.'[7]

An analysis of party membership in rural districts of Riazan province in 1922 showed that 78 per cent held posts in the local soviets, party or cooperative network. The situation was said to be similar in other provinces.[8] A breakdown of members of peasant cells in 1922 showed that only a quarter were engaged in farming, while two-thirds were employed as officials of state, party or cooperatives.[9]

In the countryside many party members were former officials who had been civil servants under the Tsarist regime. Thus in 1922, 42 per cent of party members on the executive committees of rural soviets had been serving for longer than three years, which meant since before 1919. This seems to confirm the suggestion that they were the old civil servants, Zemstvo employees, who carried on the main business of administration as they had done in earlier years.[10]

In the Red Army the proportion of party members who were highly ranked increased. This process accelerated especially after the end of the civil war, when the army was run down. Then army party cells came to consist overwhelmingly of officers and political staff. At the end of 1921 privates and NCOs constituted 50 per cent of all army communists, but by 1924 they had fallen to 20 per cent.[11]

Preventing Careerists from Joining the Party

The sacrifices associated with party membership during the civil war discouraged careerists from joining. During the civil war, when communists fell into the hands of the Whites, which happened very often, they paid with their lives. As the written report of the Central Committee to the Eighth Party Conference put it: 'a party membership ticket under these circumstances meant something approaching a candidature for Denikin's gallows'.[12]

Hence whenever the military circumstances of the Soviet republic were grim, Lenin proposed opening the doors of the party wider than usual. In the autumn of 1919, when Denikin and Iudenich threatened the downfall of the Soviet regime, and it seemed very probable that Petrograd would be taken by the Whites, the party tried to attract new members, and organized a

'Party Week' in October: 'During Party Week in Moscow, 13,000 people were enrolled in the party.'[13]

The party expanded massively. In numerical terms, 'Party Week' was a striking success. New recruits numbered at least 160,000. This expansion continued in the following months. Membership rose from 430,000 at the beginning of 1920 to over 600,000 by the Ninth Congress in March 1920.[14]

Most of those who took on the risks of party membership when the regime was under such pressure must have been convinced supporters of communism. But Lenin was still worried about careerists managing to join the party. On 16 August 1918 he said: 'We must not accept people who try to join from careerist motives; people like this should be driven out of the party.'[15]

Lenin returned to the same theme again and again, till the end of his life. We have quoted in Chapter 11 his statement to the Petrograd Soviet in March 1919 about the 'old bureaucrats' who called themselves 'commonists' when they could not bring themselves to say the word 'communist', and 'wear a red ribbon in their buttonholes and creep into warm corners . . . the scum has crawled back,' he said.[16] At the Ninth Party Congress, March-April 1919, Lenin spoke about the danger of 'the worst elements, the officials of the old capitalist system . . . creeping into the government party . . . fastening themselves onto it . . . for it is the government party, and as such opens the way to power'.[17]

On 3 April 1919, in a speech to the Moscow soviet, Lenin returned to the same theme: 'And what is going on in the rural districts? There, people who call themselves members of the party are often scoundrels, whose lawlessness is most brazen.'[18] On 21 April 1921, he drew attention to the 'abuses committed by former government officials, landowners, bourgeois and other scum who play up to the communists and who sometimes commit abominable outrages and acts of tyranny against the peasantry'.[19] Lenin proposed making it as difficult as possible for careerists to join the party.

The Eleventh Congress (March-April 1922) established three recruitment categories: (1) workers and Red Army men of worker or peasant origin; (2) peasants and handicraftsmen other than those serving in the army; and (3) others – white collar workers, etc. Category (1) was required to spend six months as candidates, category (2) a year, and category (3) two years.[20]

Lenin was unhappy with these arrangements, doubting whether they would improve the proletarian composition of the party. In two letters addressed to the Central Committee secretary, Molotov, on the eve of the Eleventh Congress, he wrote:

> I consider it extremely important to lengthen the probation period for new members of the party. Zinoviev proposes that the probation period should be six months for workers and twelve months for other categories. I propose a period of six months only for those workers who have actually been employed in large industrial enterprises for not less than ten years. A probation period of eighteen months should be established for all other workers, two years for peasants and Red Army men, and three years for other categories.[21]

To get rid of careerists Lenin supported the proposal that the party should be purged of corrupt elements. The Eighth Party Congress (March 1919) resolved:

> Elements which are not sufficiently communist, or even directly parasitic, are flowing into the party in a broad stream. The Russian Communist Party is in power, and this inevitably attracts to it, together with the better elements, careerist elements as well. A serious purge is indispensable in Soviet and Party organizations.[22]

Following the Congress, between 10 and 15 per cent of the membership in the towns, and a higher proportion in some parts of the countryside, were expelled.[23] Lenin thought that this purge should have been far more radical. Thus, in a pamphlet he wrote in June 1919, he stated,

> it was absolutely inevitable that adventurers and other pernicious elements should hitch themselves to the ruling party. There never has been, and there never can be, a revolution without that. The whole point is that the ruling party should be able, relying on a sound and strong advanced class, to purge its ranks.

Hence the purge should be very radical. About half the members should be expelled.[24]

In 1921 a large-scale purge was carried out, resulting in the expulsion of 136,386 members, a fifth of the total membership.

34 per cent of those expelled suffered this penalty for 'passivity', 25 per cent for careerism, drunkenness, etc., 9 per cent for bribe taking, extortion, etc.[25]

However, all the obstacles Lenin and the party leadership put in the way of non-workers joining the party, and the repeated purges of corrupt elements, did not stop careerists from climbing onto the bandwagon. With the fusion of party and state, a party card became an asset in the scramble for jobs. This is illustrated by the following passage in Zinoviev's Report to the Eighth Party Congress: 'There have been cases in Moscow where a man turns up at the district committee at 8 p.m. to take out party membership, and when he is told to come back the next day he replies: "Do me a good turn, I am going for a job tomorrow, and I need a party card right away." '[26]

The erosion of the proletarian composition of the party continued, above all because former Bolshevik workers ceased to be workers.

Very Few Old-Timers

To add to the weakness of the party, the proportion of old Bolsheviks in it was extremely small. In October 1919 only 20 per cent of members had been members before the October revolution; and only 8 per cent had joined before February 1917.[27] Zinoviev told the Eleventh Congress that only 2 per cent of the members in 1922 were party members before February 1917.[28]

In a letter Lenin wrote to Molotov on 26 March 1922 he said:

If we do not close our eyes to reality we must admit that at the present time the proletarian policy of the party is not determined by the character of its membership, but by the enormous undivided prestige enjoyed by the small group which might be called the old guard of the party.

The danger inherent in the situation was very great indeed: 'A slight conflict within this group will be enough, if not to destroy this prestige, at all events to weaken the group to such a degree as to rob it of its power to determine policy.'[29]

Increasing Centralization of Power in the Party

The Central Committee, originally a small compact body

and in actuality the *decision-making body* of the party, came increasingly to ratify rather than to make decisions.

At first it was required to meet twice a month (Resolution of the Eighth Party Congress and the 1919 Party Rules).[30] In 1921 the Tenth Congress modified the requirement to once in two months.[31]

Which body or bodies in practice replaced the Central Committee? Formally the Political Bureau was subordinate to the Central Committee. Its function was to 'take decisions on questions not permitting of delay', and to report to the fortnightly meeting of the Central Committee. But the formal restriction of the competence of the Politburo to urgent questions, like the similar restriction of the power of Sovnarkom *vis-à-vis* the All-Russian Soviet or VTsIK, was in fact unreal. The Central Committee met less and less frequently and the Politbureau became the principal source of policy decisions which were executed by the state machinery.

Immediately after the October revolution, the Central Committee met very frequently. We have the minutes of 17 such meetings for a period of a little over three months;[32] (the minutes of a number of other meetings of this body held in the same period have not survived). Subsequently, during the civil war, meetings became less frequent. There were only six between April and July 1918, and between July and November 1918 the Central Committee did not meet at all. (This was complained of at the Eighth Congress in March 1919.) Later the meetings became more regular: April-October 1919, 6 times; April 1920 to March 1921, 29 times.[33] But they were still far less frequent than those of the Political Bureau (or the Organizing Bureau).

The Central Committee met only six times between March and December 1919, while the Politburo and Orgburo had 29 and 110 meetings respectively. During this period there were also 10 joint Politburo–Orgburo meetings. From December 1919 to September 1920 the Central Committee met only nine times, while the Politburo and Orgburo met 77 and 64 times respectively. Between September 1920 and March 1921 the Central Committee held 24 meetings, almost one a week, while the Orgburo and Politburo had 47 and 26 sessions respectively. Between May and

August 1921 the Central Committee held nine meetings and the Orgburo and Politburo 48 and 39 respectively. Between September and December 1921 the Central Committee met only 5 times, while the Orgburo and Politburo met 63 and 44 times respectively.[34]

In practice the Politburo and the Orgburo increasingly usurped the power of the Central Committee. In his report to the Ninth Party Congress, Lenin said:

> The Political Bureau adopted decisions on all questions of foreign and domestic policy . . . During the year under review the current daily work of the Central Committee has been conducted by the two collegiums elected by the plenary meeting of the Central Committee – the Organizing Bureau of the Central Committee and the Political Bureau of the Central Committee . . . In practice it has become the main and proper function of the Organizing Bureau to distribute the forces of the party, and that of the Political Bureau to deal with political questions. It goes without saying that this distinction is to a certain extent artificial; it is obvious that no policy can be carried out in practice without finding expression in appointments and transfers.[35]

Another party institution whose power continued to increase was the secretariat. To achieve coordination between the Politburo and the Orgburo, the secretary to the party was a member of both.

To start with, in March 1919, the secretariat consisted of one responsible secretary and five technical secretaries. A year later it was decided to strengthen it by bringing into it three members of the Central Committee, and 'to transfer to the jurisdiction of the secretariat as thus composed current questions of an organizational and executive nature, while preserving for the Orgburo . . . the general direction of the organizational work of the Central Committee.'[36]

The secretariat was originally defined as a purely 'executive organ of the party'. As Lenin put it to the Eighth Congress:

> It must be emphasized from the very outset, so as to remove all misunderstanding, that only the corporate decisions of the Central Committee adopted in the Organizing Bureau or the Political Bureau, or by a plenary meeting of the Central Committee – only these decisions were carried out by the Secretary of the Central Committee of the party.[37]

In practice the secretariat usurped far more power, especially after Stalin was appointed as General Secretary in May 1922. From 1922 onwards Stalin was the only person who was a member of all four party bodies: the Central Committee, the Politburo, the Orgburo and the secretariat.

The secretariat greatly expanded its staff; from 15 in March 1919 it grew in November 1919 to 80 officials in eight departments (general administration, finance, information, organization, distribution, inspection, peasantry, women's work).[38] In March 1920 its staff rose to 150 and a year later it totalled 602 (besides a military detachment of 140 men to act as guards and messengers).[39]

One of the most important powers controlled by the secretariat was the appointment of personnel. Since 1920 one of the three party secretaries had been in charge of what was called the 'accounts and distribution section' (Uchraspred), which kept account of party manpower and supervised its distribution. In its report to the Tenth Congress (March 1922), it showed that in a period of less than twelve months it had been responsible for transfers and appointments of 42,000 party members.[40] Uchraspred had become a powerful organ of control over state and party institutions.

Zinoviev explained at the Twelfth Party Congress (1923) that the presidents of the executive committees of provincial soviets were appointed by the Central Committee of the party and that this was necessarily so.[41] In fact it was the secretariat that had this power of nomination.

Appointment of Secretaries

There were also widespread appointments in internal party bodies. During the civil war, when local party committees, including those representing quite large territorial units, expressed opposition to the Central Committee in Moscow, they were quite often summarily sacked. In the spring of 1919, for instance, the Central Committee dissolved the elected Central Committee of Ukraine and appointed a new one. Between March 1922 and March 1923 the secretariat appointed 42 secretaries of provincial committees.[42]

Again and again party congresses and conferences emphasized the need to avoid appointments instead of elections to leading party bodies. Thus the Ninth Party Conference of September 1920 resolved:

> While it is admitted in principle that it is necessary in exceptional cases to appoint people to elective positions, the Central Committee is none the less advised, as a general rule, to use recommendations instead of appointments.

It added, as an afterthought, throwing a sharp light on the existing situation:

> Attention is drawn to the fact that it is impermissible that party bodies and individual comrades, in mobilizing comrades, be guided by considerations other than those deriving from the job at hand. Repressions of any sort whatsoever against comrades for the fact that they hold divergent views on certain questions resolved by the party, are impermissible.[43]

Even delegates to party congresses were quite often not elected, but nominated. About 50 delegates from the Samara *guberniia* to the Eleventh Party Congress (27 March-2 April 1922) were selected by the plenum of the *guberniia* committee instead of being elected by the *guberniia* conference. In this case, as the mandate commission report of the Eleventh Congress put it, 'the Central Committee allowed it as a result of those objective conditions in which the Samara *guberniia* found itself' – a rather oblique reference to the fact that Samara was a stronghold of the Workers' Opposition and, had elections been held, the delegations would have been composed of the (by now outlawed) oppositionists. While this practice was permitted at the congress only in this one instance, it was also used elsewhere at the time.[44]

The result, of necessity, was a corrosion of inner-party democracy.

Appointments in the Trade Unions

With the fusion of state and party, and with the increasing substitution of appointments for elections in the party, it is not surprising that there were more and more cases of appointments in other organizations. Such was the case in the trade unions.

Let us look at what happened at the Fourth Trade Union

Congress. On 17 May 1921, just a few hours before the opening of the congress, the party fraction in the congress met. Tomsky, Chairman of the All-Russian Central Council of Trade Unions, introduced the Politburo report, 'On the Role and Tasks of the Trade Unions'. Fraction members, noticing that the section on the election of trade union officers did not contain the term 'normal methods of proletarian democracy', decided to amend the resolution. Under Riazanov's leadership, and against the formal objection of Tomsky, they voted by more than 1,500 to 30 to include in the Politburo's statement a section providing for democratic procedures.[45] The Politburo immediately removed Tomsky from the Central Council for exhibiting weakness. He was not even elected to the Presidium of the congress. (He was subsequently sent away, ostensibly on a 'mission' to Turkestan.)

In the same month of May 1921, the Central Committee of the party also intervened heavily in the affairs of the important metalworkers' trade union. The Central Committee submitted to the communist fraction of the union a list of candidates to be elected to key positions in the union. The list contained new and 'loyal' substitutes for those who had supported the Workers' Opposition. By an overwhelming vote of 120 to 40 the fraction rejected the Central Committee list. Incensed by this infringement of discipline, the Central Committee ignored the vote and appointed people of its own choice. It then proceeded to reorganize the union.[46]

'The Old Crap Revives...'

The party was not immune from the rot of corruption. It is true that during War Communism severe egalitarianism prevailed, as we saw in Chapter 7, but these rules were often evaded. Equality does not accord well with general poverty. As the young Marx put it two years before the *Communist Manifesto*: 'this development of the productive forces . . . is absolutely necessary as a practical premise [of communism], because without it only *want* is made general, and with want the struggle for necessities, and that means that all the old crap must revive'.[47]

Behind the façade of extreme equality, despite the very strong moral pressure of Bolshevism, the 'old crap' did rise again in the midst of War Communism. And this corruption ate into the party. One only needs to read the description of a communist bureaucrat during the civil war in Boris Pilnyak's story 'Riazan Apples':

> near the telephone in his room stood an armchair, and when he talked to his subordinates, he sprawled in the armchair, legs spread wide; when he talked to his equals he sat like an ordinary human being; when he talked to those in authority he jumped to attention and jingled his spurs: these were three distinct voices.[48]

Another example is provided by the Soviet author Iury Libedinsky, in his book *A Week* (1922). This is an account of a single week in a small town in the foothills of the Urals, in the spring of 1921. In it he describes a Soviet official, Matusenko, secretary of the political department, a man who would be a communist under one regime and a devout Orthodox churchman under another, but will get a soft job under either, caring only for his personal welfare.

> Today was Sunday, and the typists and shorthand writers, a merry noisy lot of people, would come to the Politdep only at eleven. But Matusenko always held himself aloof from them, or rather, simply did not notice them, did not consider their existence, just as he did not consider the existence of objects and animals that did not concern him, or that of all the people whom he considered below him in rank, like the Red Army soldiers and the school teachers who came to the Politdep.
> But to make up for that, Matusenko thought a great deal about those who stood above him in the service, beginning with Golovlev, the Chief of the Politdep, and ending with Lenin and Trotsky.[49]

While millions were starving Matusenko had 'yellow, creamy butter', 'white bread' and 'perfumed sweetened tea with cream'.[50]

Another passage in Libedinsky's book describes the starving crowd in the railway station and the elegant, cake-eating commissar:

> At one railway station there was a sort of big staircase, and from top to bottom it was covered with people. Men, women, children lying on the steps, together with their pitiable dirty belongings, and on all their faces thin spider's webs of wrinkles

of care and misery, under a veil of many days' dirt. And close by in the buffet there was a speculator eating cakes while a hungry, homeless little boy watched his mouth greedily, and when he was given something for charity, went down on the floor to count the dirty scraps of paper money to see if he had enough money for cigarettes. And down that terrible staircase, stepping squeamishly . . . squeamishly is the word . . . came some smart commissar or other with a communist star glittering on his breast, and he put down his lacquered boots so carefully among those weary, dirty bodies, and came down and ate cakes with the speculator. And in that crowd there were louse-ridden, starving children.[51]

In another Soviet novel, *Cement*, by Fedor Gladkov, one can read how Badin, chairman of a soviet Executive Committee, sitting on the party purge committee, expelled from the party a woman he himself had raped, using his superior physical strength (and his high office).

During the civil war, when the masses were performing acts of heroism, and the traditions of Bolshevism were still very strong, the privileged and corrupt had to keep their affluence more or less concealed. But the rot had started to attack the foundations of the party, the state and society in general.

The Fight to Defend Party Democratic Traditions Continues ...

The undermining of inner party democracy did not take place without vigorous protests from party members. K.K.Iurenev, for example, spoke at the Ninth Congress of the methods used by the Central Committee to suppress criticism, including the virtual exile of the critics: 'One goes to Christiana, another sent to the Urals, a third – to Siberia.'[52] He said that in its attitude toward the party, the Central Committee had become 'not accountable ministry, but unaccountable government'. At the same congress, V.N.Maksimovsky counterposed 'democratic centralism' to the 'bureaucratic centralism' for which the centre was responsible. 'It is said', he commented, 'that fish begin to putrefy from the head. The party begins to suffer at the top from the influence of bureau-cratic centralism.'[53] Iakovlev stated: 'Ukraine has become a place of exile. Comrades unwanted for one reason or another in Moscow are exiled there.'[54] And Sapronov declared: 'However much you talk about electoral rights, about the dictatorship of the proletariat, the striving of the Central Committee for party dictatorship in fact leads to the dictatorship of the party bureaucracy.[55]

Nevertheless, throughout the civil war the atmosphere of free discussion in party conferences and congresses was maintained. During the debate on the Brest-Litovsk Peace Treaty, the party enjoyed, in the words of E.H.Carr, 'a freedom and publicity of discussion rarely practised by any party on vital issues of public policy'.[56] Bukharin's pamphlet defending 'Left Communism' against Lenin's position was published in May 1918 in one million copies.[57]

In the trade union debate* the democratic traditions of Bolshevism remained clear. As a historian not sympathetic to Bolshevism, Robert V. Daniel, put it: 'The fall of 1920 was the high point of open discussion in the Communist Party, and of free oposition to the leaders' authority.'[58]

Victor Serge wrote of the situation in the party during the civil war:

> The party's old democratic customs now give way to a more authoritarian centralization. This is necessitated by the demands of the struggle and by the influx of new members who have neither a Marxist training nor the personal quality of the pre-1917 militants: the 'old guard' of Bolshevism is justly determined to preserve its own political hegemony.

But the party still retains its democratic traditions.

> The party is truly the 'cohort of steel' . . . All the same, its thinking is still very lively and free. It welcomes the anarchists and Left SRs of yesterday . . .
> Nobody is afraid to contradict Lenin or to criticize him. His authority was so little imposed, the democratic manners of the revolution were still so natural, that it was a matter of course for any revolutionary, no matter how recent a recruit, to express himself frankly in the presence of the man who headed the party and the state. Lenin was more than once criticized unsparingly, in factories or conferences, by totally unknown

* See Volume 4, Chapter 9.

people. He listened to his contestants coolly and replied to them in a commonsense manner.[59]

Lenin, the Party and the Proletariat

In Chapter 8 of Volume 2, which has the same title as this section, I wrote about Lenin in 1917:

> Throughout all the zigzags in tactics, Lenin's leitmotif was constant: to raise the level of consciousness and organization of the working class, to explain to the masses their own interests, to give clear political expression to the feelings and thought of the people . . . The proletariat made the party and made Lenin. And Lenin helped to shape the party and the proletariat.
>
> By drawing ever broader masses of workers, soldiers and peasants into the struggle under the banner of the revolution, by increasing the scope of the party's influence, by raising the level of self-activity and consciousness of the masses, by constant self-education of the proletariat, the party and the leadership, Bolshevism led the people to victory in October.[60]

The party was the vanguard of the proletariat, and Lenin was in the vanguard of the party. The party advanced slogans which the masses made their own, and elaborated strategy and tactics that helped the masses to organize themselves, to act for themselves.

Now, at the end of a terrible civil war, the situation was radically different. The proletariat had disintegrated; the party did not feel itself to be the leader of an active class, but mainly an administrator of affairs. Lenin could not 'go to the sailors' in order to sort out the 'committeemen', as he had done again and again in 1917, and before that in 1905. The masses in floodtide, as in 1917, bore up the party and the leadership; in the ebb, the masses, with different moods and objectives, had the opposite effect. The contrast between the dream of 1917, with Lenin's 'absolute confidence in the magnificent potential of the proletariat', and the actuality of the atomized working class and largely non-proletarian party, provided the elements of the human tragedy, demonstrating the impotence of the individual (and individuals) in the face of fate, of social forces far larger than themselves.

The magnificent success of the Bolshevik Party before the revolution, during the revolution and in the heroic years of the civil war did not mean that its organization on Leninist lines was in itself any guarantee for the consolidation of achievements. It was not an organizational key to all the doors of history. The revolutionary party is indispensable, but is not sufficient for revolutionary advance. Lenin's genius was that he was able, again and again, to appeal to the masses, so as to make the party respond to their aspirations and at the same time use the party to raise the level of activity and consciousness of the proletariat. In the final analysis the party remained always subordinated to and dependent on the working class. The party can affect the class only to the extent that its words, its propaganda, produce the desired activity by the class; without working class action the party is impotent.

14
Lenin and the Military Front

In Stalin's time and after his death, official Russian historians eliminated Trotsky from their account of the conduct of the Red Army during the civil war. All the successes of this army were attributed to Lenin (and Stalin). Such hagiography is an insult to Lenin. In this chapter Lenin's secondary role to Trotsky in leading the Red Army will be made clear.

Lenin and the Employment
of Tsarist Officers in the Red Army

Trotsky met with great opposition to his employment of ex-Tsarist officers. Most of the 'left communists' who rejected the Peace of Brest-Litovsk and opposed Lenin's economic policy repudiated Trotsky's policy in the name of 'Old Bolshevism'. They refused to accept a centralized standing army, let alone one commanded by Tsarist officers. Led by Smirnov, Bukharin, Radek and Bubnov, the 'left communists' came out strongly and bitterly against Trotsky. Another opposition element was made up of those who did not oppose centralized authority, but only the ex-Tsarist officers, of whom they were suspicious and jealous. They were leaders of guerrilla groups made up of workers, soldiers and sailors, who in the early days after October managed to establish the Soviet regime in various localities where they met very little armed resistance. This was the so-called 'Tsaritsyn opposition' which had its roots in a plebeian hatred of specialists. The leaders of this opposition were Voroshilov, Commander of the Tenth Army, Ordzhonikidze, Political Commissar of the same army, Gusev and, behind the scenes, Stalin. (The Tsaritsyn group became the nucleus of the Stalinist faction of later times.)

The combination of the two groups opposing Trotsky's policy was all the more formidable because Lenin for a long time reserved judgement on the employment of Tsarist officers.

Trotsky had to appeal to Lenin repeatedly to support him. In August 1918 Lenin asked Trotsky's opinion about a proposal introduced by Larin to replace all officers of the general staff with communists. Trotsky replied sharply in the negative:

> Many of them [ex-Tsarist officers] commit acts of treachery. But on the railways, too, instances of sabotage are in evidence in the routing of troop trains. Yet nobody suggests replacing railway engineers by communists. I consider Larin's proposal as being utterly worthless . . . Those who clamour the loudest against making use of officers are either people infected with panic or those who are remote from the entire work of the military apparatus or such party military figures as are themselves worse than any saboteur – such as are incapable of keeping an eye on anything, behave like satraps, spend their time doing nothing and, when they meet with failure, shuffle off the blame on to the General Staff Officers.[1]

On 24 November 1918 Lenin could still say in a speech to Red Army officers: 'in building our new army now, we must draw our officers solely from among the people. Only Red officers will have any respect among the soldiers and be able to strengthen socialism in our army. Such an army will be invincible.'[2]

Not until the eve of the Eighth Party Congress, in March 1919, did he have a clear idea of the extent to which military specialists were being used. At the beginning of March 1919, Trotsky narrates,

Lenin wrote me a note: 'What if we fire all the specialists and appoint Lashevich as commander-in-chief?' Lashevich was an old Bolshevik who had earned his promotion to the rank of a sergeant in the 'German' war. I replied on the same note: 'Child's play!' Lenin looked slyly at me from under his heavy brows, with a very expressive grimace that seemed to say: 'You are very harsh with me.' But, deep down, he really liked abrupt answers that left no room for doubt. We came together after the meeting. Lenin asked me various things about the front.

'You ask me,' I said, 'if it would not be better to kick out all the old officers? But do you know how many of them we have in the army now?'

'No.'

'Not even approximately?'

'I don't know.'

'Not less than thirty thousand.'

'What?'

'Not less than thirty thousand. For every traitor, there are a hundred who are dependable; for every one who deserts, there are two or three who get killed. How are we to replace them all?'[3]

A few days later, Lenin was making a speech on the problems of constructing the socialist commonwealth. This is what he said:

> When Comrade Trotsky informed me recently that the number of officers of the old army employed by our War Department runs into several tens of thousands, I perceived concretely where the secret of using our enemy lay, how to compel those who had opposed communism to build it, how to build communism with the bricks which the capitalists had chosen to hurl against us![4]

The above conversation clearly shows how far Lenin was from influencing the organizational structure of the Red Army, and how he took second place to Trotsky in the field of military affairs.

What about the military strategy of the Red Army?

Disagreement on War Strategy

There were four occasions on which the Central Committee of the party was split by disagreements on strategy. In other words there were as many disagreements as there were military fronts. In one of the cases Lenin was right against Trotsky: in all the others Trotsky was proved right and Lenin wrong.

The first acute disagreement, in the summer of 1919, was about the situation on the eastern front. Trotsky supported the position of Vatzetis, the commander-in-chief of the Red Army, who argued that once Kolchak was pushed to the east of the Urals the Red Army should not pursue him further, but should stay in the mountains for the winter. This would have enabled the Red Army to withdraw a few divisions from the east and switch them to the south where Denikin was becoming very dangerous. This plan, however, met with vigorous opposition from S.S.Kamenev, the commander of the eastern front and colonel of the general staff in the Tsar's army, as well as from two members of the Military Council, both old Bolsheviks – Smilga and Lashevich. They were supported by Lenin. They insisted that Kolchak was so near to being defeated that only a few men were needed to follow him, and that the most important thing was that he be prevented from taking a breathing-spell, because in that case he would recover during the winter and the eastern campaign would have to start all over again in the spring. The entire question hinged, therefore, on a true estimate of the condition of Kolchak's army and rear.

Trotsky goes on to admit that he was wrong: 'it proved to be the command of the eastern front that was right in appraising Kolchak's army . . . The eastern armies released some troops for the southern front and continued, at the same time, their advance on the heels of Kolchak into the heart of Siberia.'[5]

The second disagreement in the Central Committee was over the southern front. In this case Trotsky proved right, against Lenin and the majority of the Central Committee, who supported the plan of S.S.Kamenev, newly appointed commander-in-chief. In the south, the enemy forces were composed of two separate and antagonistic groups: the Cossacks, particularly in the province of Kuban, and the volunteer White Army. Trotsky believed that it was necessary to use the antagonism between the two uneasy partners. Kamenev, however, thought only in logistic terms, without taking into account the socio-political implications, and suggested that as Kuban province was the chief base for the volunteers, it was necessary to deliver the decisive blow at this base from the Volga. The result of Kamenev's strategy was a terrible defeat for the Red Army. Trotsky writes:

Whereas Denikin had failed to persuade the Cossacks to a long marching campaign against the north, he . . . was helped by our striking at the Cossack nests from the south. After this, the Cossacks could no longer defend themselves on their own land; we had ourselves bound up their fate with that of the volunteer army.

In spite of the careful preparation for our operations and the concentration of forces and technical means, we had no success. The Cossacks formed a formidable bulwark in Denikin's rear. They seemed to be rooted to their land, and held on with their claws and teeth. Our offensive put the whole Cossack population on their feet. We were expending our time and energy and managing only to drive all those capable of bearing arms directly into the White Army. In the meantime, Denikin swept the Ukraine, filled his ranks, advanced toward the north.[6]

On 25 June 1919 the volunteer army occupied Kharkov, the chief city of the Ukraine. By the end of the month the Don Cossack army had cleared the Don country of Soviet forces and the Kuban Cossacks had captured Ekaterinoslav on the lower Dnieper. On 30 June Denikin, with the help of British planes and tanks, captured Tsaritsyn. On 31 July Poltava was captured. Kherson and Nikolaev on the Black Sea coast were taken on 18 August, and five days later Odessa fell. On 31 August the volunteer army marched into Kiev. Throughout September Denikin's army continued to advance. On 20 September he occupied Kursk; on 6 October Voronezh; on 13 October Orel, less than 250 miles from Moscow. Carr described those weeks as 'the crucial point at which the continued existence of the regime hung by a thread'.

Now Trotsky's plan, which he had fought for from the beginning, was accepted by the leadership. He

demanded that with our first blow we cut the volunteers off from the Cossacks, and, leaving the Cossacks to themselves, concentrate all our strength against the volunteers. The main direction of the blow, according to this plan, would be not from the Volga toward Kuban, but from Voronezh toward Kharkov and the Donetsk region. In this section of the country which divides the northern Caucasus from the Ukraine, the peasants and workers were wholly on the side of the Red Army. Advancing in this direction, the Red Army would have been moving like a knife through butter. The Cossacks would have remained in their places to guard their borders from strangers, but we would not have touched them . . . In the end, it was this plan that was eventually adopted, but not before Denikin had begun to threaten Tula, whose loss would have been more dangerous than that of Moscow. We wasted several months, suffered many needless losses and lived through some very menacing weeks.'[7]

Trotsky's plan for the campaign against Denikin was, as events proved, brilliant in every respect. He took into account two socio-political factors: first, the pro-Bolshevik stance of the Don proletariat; and secondly, the antagonism between the Kuban Cossacks and the White volunteers of Denikin. In both cases his calculation was based on indisputable facts.

On 14 September the Politbureau changed the orders for the southern front, accepting Trotsky's original plan completely. Denikin's army now started to be pushed back. On 20 October the Red Army captured Orel, and four days later Budenny defeated Denikin's cavalry forces. On 15 November Denikin was defeated at Kastornaia, near Voronezh; on 17 November at Kursk; during December the retreat of his armies continued unabated. On 3 January 1920 Denikin lost Tsaritsyn, on 8 January Rostov. After a closely fought battle round Rostov it fell into Denikin's hands again on 20 January, but was recaptured three days later. The White armies continued to retreat. On 15 March Denikin lost Ekaterinodar; on 4 April he gave up the command of the Whites and left for Britain.

The third dispute Trotsky had with Lenin related to Petrograd. In October 1919, while Denikin was threatening Moscow, Iudenich, backed by the British navy in the Bay of Finland, was advancing rapidly from Estonia towards Petrograd. On 12 October his troops captured Iamburg, 10 miles from Petrograd. By 16 October they had reached Gatchina, more than 60 miles on, and shortly afterwards they were in Tsarskoe Selo, a suburban resort near Petrograd. The White generals were so confident that their operational commander is said to have declined an offer to look at Petrograd through field glasses, saying that next day he would be walking down the Nevsky Prospekt, the central thoroughfare of the city.

On 15 October the Politbureau met. Facing the threat to both capitals, Lenin proposed to abandon Petrograd, and to gather all available strength around Moscow. (He even envisaged the possibility of giving up Moscow and withdrawing to the Urals.) Trotsky disagreed, and after some discussion the Central Committee sided with him. On 16 October Trotsky rushed in his armoured train to Petrograd. He believed that they might have to defend the city street by street.

> Having broken through this gigantic city, the White Guards would get lost in this labyrinth of stone, where every house will present them with an enigma, a threat or a deadly danger. From where should they expect a blow? From a window? From a loft? From a cellar? From behind a corner? From everywhere! ... We can surround some streets with barbed wire, leave others open and transform them into traps. All that is needed is that a few thousand people should be firmly resolved not to surrender ... Two or three days of such fighting would transform the invaders into a frightened and terrified bunch of cowards, surrendering in groups or individually to unarmed passers-by and women.[8]

All Trostky's driving energy, all his gifts of organization and oratory were put to effect. 'The city which has suffered so much, which has burnt with so strong an inward flame ... this beautiful Red Petrograd remains what it has been, the torch of the revolution,' he proclaimed to the Petrograd Soviet. On horseback, he personally stopped retreating soldiers and led them back into line. With determination and daring the Red Soldiers routed Iudenich's army.

As it happened, the turning point on the Petrograd front occurred on the same day as that on the southern front: on 20 October the Red Army recaptured Orel.

The fourth disagreement Trotsky had with Lenin over military strategy was about the march on Warsaw. On 25 April 1920 Poland started a military offensive against Soviet Russia. The Ukraine was invaded. The Polish troops advanced rapidly, and on 6 May they entered Kiev, capital of Ukraine, and occupied the whole of the western part of the country. On 26 May the Soviet counter-offensive started. On 5 June Budenny's Red cavalry broke through. On 12 June the Poles evacuated Kiev, and afterwards they were quickly pushed back to the Soviet borders.

Up to this point, so long as the war was defensive, there

were no differences between Lenin and Trotsky regarding its conduct. Now the question was posed: should the Red Army go on to invade and occupy Poland? Lenin said 'Yes', Trotsky 'No'. Other members of the Bolshevik leadership on the whole sided with Lenin. Stalin, who showed no enthusiasm for the war so long as it was not going too well,[9] now, as a result of success, became quite enthusiastic.

The Polish communist leaders were split. Dzerzhinsky, Markhlevsky, and above all Radek, argued against Soviet advance into Poland. Unschlicht, Lensky and Bobinsky took the opposite standpoint. Lenin did not hesitate. Indeed, so long as the Polish war was progressing favourably, his confidence increased. On 17 July he forced the decision to march on to Warsaw on the Politbureau without much difficulty. He overruled Trotsky's advice, proferred on behalf of the Supreme Command, to halt the offensive. He carried the five other members with him.

Lenin's policy turned out to be wrong and very costly. Radek was proved absolutely right when he said that the Red Army would not be welcomed by the workers and peasants of Poland. On 15 August the Soviet troops were beaten at the gates of Warsaw, and were rapidly pushed back 400 kms. or more, out of Polish territory.

There were other factors which played a part in the Soviet defeat. For instance, there was an astonishing absence of co-ordination between the Soviet western and southwestern commands: despite an order to the southwestern command on 13 August to join the western front, it played no significant part in the battle whatever. Trotsky's explanation for the behaviour of the southwestern command was simple and convincing: the private ambitions and petty jealousies of Stalin, political commissar of the southwestern army. Stalin could not bear either to watch Tukhachevsky's triumph in Warsaw or to be overshadowed by the success of Tukhachevsky's political officer, Smilga. He wanted at all costs to enter Lvov at the same time as Tukhachevsky and Smilga were to enter Warsaw.

> Stalin was waging his own war. When the danger to Tukha-
> chevsky's army became clearly evident and the commander-in-
> chief ordered the southwestern front to shift its direction sharply

toward Zamostye-Tomashev, in order to strike at the flanks of the Polish troops and Warsaw, the command of the south-western front, encouraged by Stalin, continued to move to the west: Was it not more important to take possession of Lvov itself than to help 'others' to take Warsaw? For three or four days our general staff could not secure the execution of this order. Only after repeated demands reinforced by threats did the southwestern command change direction, but by then the delay of several days had already played its fatal role. On the 16th of August the Poles took the counter-offensive and forced our troops to roll back. If Stalin and Voroshilov and the illiterate Budenny had not 'had their own war' in Galicia and the Red Cavalry had been at Lublin in time, the Red Army would not have suffered the disaster.[10]

(This is not really the place to discuss whether the march on Warsaw was in any case condemned to failure for logistic reasons, because of the poor communications backing the Red Army, the lack of support services, etc.) The whole concept of the march on Warsaw was a political mistake. After the failure of the march on Warsaw Lenin said: 'Our offensive, our too swift advance almost as far as Warsaw, was undoubtedly a mistake.'[11] The Poles were bound to see in this invasion an attack by their hereditary enemies. And Lenin was not one to hide his mistakes. He told Klara Zetkin:

> in the Red Army the Poles saw enemies, not brothers and liberators. The Poles thought, and acted, not in a social, revolutionary way but as nationalists, as imperialists. The revolution in Poland which we counted on did not take place. The workers and peasants, deceived by Pilsudski and Daszynski, defended their class enemy and let our brave Red soldiers starve, ambushed them, and beat them to death ... Radek predicted how it would turn out. He warned us. I was very angry and accused him of 'defeatism' ... But he was right in his main contention.[12]

Despite all the tactical differences between Lenin and Trotsky regarding the management of the Red Army, their relations were extremely close. To see this, one has only to read the massive correspondence between the two in those years, which were largely confined to matters relating to the civil war; the innumerable short notes and long telegrams.[13]

Their differences in these civil war episodes – the struggles against Kolchak, Denikin, Iudenich and Pilsudski – were of great practical importance, but they did not involve differences of principle. They were arguments about expediency – the best way of fighting the enemy at a given moment at a given place. No doubt if it had been Trotsky and not Lenin who argued for the evacuation of Petrograd, or for the failed march on Warsaw, the Stalinists would have managed to construct legends about Trotsky's capitulations and adventurism, rather than Lenin's. On the whole Trotsky's strategic judgement in military affairs proved far more reliable than Lenin's. Lenin was too absorbed in the conduct of political and economic affairs to visit the front or take part in the everyday work of the military department. His grasp of military affairs was therefore not so sure. As in the technical organization of the October insurrection, Trotsky had a far better understanding than Lenin of what was needed.[14]

At the same time, Trotsky's success at the head of the Red Army no doubt depended very much on the support of Lenin, as Chairman of the Council of People's Commissars and of the Council of Labour and Defence.

The closeness of Lenin and Trotsky during the civil war was reflected in the hyphenating of their names. The government was usually referred to as the government of Lenin–Trotsky, and so was the party, first in Russia and then throughout the world. One symbol of the confidence Lenin had in Trotsky was the blanket endorsement he gave to any order he might issue. Thus at the bottom of a blank sheet of paper Lenin wrote:

> Comrades! Knowing the strict character of the instructions issued by Comrade Trotsky, I am so convinced, supremely convinced that the instruction issued by Comrade Trotsky is correct, to the point, and essential for the good of the cause, that I wholly support this instruction. V.Ulianov (Lenin).[15]

In military affairs Lenin was always convinced that Trotsky's role was crucial. Gorky reported some remarks made by Lenin about Trotsky in private conversation. 'Show me any other man,' he said, 'capable of organizing an almost model army in one year and moreover of winning the sympathy of professional soldiers. We have that man. We have everything. You will see miracles.'[16]

Trotsky was the father of the Soviet victory. He was the founder of the Soviet army and the artisan of its victories. He undertook to create a massive and powerful army out of practically nothing. He galvanized the huge numbers of workers and peasants in the Red Army, strengthened their will for victory, stiffened their morale and led them to victory.

The symbol of the new army was Trotsky's armoured train. It was a flying apparatus of administration, including a secretariat, a printing press, a telegraph station, a radio station, an electric power station, a library, a garage, a bath. It seems to have covered a distance, during the three years of civil war, some 5½ times the length of the equator.[17]

It was a centre of inspiration, propaganda, organization and revolutionary example which transformed a vacillating, unstable mass into a real fighting army. Trotsky's gifts were a rare combination of organization and improvisation, coupled with a genius for making the soldiers know and love what they were fighting and dying for.

The international nature of the Russian revolution

At the end of the civil war Lenin knew that Bolshevism had stood the acid test and that it had triumphed.

But at what a price! How far different was the social-political regime of 1920 from the ideals the Bolsheviks had put forward in 1917! The *end* of the revolution was the establishment of a socialist society without class obstructions, a society administered by its members as a whole, a society with no bureaucracy. In such a society the well-being of all citizens would from the *beginning* foster the independence, initiative and creative powers of the human personality. Russia of the civil war was a very different kind of society. While the revolution managed to defeat the counter-revolutionary forces by relying on popular support, enthusiasm and sheer will power, it paid for victory with the destruction of the proletariat that had made the revolution, while leaving intact the state apparatus built by it. The socialist state of 1917 had become the single-party state. The soviets that remained had become a front for bureaucratically controlled Bolshevik power. The party itself had changed radically from a working class party to one highly centralist party of officials controlled by the Politburo, the Ogburo and the Secretariat.

Nobody was more aware than Lenin of the contradiction between the ideals of 1917 and the reality of 1920. But he knew that bolshevism had to proceed from the *facts*, however unpleasant they were. The only escape from the impasse was, Lenin believed, in the victory of the international revolution.

Lenin made it clear again and again that the fate of the Russian revolution would be determined by the development of the world revolution. As he told the Third Congress of Soviets on 11 (24) January 1918: 'The final victory of socialism in a single country is of course impossible. Our contingent of workers and peasants which is upholding soviet power is one of the contingents of the great world army' (18) '. . . no matter what difficulties we experienced, no matter what defects were in store for us, the world socialist revolution would come' (19) '. . . it is the absolute truth that without a German revolution we are doomed' (20)

And in fact the Russian revolution did send shock waves through the world. A Communist International made up of mass parties rose swiftly. The fate of Russian bolshevism and world communism became highly intertwined. The success, and failure, of world communism and their interaction with Russian developments will be the subject of our next volume.

Notes

Chapter 1: The Bolshevik Government's First Steps

1. L.Trotsky, *My Life*, New York 1960, p.37
2. R.P.Browder and A.F.Kerensky, *The Russian Provisional Government 1917 – Documents*, Stanford 1961, Vol.3, p.1801
3. P.N.Miliukov, *Istoriia vtoroi russkoi revoliutsii*, Sofia 1923, Part 3, p.296
4. V.B.Stankevich, *Vospominaniia, 1914-1919 g.*, Berlin 1920, p.267
5. A.Kopp, *Town and Revolution*, London 1967, pp.1-2
6. I.V.Gessen, 'In Two Revolutions: Life Experience', *Arkhiv russkoi revoliutsii*, Vol.22, Berlin 1937, p.382
7. J.Bunyan and H.H.Fisher, *The Bolshevik Revolution, 1917-1918: Documents and Materials*, Stanford 1934, p.148
8. J.Reed, *Ten Days that Shook the World*, London 1961, p.97
9. N.N.Sukhanov, *The Russian Revolution 1917, A Personal Record*, London 1955, p.648
10. I.Getzler, *Martov*, Cambridge (Mass.) 1967, p.172
11. Reed, *op.cit.*, p. 28
12. Sukhanov, *op.cit*, p. 636
13. *ibid.* pp.639-40
14. V.I.Lenin, *Collected Works*, translated from the fourth Russian edition (henceforth referred to as *Works*), Vol.29, p.209
15. L.Trotsky, *On Lenin*, London 1971, p.122
16. Lenin, *Works*, Vol.44, p.206
17. Trotsky, *On Lenin*, *op.cit.* p.127
18. S.S.Pestovsky, 'On October Days in Peter', *Proletarskaia revoliutsiia*, No.10, 1922; Bunyan and Fisher, *op.cit.* pp.186-7
19. Reed, *op.cit.* p.102
20. *Vospominaniia o Vladimire Ilyiche Lenine*, Moscow 1963, Vol.3, pp.160-6
21. Bunyan and Fisher, *op.cit.* p.186
22. Lenin, *Works*, Vol.26, pp.249-50
23. *ibid.* pp.258-60
24. *ibid.* Vol.30, p.265
25. Y.Akhapkin, *First Decrees of Soviet Power*, London 1970, p.32
26. *ibid.* pp.36-8
27. *ibid.* pp.42-3
28. *ibid.* pp.63-5, 69-71
29. *ibid.* pp.88-9
30. W.H.Chamberlin, *The Russian Revolution*, New York 1965, Vol.1, p.355
31. Lenin, *Works*, Vol.44, pp.71-2
32. J.L.H.Keep, 'Lenin's Letters as an Historical Source', in B.W.Eissenstat (ed.), *Lenin and Leninism*, Lexington (Mass.) 1971, p.258
33. G.S.Ignatiev, *Oktiabr 1917 goda v Moskve*, Moscow 1964, p.4

34. J.Keep, 'October in the Provinces', in R.Pipes (ed.) Revolutionary Russia, Cambridge (Mass.) 1967, p.194
35. ibid. pp.195-6
36. ibid. p.197
37. R.W.Pethybridge, The Spread of the Russian Revolution: Essays on 1917, London 1971, p. 77
38. Reed, op.cit. pp.161-2
39. ibid. p.164
40. Pethybridge, op.cit. p. 17
41. ibid. p.22
42. ibid. p.23
43. Lenin, Works, Vol.26, p.294
44. V.Serge, Year One of the Russian Revolution, London 1972, p.79
45. Trotsky, On Lenin, op.cit. pp.151, 118
46. Lenin, Works, Vol.27, p.519
47. M.Latsis, Chrezvychainaia komissiia po borbe s kontr-revoliutsiei, Moscow 1920
48. Serge, op.cit. p.307
49. E.H.Carr, The Bolshevik Revolution, 1917-1923, Vol.1, London 1950, p.168
50. Serge, op.cit. p.189
51. Lenin, Works, Vol. 30, p. 223
52. Vospominaniia o Vladimire Ilyiche Lenine, op.cit. Vol.2, pp.435-8
53. Lenin, Works, Vol.26, pp.409, 415
54. ibid. p.261
55. ibid. p.288
56. ibid. p.365
57. ibid. p.459
58. ibid. p.404
59. Reed, op.cit. p.179
60. ibid. p.150

Chapter 2: The Consolidation of Power

1. The Bolsheviks and the October Revolution: Minutes of the Central Committee of the Russian Social Democratic Labour Party (bolsheviks) August 1917-February 1918 (hereafter referred to as CC Minutes), London 1974, p.127
2. ibid. pp.129-34
3. L.Trotsky, The Stalin School of Falsification, New York 1962, pp.109-22
4. CC Minutes, op.cit. pp.136-8, 300
5. ibid. pp.139-41
6. ibid. p.150
7. O.H.Radkey, The Sickle under the Hammer, New York 1963, pp.66-7
8. Bunyan and Fisher, op.cit. p.190

Chapter 3: The Dissolution of the Constituent Assembly

1. Lenin, Works, Vol.24, p.99
2. ibid. Vol.26, p.20
3. Browder and Kerensky, op.cit. Vol.3, p.1695
4. ibid. p.1729
5. Trotsky, On Lenin, op.cit. pp.105-6
6. O. H. Radkey, The Elections to the Russian Constituent Assembly of 1917, Cambridge (Mass.) 1950, pp.16-17
7. ibid. p.20
8. ibid. p.36
9. ibid. p.37

10. Radkey, *The Sickle under the Hammer*, op.cit. p.344
11. Radkey, *The Elections to the Russian Constituent Assembly of 1917*, op.cit. p.38
12. Lenin, *Works*, Vol.26, p.380
13. Radkey, *The Sickle under the Hammer*, op.cit. p.301
14. See T.Cliff, *Lenin*, London 1975, Vol.1, p.116
15. Lenin, *Works*, Vol.26, pp.379-83
16. *ibid*. Vol.30, pp.257-8
17. *ibid*. p.263
18. *ibid*.
19. *ibid*. pp.266-7
20. K.Marx and F. Engels, *Selected Correspondence*, London 1942, pp.433-4
21. K.Marx, 'Address to the Communist League, 1850', Appendix to F.Engels, *Revolution and Counter Revolution in Germany*, London 1933

Chapter 4: The Peace of Brest-Litovsk

1. Lenin, *Works*, Vol.21, p.404
2. *ibid*. Vol.26, pp.444, 447-8
3. *CC Minutes*, op.cit. p.173
4. Lenin, *Works*, Vol.26, p.451
5. *CC Minutes*, op.cit. pp.177-8
6. *ibid*. p.174
7. *ibid*. p.179
8. *ibid*. pp.189-91
9. *ibid*. p.194
10. V.I.Lenin, *Sochineniia*, 1st edition, Moscow 1924-5, Vol.15, p.626
11. J.W.Wheeler-Bennett, *Brest Litovsk: The Forgotten Peace*, London 1938, p.237
12. *CC Minutes*, op.cit p.205
13. *ibid*. pp.210-11
14. *ibid*. pp.212-15
15. Lenin, *Works*, Vol.27, p.37
16. *ibid*. p.39
17. *CC Minutes*, op.cit, p.216
18. Lenin, *Works*, Vol.27, pp.19-20
19. *ibid*. pp.23-4
20. *ibid*. p.29
21. *ibid*. p.65
22. *CC Minutes*, op.cit. pp.218-25
23. Lenin, *Works*, Vol.27, pp.68-9
24. Bunyan and Fisher, op.cit. p.523
25. *ibid*. pp.523-4
26. *Leninskii sbornik*, Vol.11, pp.59-61
27. *ibid*. p.89
28. *ibid*. p.42
29. Trotsky, *My Life*, op.cit. pp.380-1
30. Wheeler-Bennett, op.cit. p.170
31. *ibid*. p.196
32. *Piatii sozyv vserossiiskogo tsentralnogo ispolnitelnogo komiteta sovetov rabochikh, krestianskikh, krasnoarmeiskikh, kazachikh deputatov: stenograficheskii otchet*, Moscow 1919, p.248
33. Lenin, *Works*, Vol.33, p.95
34. *ibid*. p.98
35. Trotsky, *On Lenin*, op.cit. p.103-4

Chapter 5: The Transition from Capitalism to Socialism

1. Lenin, *Works*, Vol. 27, pp.230-1
2. K.Marx and F. Engels, *Selected Works*, London 1942, Vol.2, p.504
3. S.E.Cohen, *Bukharin and the*

Bolshevik Revolution, a
Political Biography 1888-
1938, London 1974, p.90
4. K.Marx, F.Engels and
F.Lassalle, Aus dem liter-
arischen Nachlass von K.
Marx, Fr. Engels und F.
Lassalle, Stuttgart 1902, Vol.3,
pp.435-9; in D.Ryazanoff (ed.),
K.Marx and F.Engels, The
Communist Manifesto, New
York 1963, pp.184-5
5. K.Marx, The Cologne Communist Trial, London 1971,
p.62
6. Lenin, Works, Vol.25, p. 329

7. ibid. pp.330-1
8. ibid. p.337
9. ibid. pp.341-2
10. ibid. Vol.27, p.148
11. ibid. Vol.28, p.214
12. ibid. pp.424-5
13. ibid. Vol.29, p.69
14. ibid. p.74
15. ibid. p.206
16. ibid. p.208
17. ibid. Vol.10, pp.253-4
18. ibid. Vol.30, pp.330-1
19. ibid. Vol.28, pp.72-3
20. ibid. Vol.30, p.202
21. ibid. p.518

Chapter 6: 'We Need State Capitalism'

1. M.Philips Price, My Reminiscences of the Russian
Revolution, London 1921,
p.212
2. Chamberlin, op.cit. Vol.1,
p.416
3. Serge, op.cit. p.212
4. ibid. p.236
5. Chamberlin, op.cit. Vol.1,
p.418
6. Bunyan and Fisher, op.cit.
pp. 649-50
7. See T.Cliff, State Capitalism
in Russia, London 1974
8. Lenin, Works, Vol.27, p.301
9. Carr, op.cit. Vol.2, pp.88-9;
Bunyan and Fisher, op.cit.
pp.621-2
10. Lenin, Works, Vol.27,
pp.245-6
11. ibid. p.248
12. ibid. pp.248-50
13. ibid. pp.249, 350
14. ibid. pp.268-9

15. ibid. p.212
16. ibid. p.349
17. ibid. p.271
18. ibid. p.212
19. ibid. Vol.26, p.500
20. ibid. Vol.27, p.231
21. ibid. p.515
22. ibid. pp.258-9
23. ibid. Vol.20, pp.152-4
24. ibid. Vol.27, pp.335-6
25. ibid. p.294
26. ibid. p.337
27. ibid. pp.338-9
28. ibid. pp.295-6
29. ibid. p.340
30. ibid. p.301
31. ibid. pp.213-4
32. ibid. p.396
33. ibid. p.475
34. ibid. p.218
35. Marx and Engels, Selected
Correspondence, op.cit p.493
36. Cliff, State Capitalism in
Russia, op.cit pp.124-41

Chapter 7: War Communism (1918-1921)

1. V.Brügmann, Die russischen
Gewerkschaften in Revo-
lution und Bürgerkrieg 1917-
1919, Frankfurt a/M 1972,
p.140
2. M.Dobb, Soviet Economic

Development Since 1917, London 1948, pp.84-5

3. Serge, op.cit p.137
4. Dobb, op.cit. p.90
5. V.P.Miliutin, Istoriia ekonomicheskogo razvitiia SSSR, Moscow–Leningrad 1929, p.115
6. Brügmann, op.cit. p. 247
7. L.N.Kritzman, Die heroische Periode der grossen russischen Revolution, Frankfurt a/M 1971, pp.101-2, 208
8. ibid. pp.97-8
9. ibid. p.80
10. ibid. p.293
11. K.Leites, Recent Economic Development in Russia, Oxford 1922, pp.152, 199
12. J.Bunyan, The Origin of Forced Labor in the Soviet State: 1917-1921, Baltimore 1967, pp.173-4
13. Brügmann, op.cit. p.151
14. Kritzman, op.cit. p.252
15. ibid. p.254
16. ibid. p.283
17. ibid. p.265
18. ibid. p.273
19. ibid. p.276
20. ibid. p.216
21. Chamberlin, op.cit. Vol.2, pp.100-1
22. Dobb, op.cit. p.100
23. Chamberlin, op.cit. Vol.2, p.105
24. Kritzman, op.cit. p.287
25. Lenin, Works, Vol.30, p.228
26. F.Lorimer, The Population of the Soviet Union, History and Prospects, Geneva 1948, p.41
27. Kritzman, op.cit. p.288
28. Lenin and Gorky: Letters, Reminiscences, Articles, Moscow 1973, p.163
29. V.Serge, Conquered City, London 1976, pp.89-90
30. V.Serge, Memoirs of a Revolutionary, 1901-1941, London 1963. p.79
31. ibid. p.101
32. Lenin, Works, Vol.35, p.333
33. A.Ransome, Six Weeks in Russia in 1919, London 1919, pp.68-9
34. Lenin, Works, Vol.32, p.22
35. Dobb, op.cit. p.114
36. Lenin, Works, Vol.29, pp.137-8
37. ibid. Vol.30, pp.108-9
38. ibid. pp.284-5
39. N.I.Bukharin, Economics of the Transformation Period, New York 1971, p.146
40. C.Clark, The Conditions of Economic Progress, London 1940, pp.79, 83, 91, 98
41. Lenin, Works, Vol.33, pp.62-3
42. ibid. p.58
43. ibid. p.57
44. ibid. pp.84-6
45. L.Trotsky, The First Five Years of the Communist International, London 1953, Vol.2, p.266
46. Lenin, Works, Vol.32, pp.233-4
47. ibid. p.343

Chapter 8: The Heroic and the Tragic Intertwine

1. Lenin, Works, Vol.30, p.437
2. ibid. p.454
3. ibid. p.288
4. ibid. p.297
5. ibid. Vol.32, p.154
6. L. Trotsky, Problems of Everyday Life, New York 1973, p.163

7. Reed, *op.cit.* p.12
8. Serge, *Year One of the Russian Revolution, op.cit.* p.362
9. Chamberlin, *op.cit.* Vol.2, p.340
10. J. Maynard, *The Russian Peasant: and Other Studies*, London 1942, pp.102, 139
11. L.Trotsky, *The Revolution Betrayed*, New York 1937, p.181
12. K.Marx and F.Engels, *Collected Works*, London 1976, Vol.3, p.263
13. Trotsky, *Problems of Everyday Life, op.cit.* p.53
14. Trotsky, quoted in I.Deutscher, *The Prophet Armed*, London 1954, p.407
15. Lenin, *Works*, Vol.29, p.74
16. *ibid.* pp.154-5
17. *ibid.* Vol.30, p.518
18. *ibid.* Vol.33, p.24
19. *ibid.* Vol.32, p.361
20. *ibid.* p.327
21. Bunyan, *The Origin of Forced Labor in the Soviet State, op.cit.* p.98
22. K.Marx, *The German Ideology*, London 1940, p.69
23. Trotsky, *Problems of Everyday Life, op.cit.* p.54
24. Trotsky, *The First Five Years of the Communist International, op.cit.* Vol.2, p.120
25. Lenin, *Works*, Vol.28, p.72
26. *ibid.* Vol.27, p.341
27. *ibid.* p.498
28. *ibid.* Vol.33, p.306
29. *ibid.* p.605
30. *ibid.* p.279
31. *ibid.* Vol.32, p.224
32. Shakespeare, *Macbeth*

Chapter 9: The Proletariat under War Communism

1. Ia.S.Rosenfeld, *Promyshlennaia politika SSSR*, Moscow 1926, p.37
2. Brügmann, *op.cit.* pp.215-6
3. *Vtoroi vserossiiskii sezd professionalnykh soiuzov*, Moscow 1921, p.138
4. Lenin, *Works*, Vol.29, p.158
5. *ibid.* Vol.33, p.26
6. *ibid.* p.256
7. Kritzman, *op.cit.* p.217
8. *Trudy II vserossiiskogo sezda sovetov narodnogo khoziaistva*, Moscow 1919, p.251
9. Kritzman, *op.cit.* p.218
10. *Trudy I vserossiiskogo sezda sovetov narodnogo khoziaistva*, Moscow 1918, p.434
11. *Chetvertii vserossiiskii sezd professionalnykh soiuzov*, Moscow 1921, p.119
12. M.H.Dobb and H.C.Stevens, *Russian Economic Development Since the Revolution*, London 1928, p.189
13. Lenin, *Works*, Vol.29, p.555
14. *ibid.* Vol.33, p.65
15. *ibid.* Vol.32, p.199
16. *ibid.* p.411
17. *ibid.* Vol.33, pp.23-4
18. R.Arskii, 'Trade Unions and Factory Committees', *Vestnik narodnogo kommissariata truda*, February-March 1918. Quoted in F.I.Kaplan, *Bolshevik Ideology and the Ethics of Soviet Labour*, London 1969, pp.129-30
19. A.Pankratova, *Fabzavkomy i profsoiuzy v revoliutsii 1917 goda*, Moscow–Leningrad 1927, p.238
20. *Izvestiia*, 27 April 1918.

Quoted in Bunyan and Fisher, *op.cit.* p.619

21. Bunyan, *Origin of Forced Labor in the Soviet State*, *op.cit.* pp.20-1
22. *ibid.* p.26
23. P.N.Amosov *et al.*, *Oktiabrskaia revoliutsiia i fabzavkomy*, Moscow 1927, Vol.2, p.188
24. *Pervii vserossiiskii seze professionalnykh soiuzov*, Moscow 1918, p.235
25. *ibid.* p.243
26. *ibid.* pp.369-70
27. *ibid.* p.374
28. Akhapkin, *op.cit.* p.50
29. J.Bunyan, *Intervention, Civil War and Communism in Russia, April-December 1918*, Baltimore 1936, pp.405-6
30. *Trudy I vesrossiiskogo sezda sovetov narodnogo khoziaistva*, *op.cit.* p.10
31. *Chetvertii vesrossiiskaia konferentsiia professionalnykh soiuzov*, Moscow 1923, p.28
32. Kritzman, *op.cit.* p.135

33. N.Bukharin and P.Preobrazhensky, *The ABC of Communism*, London 1969, p.448
34. *Sobranie uzakonenii i rasporiazhenii rabochego i krestianskogo pravitelstva*, 1919, No.14, Art.163 (hereafter sited as SUR)
35. *SUR*, 1919, No.18, Art.204
36. Bunyan, *Origin of Forced Labor in the Soviet State*, *op.cit.* pp.163-4
37. M.Dewar, *Labour Policy in the USSR: 1917-1928*, London 1956, pp.48-9
38. Lenin, *Works*, Vol.30, p.312
39. *ibid.* pp.333-4
40. Kaplan, *op.cit.* p.359
41. Lenin, *Works*, Vol.29, pp.423-4, 426-7
42. Dewar, *op.cit.* p.61
43. Lenin, *Works*, Vol.30, p.499
44. *ibid.* Vol.32, p.412
45. *Odinnadtsatii sezd RKP(b)*, Moscow 1936, p.109
46. Lenin, *Works*, Vol.31, pp.364-5

Chapter 10: War Communism and the Peasantry

1. Cliff, *Lenin*, *op.cit.* Vol.1, pp.211ff., 224-5
2. Lenin, *Works*, Vol.10, p.191
3. *ibid.* Vol.32, p.251
4. *ibid.* Vol.30, p.506
5. *ibid.* Vol.29, p.359
6. *ibid.* Vol.27, p.232
7. *ibid.* Vol.24, p.23
8. *Kommunisticheskaia partiia sovetskogo soiuza v rezoliutsiiakh i resheniiakh sezdov, konferentsii i plenumov TsK*, 7th edition, Moscow 1953 (hereafter cited as *KPSS v Rezoliutsiiakh*), Vol.1, pp.341-2
9. *O Zemle*, Moscow 1921, p.9

10. Lenin, *Works*, Vol.28, pp.175-7
11. *ibid.* p.342
12. *SUR*, 1919, No.4
13. J.L.H.Keep, *The Russian Revolution: A Study in Mass Mobilization*, London 1976, p.414
14. A.M.Bolshakov and N.A.Rozhkov, *Istoriia khoziaistva rossii v materialakh i dokumentakh*, Leningrad 1926, Vol.3, p.248
15. P.Lezhnev-Finkovskii, *Sovkhozy i kolkhozy*, Moscow–Leningrad 1928, p.61
16. Lenin, *Works*, Vol.27, p.337

17. Keep, *The Russian Revolution*, op.cit. p.462
18. *Izvestiia TsK RKP(b)*, No.8, 2 December 1919. Quoted in R.H.Rigby, *Communist Party Membership in the USSR, 1917-1967*, Princeton 1968, p.106
19. O.A.Narkiewicz, *The Making of the Soviet State Apparatus*, Manchester 1970, p.60
20. Ia.A.Iakovlev (ed.), *K voprosu o sotsialisticheskom pereustroistve selskogo khoziaistva*, Moscow 1928, pp. 3, 7
21. Kritzman, *op.cit.* p.73
22. Lenin, *Works*, Vol.32, p.277
23. *ibid.* p.341
24. *ibid.* Vol.26, p.503
25. *ibid.* pp.503-4
26. *SUR* 1917-1918, No.35; Bunyan, *Intervention, Civil War and Communism in Russia*, op.cit. pp.460-2
27. *ibid.* p.464
28. Lenin, *Works*, Vol.27, p.397
29. *ibid.* pp.437-9
30. *SUR*, 1917-1918, No.43; Bunyan, *Intervention, Civil War and Communism in Russia*, op.cit. pp.472-3
31. Lenin, *Works*, Vol.29, p.157
32. Kritzman, *op.cit.* pp.135-9
33. A. S. Pukhov, *Kronstadtskii Miatezh 1921 g*, Leningrad 1931, p.8
34. C.Betelheim, *Class Struggles in the USSR: First Period: 1917-1923*, New York 1976, p.233
35. B. Pilnyak, *Mother Earth and other Stories*, London 1972, p.20
36. Lenin, *Works*, Vol. 29, p.299
37. Maynard, *op.cit.* p.104
38. Marx and Engels, *Collected Works*, op.cit. Vol.7, p.520
39. *The Trotsky Papers*, edited by J.M.Meijer, The Hague 1971, Vol.2, pp.485-565
40. *Kolkhozy vo vtoroi stalinskoi piatiletke*, Moscow 1939, p.1
41. *ibid.*
42. Lenin, *Works*, Vol.30, p.112
43. *ibid.* Vol.29, pp.359, 369

Chapter 11: The Withering Away of the State?

1. Lenin, *Works*, Vol.25, p.402
2. *ibid.* pp.412, 463
3. *ibid.* pp.487-8
4. *ibid.* p.472
5. *ibid.* p. 489
6. *ibid.* p.429
7. *ibid.* p.448
8. Akhapkin, *op.cit.* p.157
9. *Sezdy sovetov RSFSR v postanovleniakh i rezoliutsiiakh*, Moscow 1939, p.218
10. J.Towster, *Political Power in the USSR: 1917-1947*, New York 1948, p.209
11. *ibid.* pp.157-9
12. Lenin, *Works*, Vol.30, p.237
13. *Sedmoi vserossiiskii sezd sovetov rabochikh, krestianskikh, krasnoarmeiskikh, i kazachikh deputatov*, Moscow 1920, pp.261-2
14. Towster, *op.cit.* p.246
15. G.V.Vernadsky, *A History of Russia*, New York 1944, p.319
16. *SUR*, 1917-1918, No.12, Art.79
17. *SUR*, 1919, No.53, Art.508
18. O.Anweiler, *The Soviets: The Russian Workers, Peasants and Soldiers' Councils, 1905-1921*, New York 1974, p.235
19. J.V.Stalin, *Works*, Moscow 1952-5, Vol.4, p.220

20. Latsis, *op.cit.*
21. W.Pietsch, *Revolution und Statt: Institutionen als Träger der Macht in der Sowjetrussland (1917-1922)*, Cologne 1969, p.94
22. *ibid.* p.95
23. *ibid.* p.96
24. *ibid.* pp.114-5
25. Lenin, *Works*, Vol.33, p.176
26. *SUR*, 1922, No.4, Art. 42
27. Lenin, *Works*, Vol.25, p.389
28. *ibid.* Vol.26, p.272
29. *ibid.* Vol.24, pp.100-1
30. Bunyan and Fisher, *op.cit.* pp.298-9
31. Rigby, *op.cit.* pp.417-18 *Growth of the Red Army*, Princeton 1944, p.102
32. *The Trotsky Papers*, *op.cit.* Vol.1, pp.799-800
33. Fedotoff-White, *op.cit.* p.105
34. *ibid.* p.99
35. *ibid.* p.91
36. *The Trotsky Papers*, *op.cit.* Vol.1, p.29
37. *ibid.* p.208
38. *ibid.* p.118
39. L.Trotsky, *Kak vooruzhalas revoliutsiia*, Moscow 1923, Vol.1, p.235
40. Fedotoff-White, *op.cit.* p.90
41. Pietsch, *op.cit.* p.137
42. Lenin, *Works*, Vol.31, p.178
43. Kritzman, *op.cit.* p.233
44. Lenin, *Works*, Vol. 29, pp.32-3
45. *ibid.* p.183
46. *ibid.* Vol.33, p.77
47. *ibid.* Vol.36, p.557
48. *ibid.* p.566
49. *ibid.* Vol. 33, pp.428-9
50. Bukharin and Preobrazhensky, *op.cit.* p.240

Chapter 12: The Establishment of the Bolsheviks' Political Monopoly

1. Lenin, *Works*, Vol.23, pp.325-6
2. *ibid.* Vol.25, p.450
3. *ibid.* p.440
4. *ibid.* p.404
5. *ibid.* pp.487-8
6. Sukhanov, *op.cit.* pp.528-9
7. Carr, *op.cit.* Vol.1, p.183
8. Bunyan and Fisher, *op.cit.* p.359
9. *ibid.* p.361
10. *ibid.* p.220
11. Radkey, *The Sickle under the Hammer*, *op.cit* p.291
12. *ibid.* p.491
13. Serge, *Year One of the Russian Revolution*, *op.cit.* p.230
14. *SUR*, 1917-1918, No.44, Art.536
15. Lenin, *Works*, Vol.28, pp.190-1
16. M.Gorky, *Untimely Thoughts: Essays on Revolution, Culture and the Bolsheviks, 1917-18*, New York 1968, pp.85-6
17. *ibid.* p.88
18. Stalin, *op.cit.* Vol.4, p.138
19. Carr, *op.cit.* Vol.1, p.171
20. Lenin, *Works*, Vol.28, pp.212-3
21. *ibid.* Vol.29, p.151
22. Getzler, *op.cit.* p.200
23. L.Schapiro, *The Origin of the Communist Autocracy*, New York 1965, pp.123, 125-6
24. P.Avrich, *The Russian Anarchists*, Princeton 1971, pp.195-6
25. Bukharin and Preobrazhensky, *op.cit.* p.436
26. Serge, *Year One of the Russian Revolution*, *op.cit.* p.336

27. *KPSS v rezoliutsiakh*, Vol.1, pp.446-7
28. *ibid.* pp.600-1
29. *ibid.* p.627
30. *ibid.* p.469
31. Rigby, *op.cit.* pp.417-18
32. *ibid.* pp. 470-1
33. Lenin, *Works*, Vol.33, p.135
34. *ibid.* Vol.26, p.260
35. *ibid.* Vol.29, p.183
36. *ibid.* p.559
37. *ibid.* Vol.36, p.561
38. *Dvenadtsatii sezd RKP(b)*, Moscow 1923, pp.41, 207
39. Bunyan, *The Origin of Forced Labor in the Soviet State*, op. cit. p.251
40. *Vosmoi sezd RKP(b)*, Moscow 1933, p.250
41. *Deviagii sezd RKP(b)*, Moscow 1934, p.307
42. Trotsky, *The First Five Years of the Communist International*, op.cit. Vol.1, pp.99-100
43. M. A. Waters (ed.) *Rosa Luxemburg Speaks*, New York 1970, p.394
44. *ibid.* pp.389-90
45. *ibid.* p.391
46. *ibid.* p.375
47. *ibid.* p.369
48. *ibid.* p. 394
49. *ibid.*
50. Lenin, *Works*, Vol.32, p.25
51. *ibid.* Vol.33, pp.306-7, 314
52. Serge, *Year One of the Russian Revolution*, op.cit. p.264

Chapter 13: The Transformation of the Party

1. See Cliff, *Lenin*, op.cit. Vol.2, pp.160-1
2. Rigby, *op.cit.* pp.241-2
3. Lenin, *Works*, Vol.30, p.498
4. *Izvestiia TsK RKP(b)*, 24 March 1920
5. *Desiatii sezd RKP(b)*, Moscow 1933, pp.29-30, 76
6. *Odinnadtsatii sezd RKP(b)*, op.cit. p.443
7. *ibid.* p.422
8. Rigby, *op.cit.* p.109
9. *Izvestiia IsK RKP(b)*, January 1923
10. Narkiewicz, *op.cit.* p.61
11. Rigby, *op.cit.* p.245
12. *Izvestiia TsK RKP(b)*, 2 December 1919
13. Lenin, *Works*, Vol.30, p.71
14. Rigby, *op.cit.* p.78
15. Lenin, *Works*, Vol.28, p.61
16. *ibid.* Vol.29, pp.32-3
17. *ibid.* Vol.30, p.485
18. *ibid.* Vol.29, p.265
19. *ibid.* Vol.32, p.355
20. *KPSS v rezoliutsiiakh*, op.cit. Vol.1, pp.623-4
21. Lenin, *Works*, Vol.33, p.254
22. *KPSS v rezoliutsiiakh*, op.cit. Vol.1, pp.446-7
23. Rigby, *op.cit*, p.77
24. Lenin, *Works*, Vol. 24, pp.432-3.
25. *Izvestiia TsK RKP(b)*, March 1922
26. Pietsch, *op.cit.* p.133
27. *Izvestiia TsK RKP(b)*, 24 March 1920
28. *Odinnatsatii sezd RKP(b)*, op.cit. p.420
29. Lenin, *Works*, Vol.28, p.257
30. *KPSS v rezoliutsiiakh*, op.cit. Vol.1, pp.442, 463
31. *ibid.* p.525
32. *CC Minutes*, op.cit. pp.126-251
33. Pietsch, *op.cit.* p.153
34. R.H.McNeal (ed.), *Resolu-*

tions and Decisions of the
Communist Party of the
Soviet Union, Toronto 1974,
Vol.2, p.13

35. Lenin, Works, Vol.30,
pp.443-4

36. KPSS v rezoliutsiiakh, op.cit.
Vol.1, p.500

37. Lenin, Works, Vol.30, p.444

38. Vosmaia konferentsiia
RKP(b), Moscow 1961, p.221

39. Desiatii sezd RKP(b), op.cit.
p.56

40. Izvestiia TsK RKP(b), 5
March 1921

41. Dvenadtsatii sezd RKP(b)
op.cit. p.207

42. Izvestiia Tsk RKP(b), March
1923

43. KPSS v rezoliutsiiakh, op. cit.
Vol.1, p.509

44. McNeal, op.cit. Vol.2,
pp.11-12

45. Odinnadtsatii sezd RKP(b),
op.cit. pp.277-8

46. J.B.Sorenson, The Life and
Death of Soviet Trade
Unionism, 1917-1928, New
York 1969, pp.167-9

47. K.Marx and F.Engels,
Sochineniia, Moscow 1955,
Vol.3, p.33

48. Pilnyak, op.cit. p.145

49. I.Libedinsky, A Week,
London 1923, p.42

50. ibid. p.47

51. ibid. p.99

52. Desiatii sezd RKP(b), op.cit.
p.52

53. ibid. p.54

54. ibid. pp.62-3

55. ibid. pp.56-7

56. Carr, op.cit. Vol.1, p.188

57. A.G.Löwy, Die Weltges-
chichte ist das Weltgericht,
Vienna 1968, p.111

58. R.V.Daniels, The Conscience
of the Revolution: Com-
munist Opposition in Soviet
Russia, Cambridge (Mass.)
1965, p.129

59. Lenin, Works, Vol.31, p.336;
Serge, Year One of the
Russian Revolution, op.cit.
pp.366-7

60. Cliff, Lenin, op.cit. Vol.2,
p.169

Chapter 14: Lenin and the Military Front

1. The Trotsky Papers, op.cit.
Vol.1, pp.107-9

2. Lenin, Works, Vol.28, p.195

3. Trotsky, My Life, op.cit.
p.447

4. Lenin, Works, Vol.29, p.71

5. Trotsky, My Life, op.cit p.452

6. ibid. p.454

7. ibid. pp.454-5

8. Trotsky, Kak vooruzhalas
revoliutsiia, op.cit. Vol. 2,
Book 1, pp.388ff.

9. Stalin, op.cit. Vol.4, pp.345-6

10. L.Trotsky, Stalin, London
1947, pp.329, 332

11. Lenin, Works, Vol.32, p.173

12. C.Zetkin, Reminiscences of
Lenin, London 1929, p.20

13. The Trotsky Papers, op.cit.
Vols.1 and 2

14. See Cliff, Lenin, op.cit. Vol.2
pp.369-75

15. The Trotsky Papers, op.cit.
Vol. 1, p.589

16. B.Souvarine, Stalin, London
1939, pp.222-3

17. Trotsky, My Life, op.cit.
p.414

18. Lenin, Works, Vol.26,
pp.470-1

19. ibid. Vol.27, p.95

20. ibid. p.98

Chronology

Events occurring before 1 February 1918 are dated according to the Julian as well as the (western) Gregorian calendars; events occurring later are dated according to the Gregorian calendar only.

1917

25 October / 7 November: Overthrow of the Provisional Government in Petrograd; Kerensky flees. Second Congress of Soviets, with Bolshevik majority, opens in Petrograd.

26 October / 8 November: Organization of new Government of People's Commissars, consisting exclusively of Bolsheviks; promulgation of decrees nationalizing the land and proposing immediate peace negotiations to all belligerent powers.

27 October / 9 November: Kerensky starts to move on Petrograd with General Krasnov, who commands a force of a few hundred Cossacks. Beginning of fighting between the forces of the Provisional Government and of the Soviet in Moscow.

29 October / 11 November: Unsuccessful uprising of Junkers in Petrograd.

30 October / 12 November: Fighting with Kerensky's troops on the outskirts of Petrograd.

1 November / 14 November: Flight of Kerensky and capture of Krasnov.

2 November / 15 November: Victory of the Bolsheviks in Moscow. General Alekseev, former Commander-in-chief of the Russian Army arrives in the Don Cossack capital, Novo-Cherkassk, and sets about forming the Volunteer Army, which later becomes the most formidable of the anti-Bolshevik military forces.

4 November / 17 November: Withdrawal of some prominent Communists from the Council of People's Commissars and from the Central Committee of the Communist Party as a protest against Lenin's uncompromising attitude toward inclusion of representatives of other Socialist parties in the Government.

7 November / 20 November: Ukrainian Rada, which has seized power in Ukraine, publishes Third Universal, asserting its right to exercise state power until the convocation of the Constituent

Assembly. Soviet Government orders Commander-in-chief Dukhonin to begin peace negotiations.

9 November / 22 November: Dukhonin dismissed for refusing to obey orders of Soviet Government; Bolshevik Ensign Krilenko appointed Commander-in-chief.

13 November / 26 November: Decree establishing workers' control over all industrial enterprises.

18 November / 1 December: Agreement between Bolsheviks and Left Socialist Revolutionaries, as result of which representatives of latter Party enter the Government.

19 November / 2 December: Kornilov, Denikin and other Generals, imprisoned in Bikov, near Moghilev, for participation in the Kornilov revolt, escape and make for the Don Territory, where they become leaders of Alekseev's Volunteer Army.

22 November / 5 December: Preliminary armistice agreement signed.

2 December / 15 December: Conclusion of armistice with Central Powers.

4 December / 17 December: Soviet Government addresses ultimatum to Ukrainian Rada, demanding that it cease disarming revolutionary troops and permitting Cossack units to pass through Ukraine to the Don.

7 December / 20 December: Organization of the Cheka – the All-Russian Commission for Combating Counterrevolution, Sabotage and Speculation.

9 December / 22 December: Beginning of peace negotiations in Brest-Litovsk.

13 December / 26 December: Organization of Ukrainian Soviet Government, challenging the authority of the Rada, in Kharkov.

14 December / 27 December: Decree nationalizing the banks.

23-31 December / 5-13 January 1918: Third Congress of Soviets.

1918

5 January / 18 January: The Constituent Assembly opens; reveals an anti-Bolshevik majority.

6 January / 19 January: Constituent Assembly dispersed by commander of the sailors and soldiers appointed to guard it.

7-14 January / 20-27 January: First Congress of Trade Unions.

8-9 January / 21-22 January: Extraordinary sessions of the Central Committee concerning the Brest-Litovsk parleys; both Lenin's proposal (sign annexationist peace) and Trotsky's (no peace, no war) outvoted in favour of Bukharin's proposal (wage a revolutionary war against the Germans).

10-18 January / 23-31 January: Third Congress of Soviets.

12 January / 25 January: Ukrainian Rada issues Third Universal, declaring Ukraine independent.

16-23 January / 29 January-3 February: Bolshevik rebellion in Kiev, finally suppressed by Ukrainian troops.

28 January / 8 February: Kiev occupied by Red Army.

29 January / 9 February: Representatives of the Rada sign separate peace with the Central Powers.

30 January / 10 February: Trotsky, as head of the Soviet peace delegation, issues statement refusing to sign peace, but declaring the war ended and the Russian army demobilized.

18 February: Germans, beginning broad advance, occupy Dvinsk. Extraordinary session of the Central Committee; at morning session Lenin outvoted by Trotsky and Bukharin supporters; at evening session Lenin's motion for immediate peace adopted after Trotsky swings his support to Lenin.

19 February: Soviet Government agrees to sign peace.

20 February: Decree for formation of Red Army.

22 February: At session of Central Committee, Trotsky proposes asking Allies for aid against Germans and tenders his resignation as Commissar of Foreign Affairs; Lenin, absent, sends note approving 'receipt of support and arms from Anglo-French imperialist brigands;' Trotsky's recommendation adopted by a 6 to 5 vote. Soviet Government receives new German peace conditions.

23 February: The Council of People's Commissars and the Bolshevik Party Central Committee agree to sign the peace.

25 February: Rostov and Novo-Cherkassk, the centres of the anti-Bolshevik movement in the Don Territory, occupied by Red Troops; the small Volunteer Army retreats southward and moves into the Kuban Territory.

2 March: German army occupies Kiev, restores Government of the Ukrainian Rada.

3 March. Signature of Peace of Brest-Litovsk.

6-8 March: Seventh Party Congress.

8 March: the Bolsheviks adopt the name 'Communists'.

12 March: Government moves from Petrograd to Moscow.

13 March: Trotsky appointed War Commissar.

14 March: Red troops occupy Kuban capital, Ekaterinodar, after flight of the local Cossack Government.

14-16 March: Fourth Congress of Soviets.

15 March: Fourth Congress of Soviets ratifies the Peace of Brest-Litovsk. Left Socialist Revolutionaries leave Soviet Government as protest against the signature of the Treaty.

6 April: Japenese descent in Vladivostok.

9 April: Proclamation of the independence of Trans-Caucasia.

15 April: Turks take Batum.

23 April: Decree nationalizing foreign trade.

29 April: Germans dissolve Ukrainian Rada; General Skoropadsky proclaimed Hetman of Ukraine with dictatorial powers.

6 May: Insurgent anti-Soviet Cossacks occupy Novo-Cherkassk.

8 May: Germans and Cossacks occupy Rostov.

25 May: Beginning of open hostilities between the Soviets and the Czecho-Slovaks; the latter occupy Cheliabinsk.

26 May: The Trans-Caucasian Federation breaks up into the three independent states of Georgia, Armenia and Azerbaidzhan.

28 May: Czecho-Slovaks seize a number of towns in Eastern Russia and Siberia.

29 May: All-Russian Soviet Executive Committee introduces partial conscription for the Red Army.

8 June: Czecho-Slovaks occupy Samara, making possible creation of anti-Bolshevik Government, headed by Socialist Revolutionary members of the Constituent Assembly. Anti-Bolshevik Government created in Omsk, in Siberia.

11 June: Institution of the Committees of Poor Peasants.

17-19 June: Unsuccessful rebellion against the Soviet regime in Tambov.

20 June: Assassination of prominent Petrograd Communist, Volodarsky, by a Socialist Revolutionary.

28 June: Nationalization of large industries.

4-10 July: Fifth Congress of Soviets adopts Constitution.

6 July: German Ambassador, Count Mirbach, assassinated by Left Socialist Revolutionaries in Moscow; rebellion of the Left Socialist Revolutionaries. Town of Iaroslav seized by insurgents acting under the direction of Boris Savinkov.

11 July: Muraviev, commander of Soviet troops on the Volga front, turns against the Bolsheviks and tries to send troops against Moscow; is shot when his troops refuse to follow him.

16 July: The former Tsar and members of his family shot in Ekaterinburg.

21 July: Iaroslav captured by Soviet troops.

2 August: Allied occupation of Archangel and organization of anti-Bolshevik Government of North Russia.

6 August: Czecho-Slovaks and anti-Bolshevik Russians capture Kazan, high point of their advance.

14 August: Small British force under General Dusterville occupies Baku after Bolshevik Soviet regime has been ousted by the population.

15 August: Volunteer Army, under leadership of General Denikin, captures the capital of the Kuban Territory, Ekaterinodar.

26 August: Volunteer Army occupies Novorossisk, gains access to the sea.

30 August: Fanya Kaplan fires at and wounds Lenin; Uritzky, prominent Petrograd Communist, killed by a Socialist Revolutionary.

4 September: Soviet Commissar for the Interior, Petrovsky, publishes appeal for 'mass terror' against the bourgeoisie.

8-23 September: Representatives of anti-Bolshevik Government of Siberia and Eastern Russia meet in State Conference at Ufa; agree to create central authority in the form of a Directory of five persons.

10 September: Red Army captures Kazan; turning point of campaign on Volga.

14 September: Turks occupy Baku after departure of British; great massacre of Armenians.

20 September: Execution of twenty-six Baku Commissars in the desert between Krasnovodsk and Askhabad by order of the Trans-Caspian authorities.

8 October: Red Army captures Samara.

6-9 November: Sixth Congress of Soviets.

9 November: Revolution in Germany.

13 November: Soviet Government annuls Treaty of Brest-Litovsk. Ukrainian nationalists, under leadership of Petlura, raise revolt against Hetman in town of Belaia Tserkov.

18 November: Admiral Alexander Kolchak proclaimed Supreme Ruler, vested with dictatorial powers, after military coup d'état in Omsk and arrest of Socialist Revolutionary members of the Directory.

21 November: Soviet Government nationalizes internal trade.

27 November: Provisional Soviet Government of Ukraine proclaimed, as first step toward new Bolshevik occupation of Ukraine.

14 December: Ukrainian nationalist troops under Petlura occupy Kiev; Hetman Skoropadsky flees. Red Army, moving westward into former zone of German occupation, occupies Minsk.

1919

3 January: Soviet troops, advancing in western and southern directions, take Riga, capital of Latvia, and Kharkov, the largest city of Eastern Ukraine.

16-25 January: Second Congress of Trade Unions.

6 February: Red Army captures Kiev, capital of the Ukranian nationalist regime.

15 February: General Krasnov, Ataman of the Don Territory, resigns and is succeeded by General Bogaevsky, withdrawal of Krasnov leaves Denikin in supreme command of anti-Bolshevik forces in south-eastern Russia.

2-7 March: First Congress of the Communist International in Moscow.

13 March: Kolchak's army, launching drive toward Volga, captures Uta.

18-23 March: Eighth Congress of the Communist Party.

21 March: Soviet regime established in Hungary.

6 April: Red Army enters chief Ukranian port, Odessa, after its evacuation by French forces of occupation.

10 April: Soviet troops, invading Crimean peninsula, occupy Simferopol.

26 April: Kolchak's offensive stopped before reaching Volga as a results of defeats in the Buzuluk and Buguruslan regions.

7 May: Ataman Grigoriev, leader of Soviet troops which were destined for offensive against Rumania, begins rebellion; issues anti-Bolshevik and anti-Semitic manifesto to the population.

15-17 May: Huge pogrom carried out by Grigoriev troops in town of Elizavetgrad.

19 May: Denikin takes offensive against Soviet troops on southeastern front; his cavalry breaks through Red front near Iuzovka.

4 June: Partisan leader Makhno breaks with Red Army command; dissatisfaction among Makhno's followers and other Red troops helps White Army of Denikin to win decisive victories in the Don Territory and in the Donetz coal basin.

9 June: Ufa retaken by Red troops; Kolchak's retreat continues.

12 June: Fort Krasnaia Gorka, near Petrograd, betrayed to Northwestern White Army by its commanding officers.

16 June: Krasnaia Gorka retaken; threat to Petrograd averted.

25 June: Denikin captures Kharkov.

30 June: Continuation of Denikin's advance marked by capture of Tsaritsin and Ekaterinoslav.

1 July: Soviet troops, pushing forward on Eastern Front, take Perm.

25 July: Red Army occupies Cheliabinsk; retreat of Kolchak's troops becomes increasingly disorderly.

27 July: Grigoriev killed by Makhno.

1 August: Fall of Hungarian Soviet Government.

10 August: Denikin's cavalry General, Mamontov, breaks through front, begins long raid in rear of Soviet armies on Southern Front.

18-21 August: Mamontov holds Tambov.

23 August: Denikin seizes Odessa.

30 August: Red Army evacuates Kiev; Petlurists march in.

31 August: Denikin's forces push Petlurists out of Kiev.

25 September: Anarchists throw bomb into headquarters of Moscow Committee of Communist Party; a number of Communists killed and wounded.

11 October: Iudenitch starts drive on Petrograd.

14 October: Denikin occupies Orel: high point of his advance.

20 October: Red Army retakes Orel.

22 October: Iudenitch pushed back from suburbs of Petrograd. Tsarskow Selo and Pavlovsk.

14 November: Red Army takes Kolchak's capital, Omsk.

17 November: Soviet troops on Southern Front occupy Kurks; Denikin's resistance begins to crumble all along the line.

5-9 December: Seventh Congress of Soviets.

12 December: Red Army captures Kharkov.

30 December: Red troops take Ekaterinoslav.

1920

3 January: Red Army occupies Tsaritsin.

4 January: Kolchak abdicates as Supreme Ruler in favour of Denikin.

8 January: Red Army captures Rostov, seat of Denikin's Government; Denikin's Army retreats south of the Don.

15 January: Kolchak handed over to the Political Centre in Irkutsk by Czecho-Slovaks who were guarding him.

16 January: Allies Supreme Council raises the blockade of Soviet Russia.

2 February: Signature of Peace with Esthonia.

7 February: Kolchak shot by decision of the Revolutionary Committee in Irkutsk.

10 February: Beginning of organization of 'labour armies' with a view to utilizing Red Army soldiers for productive work.

19 February: Fall of Northern Government in Archangel.

17 March: Red Army occupies Kuban capital, Ekaterinodar.

27 March: Soviet troops, pursuing demoralized White Army of Denikin, take port of Novorossisk.

4 April: Denikin resigns command of armed forces of South Russia, nominating General Baron Peter Wrangel as his successor.

3-6 April: Third Congress of Trade Unions.

27 April: Red Army captures Baku; Azerbaidjan Soviet Government organized.

29 April-5 May: Tenth Congress of Communist Party.

6 May: Poles enter Kiev.

7 May: Soviet Government concludes treaty with Georgia, recognizing its independence.

6 June: Wrangel, after reorganizing his army, begins movement northward from the Crimea.

8 June: Budenny's Cavalry Army, raiding in rear of Poles, seizes Berditchev and Zhitomir.

12 June: Red Army retakes Kiev.

11 July: Red Army, on the offensive of the Polish Front, captures Minsk.

14 July: Soviet troops occupy Vilna.

21 July / 6 August: Second Congress of Communist International.

31 July: With view to creating a Soviet regime in Poland a Revolutionary Committee, headed by communists of Polish origin, is established in Belostok.

1 August: Red Army takes Brest-Litovsk.

15 August: Polish forces south of Warsaw launch counter-offensive.

21 August: Success of Polish counterstroke marked by recapture of Brest-Litovsk and general retreat of Red Army from the Vistula.

21 September: Beginning of Russo-Polish peace negotiations in Riga.

12 October: Signature of preliminary peace treaty with Poland.

20 October: Beginning of final offensive against Wrangel.

2 November: Wrangel's Army retreats into the Crimea.

11 November: Red Army storms the Isthmus of Perekop, the approach to the Crimea.

14 November: Wrangel evacuates the Crimea.

29 November: Soviet Government issues decree nationalizing small industries.

Index

Kamenev,L.B., 18; for a coalition government of all socialist parties, 23-8; ready to exclude Lenin and Trotsky from government, 23; the party rules, 175

Kamenev,S.S., 197

Kerensky,A., 12

Kolchak, Admiral A., 38, 148, 152, 169, 197-8, 203

Kollontai,A., 23, 50

Kornilov, General L.G., 12, 16, 165

Krasnov, General P.N., 12, 17

Krestinsky,N.N., 43, 48

Kritzman,L.N., 83, 88, 92

Krupskaya,N.K., 91-2

Krylenko,N.N., 4

Kursky,D.I., 174

Labour armies, 125-6

Labour discipline, role in transition period, 59-60, 74-5, 79-80; deteriorates as result of malnutrition and exhaustion of workers, 85-6

Land decree, 8-9, 35

Larin,U., 7

Lashevich,M., 196

Latsis,M.I., 18

Left Communists, 39-51

Lenin,V.I., on prospects of Bolsheviks retaining power, 1; issues many decrees, 5-6; strict chairman of sovnarkom, 5-6; decrees part of his Collected Works, 6; did not see many decrees published over his signature, 7-8; drafts decree on peace, 8; drafts decree on land, 8-9; pinches SR programme, 9; drafts decree on right of national self-determination, 9; drafts decree on workers' control, 10; drafts decree on right of recall, 10; involved in trivial administrative matters, 11-12; aided by primitive secretarian organization, 12; on Red terror, 17-19; badly wounded in attempt on his life, 18-19, 166; robbed, 20-1; Mensheviks and SRs demand his (and Trotsky's) exclusion from coalition of all socialist parties, 23-8; opposes coalition government with Mensheviks and SRs, ibid.; in minority in Central Committee on question, 25, puts ultimatum to Right Bolsheviks, 27-8; prior to October revolution calls for early convening of Constituent Assembly, 30; hesitates whether to hold elections to Constituent Assembly, 31-2; for disposal of Constituent Assembly, 34;

on relation between Constituent and Soviets, 34-6; on towns leading countryside, 36-7; prior to October revolution argues for revolutionary war, 39; after October argues for accepting German peace terms, 39-41; for marking time until victory of German revolution, 39-40; his peace policy rejected by majority of Central Committee and Party, 41-51; rebukes Zinoviev and Stalin who used non-internationalist arguments in support of peace policy, 42-3; for accepting military aid from Britain and France, 44-5; argues in press for peace policy, 45-7; wins Central Committee for same, 48-9; wins Party for same, 49-51; opposes Stalin's suggestion of expelling Left Communist leaders from Party, 49; his peace policy – principled and realistic, 53-4; learns from Marx and Engels regarding transition period, 55-9; charting transitional demands prior to October revolution, 60-2; on workers' control, 62; on long and complicated transition period, 62-6; on human nature changing in transition period, 63-4; on creativity of masses as key to transition, 64-6; state capitalism as the content of transition period, 66-71; state capitalism and peasantry, 69, 76-7; on need for bourgeois specialists, 71-2; privileges of specialists are concessions to capitalism, 72-3; on one-man management, 73-5; on Taylorism, 75; on petty bourgeois counter-revolutionary threats during transition period, 76-7; on threat of counter-revolution from intelligentsia, 78-80; on need to strengthen proletarian dictatorship, 78-9; on lice threatening the revolution, 89-90; his very frugal life-style, 91-2; defines War Communism as real communism, 93-4; redefines War Communism as unavoidable siege economy, 96-9; on miracles of organization and heroism of proletariat, peasantry and Red Army, 100-1; on Bolsheviks' unpreparedness to govern, 104; on proletarian perseverance as guarantee for victory, 104-5; on need for realism – neither pessimism nor optimism, 104-5; on stench of old society poisoning the new, 107; on

revolution as a 'leap into freedom', 109; on means and ends – proletarian dictatorship and freedom, 110; on bureaucratic degeneration of state, 111-12; on decimation of proletariat during civil war, 113; on proletariat becoming more petty bourgeois, 113-14; on the decomposition of proletariat, 115; on militarization of labour, 125-6; on statification of trade unions, 126; on subbotniks, 127; on the proletarian nature of the state undermined by decomposition of proletariat, 128-9; on distinction between proletariat and peasantry, 130, 144; on need to organize large farms, 130-2; on organizing agricultural workers, 133-4; on food requisitioning, 133-4; on Poor Peasant Committees, 134-7; on peasantry gaining from revolution far more than proletariat, 143; on withering away of state, 144-5; on dictatorship of proletariat as consistent democracy, 145-6; on decline of VTsIK, 148; on need to limit power of Cheka, 152-3; for soldiers' committees and election of officers in army, 153; on great number of bourgeois officials in state apparatus, 158; on dictatorship of proletariat or of Party, 161-2, 174; for relaxation of measures against Right SR, 166-7; conciliatory attitude towards Mensheviks, 168-9; for tightening screws on Right SRs and Mensheviks, 169; on need of workers to defend themselves against state, 178; on distorted relationships between party and state, 178; on mobilization of party members whenever the regime threatened, 180; on need to purge party from careerists, 182-3; on scarcity of veterans in party, 184; on relation between Politburo, Orgburo and secretariat on the one hand and Central Committee on the other, 186; Lenin, the party and the proletariat, 193-4; supports Trotsky against 'military opposition', 195-6; disagrees with Trotsky on military strategy and proved largely wrong, 197-203; for evacuation of Petrograd, 199-200; for march on Warsaw, 200-2; on international nature of revolution, 204-5
Libedinsky,Iu., 190-1
Lice, threat to revolution, 89-90

Lomov,G.I., 5, 43, 44, 46, 50
Ludendorff, 52-3
Lunacharsky,A.V., 5, 23-8
Luxemburg,R., against substitution of party for proletariat in power, 176; party monopoly will lead to withering away of Soviet, 176-7; substitution of party for class caused by isolation of Russian revolution, 177-8

Maksimovsky,V.N., 191
March on Warsaw, 201-3
Markhlevsky,J., 201
Marriage law, 11
Martov,L., on popularity of Bolshevik regime, 2; calling for a coalition government of all socialist parties, 3; leaves the Soviet, 4; on helplessness of 'third camp', 169
Marx,K., on 'pure democracy', 38; on communist society, 93-5; on equality not compatible with poverty, 95; on revolution as only way to transform proletariat, 106
Mayakovsky,V.V., 108
Means and ends – proletarian dictatorship and freedom, 109-12
Mensheviks, 1-2; in Second Congress of Soviets, 3; leaving Soviet, 4; organizing strikes against Bolshevik government, 15-17; demand a coalition government of all socialist parties with exclusion of Lenin and Trotsky, 23-8; faring badly in election to Constituent Assembly,, 32-4; reject decrees on land, peace and workers' control at Constituent Assembly, 35; the press unfettered, 167-8; support Bolshevik regime critically, 168; being suppressed, 169-70
Menzhinsky,V.R., 6-7
Miliutin,V.P., 4, 23, 28
Militarization of labour, 124-6
Molotov,V.M., 184

Nogin,V.P., 4, 13, 23-8

Obolensky,V., 43
One-man management, 73-5
Ordzhonikidze,G.K., 195

Peace decree, 8, 35
Peasantry, land decree, 8-9; distinction from proletariat, 36-7, 129-30, 144; and state capitalism, 69, 76-7; compulsory requisition of grain, 87-8, 133-4; effect on Jacobin

Peasantry – (*Cont.*)
centralization of state, 105, 138-43;
and organization of large farms,
130-2; decline in stratification of,
133-4; Poor Peasant Committees,
134-8; resistance to compulsory
requisitions, 137-8; contradictions in
attitude to Bolsheviks, 138;
affecting moods of proletariat, 142-3;
affect moods in Party, 143; gained
from revolution more than the
proletariat, 143; increased social
weight compared with proletariat's,
143; being discriminated against
by electoral law
Petukovsky,S.S., 6-7
Piatakov,G.L., 43, 46, 49-50
Pilnyak,B., 138, 190
Plekhanov,,G.B., 35
Pokrovsky,M.N., 46, 50
Preobrazhensky,E.A., 43, 50
Prokopovich,S.N., 1
Proletariat, versus peasantry, 36-7,
129-30, 144; exhibits miracles of
organization and heroism, 99, 101;
thirst for culture, 101-3; its
perseverance guarantee for victory,
104-5; its being a tiny minority of
population undermines democracy,
105-6; tolerates dictatorship against
itself, 106; its heroism intertwines
with backwardness, 106-7; over-
burdened with dead of past, 106, 108;
decomposition of proletariat affects
the party, 108; decimation during
civil war, 113; becoming petty
bourgeois, 113-14; workers steal, 104-
5; decomposition of, 115; decomposition of proletariat and
collapse of workers' control, 116-18;
militarization of, 125-6; subbotniks,
126-8; its decomposition affects
socialist nature of state, 128-9;
organizing agricultural proletariat,
130-3; disappearance of agricultural
proletariat, 133-4; gained from
revolution less than peasantry, 143;
has to defend itself from state,
178; its relation to party and to
Lenin, 193-4; see factory committees,
trade unions, workers' control

Radek,K., 39, 201
Radkey,S.O., 32-4, 164-5
Railways, collapse of, 86; workers'
control over, 117-18; see Vikzhel
RCP(b), prospects of holding power,
1-2; hardly prepared to govern, 104;
affected by decomposition of

proletariat, 107-8; affected by moods
of peasantry, 143; central role of its
members in morale of Red Army,
156-7; heroism of its members in
Red Army, *ibid.*; its members as
Political Commissars in army, 157-8;
rise of its political monopoly,
161-79; becoming non-proletarian in
composition, 180-1; careerists join
it, 181-4; very few veterans in it, 184;
increasing centralization in, 184-9;
power of its Central Committee
usurped by Politburo and Orgburo,
185-6; Secretariat usurps power,
186-7; appointment in party replaces
election, 187-8; party appointment
of trade union officials, 188-9;
privileges rise in, 189-91; fight to
defend democratic traditions in,
191-3; Lenin, the party and the
proletariat, 193-4; 'Military
Opposition' in, 194-6
Recall, right of, 10
Red Army, main consumer of
industrial output, 87; miracles of
organization and heroism, 99-101;
heroism and bestiality intermingles,
106-7; decree on soldiers' committees
in army, 153-4; abolition of ranks
in army, 154; Red Guard, 154-5;
Trotsky's role in, 154-8, 194-204;
deserters from, 155; proportion of
proletariats in, 155-6, central role of
party members in morale of, 156-7;
ex-Tsarist officers in, 157; Political
Commissars in, 157-8; 'Military
Opposition' in, 194–6
Reed,J., 1-2, 16, 101
Riazanov,D.B., 23, 189
Right of National Self-determination,
decree, 9
Rudzutak,Ia.E., 113
Rykov,A.I., 4, 13, 23-8

Sabotage, 15-16
Sapronov,T.V., 192
Savinkov, 165
Schmidt,V., 121
Serge,V., 17-18, 82, 90-1, 102, 179, 192-3
Shliapnikov,A.G., 4, 28, 117-18
Skvortsov,I.I., 5
Smilga,I.T., 44
Smirnov,V.M., 43-6, 49
Socialist Revolutionaries, Left, 29, 31-2,
170-1
Socialist Revolutionaries, Right, 1, 2,
28-9; in Second Congress of Soviets,
3; leaving Soviet, 4; land programme
pinched by Lenin, 9; organized

strikes against Bolsheviks, 15-17; attempt on Lenin's life, 18-19; demand a coalition government of all socialist parties excluding Lenin and Trotsky, 23; in Constituent Assembly, 32-5; reject decrees on land, peace and workers' control in Constituent Assembly, 35; support White regimes, 38, 163-6; government relaxation of measures against them, 166-7; their conference declares opposition to intervention, 167; their suppression, 169-70

Sokolnikov,G.Ia., 23

Soviets, see State

Sovnarkom, see State

Specialists, 71-5, 78-80

Stalin,J.V., Commissar for Nationalities, 5; on Constituent Assembly, 31; supports Lenin's policy using non-internationalist argument, rebuked by Lenin, 42-3; vacillates on peace policy, 48; for expelling Left Communists from party, 49; on ex-Tsarist personnel in local soviets, 150-1; and the Military Opposition, 194-5; supports march on Warsaw, 201; role in failure of march on Warsaw, 201-2

Stankevich,V.B., 1

State, inexperience of central administration, 6-7; proletarian and bourgeois democracy, 34-6; Lenin on need to strengthen it, 78-9; backwardness undermines democracy, 105-6; peasant majority effect on democracy, 105, 138-43; proletarian dictatorship and freedom, 110; bureaucratic degeneration of, 111-12; affected by decimation of proletariat, 128-9; the notion of withering away of, 144-5; dictatorship of proletariat – consistent democracy, 145-6; Supreme Soviet replaced by VTsIK, 146-7; VTsIK replaced by Presidium, 147-9; power of Presidium usurped by Sovnarkom, 149; decline of local soviets, 149-51; numerous ex-Tsarist personnel in soviet apparatus, 150; Cheka usurps power of soviets, 151-2; massive growth of bureaucracy in, 158; anti-Bolshevik stance of state personnel, 158-9; corruption of state officials, 159-60; military-centralist structure of state, 160; dictatorship of proletariat or party? 161-2, 174; decline of democracy as result of Bolshevik party monopoly, 171-9;

fusion of party and soviets, 172-3; Lenin on need of workers to defend themselves from state, 178

State Capitalism, Lenin on state capitalism as transition form to socialism, 66-71; two opposing concepts of term, 69; and peasantry, 69; and bourgeois specialists, 71-3; and one-man management, 73-5; and petty bourgeois counter-revolutionary threat, 76-7, 79-80

Strumilin,S.G., 85-6

Subbotniks, 126-8

Sukhanov,N.N., 162

Sverdlov,Ia.M., 23, 35, 44

Taylorism, 75

Teodorovich,I.A., 5, 28

Terror, 17-19; see Cheka

Tomsky,M.P., 121, 189

Trade Unions, take over factory committees, 118-19; integrated into VSNKh, 120; and Commissariat of Labour, 121; and statification of, 121-3, 126; and the military front, 123; and militarization of labour, 124-5; appointment, not election, of officials in, 188-9

Transition period from capitalism to socialism, Marx and Engels on, 55-9; Marx on role of gradual reforms after revolution, 57-8; on changing human nature in transition period, 58-60; Lenin's transitional demand prior to October, 60-2; Lenin on transition being long and complicated, 62-6; the old can bury the new, 107; revolution as 'a leap into freedom', 109; means and ends – proletarian dictatorship and freedom, 110; see State Capitalism

Trotsky,L.D., on giddiness on coming to power, 1; opposes coalition government with Mensheviks and SRs, 4, 23-8; foreign Commissar, 5; on Soviet decrees as part of Lenin's Collected Works, 6; close relations with the masses, 21-2; Mensheviks and Right SRs demand his (and Lenin's) exclusion from coalition government of socialist parties; on Constituent Assembly, 30-1; on Brest-Litovsk, 39; opposes Lenin's peace policy, 41-4; for taking military aid from Britain and France, 43-4; grudgingly accepts Lenin's peace policy, 44-5, 48-9; differences with Lenin regarding peace purely operational, 51-3; his policy on

Trotsky – (*Cont.*)

peace and war quite realistic, *ibid*;
declares Lenin's peace policy was
right, 54; defines war communism as
a siege economy, 98; on workers'
thirst for culture, 102-3; on
revolution awakening the personality, 103; on heroism and backwardness intertwined in the masses, 107;
and militarization of labour, 125-6;
becomes People's Commissar of
War, 154; builds Red Army, 155; on
central role of party members in
morale of Red Army, 156; for
multiplicity of parties under
proletarian dictatorship, 162;
defends substitution of party for
proletariat in power, 175; on Central
Committee as actual repository of
power, 175-6; meets strong
opposition in party for appointment
of ex-Tsarist officers, 194-5; appeals
to Lenin for support against
'Military Opposition', 195-6; disagrees with Lenin regarding military
strategy, and proves in the main
right, 197-203; wrong regarding
strategy on Eastern front, 197-8, 203;
brilliant strategy on Southern front,
197-9, 203; against the evacuation
of Petrograd, 199-200, 203; against
the march on Warsaw, 200-3; gets
blanket endorsement from Lenin
for military actions, 203; the father
of victory of Red Army, 203-4
Tsiurupa,A.D., 160
Tukhachevsky,M.N., 201-2
Typhus kills millions, 89

Ulyanov, Maria, 19, 92
Uritsky,M.S., 19, 23-4, 42, 166

Vikzhel, opposes Bolshevik govern-
ment, 16-17; threatens general strike
if no coalition government of all
socialist parties is established; 22-9
Volodarsky,V., 18, 166
Von Hertling, 53
Von Kühlman, 53
Voroshilov,K.Y., 195
VSNKh, 70, 120-1
VTsIK, see State

Workers' control, decree on, 10; Lenin
on, 62; sabotaged by capitalists,
81-2; replaced by nationalization of
industry, 82-3; disintegration of,
116-18; factory committees
integrated into trade unions,
118-19, 126

Zetkin,C., 202
Zinoviev,G.E., 41, 44, 49; demands
coalition government of all socialist
parties, 23-8; resigns from Central
Committee but later capitulates, 28;
supports Lenin's peace policy, but
using non-internationalist arguments,
and rebuked by Lenin, 42-3; for
dictatorship of Central Committee,
174-5; on party card as key to
promotion, 184; on appointment of
presidents of local soviets by Central
Committee, 187